being a part of
"my life" and all
of its craziness!
My best always,
Sally Breslin

THERE'S A

TICK

IN
MY UNDERWEAR!

Sally A. Breslin

There's a Tick in My Underwear!

DEDICATED

IN MEMORY OF

My wonderful parents:

Lucien E. Roberge (1925-1984)

and

Adella "Dell" Roberge (1927-2006)

and

My dear friend

Janet Melanson Staggs (1949-2002)

CHAPTER ONE

New Hampshire—1962

Thirty-four days had passed since I'd bolted out of my seventh-grade class at Elm Park School, extended my arms toward the sky, and shouted, "Yahoo! It's summer vacation!"

Seventeen of those days had been spent in Connecticut visiting Ricky, my much-younger cousin, who was like a chubbier and brattier version of Richie Rich, and whose hobbies included pegging rocks at me, shoving me into the brook, spilling paint on my sneakers and throwing daily tantrums in a variety of octaves and decibels. Still, I really enjoyed my visit. His swimming pool, go-carts, ponies and kid-sized electric train that circled his yard, may have had something to do with it.

I'd been back from Connecticut for only a day and already I was bored. So bored, I'd spent the morning watching my mother do the laundry. I'd even begged her to let me shove the wet clothes through the wringer on our ancient green washing machine because squishing water out of shirts was more fun than listening to myself yawn. Being an only child, I couldn't even pick on a brother or sister for entertainment.

"Be a dear and go hang the clothes outside for me," Mom said after I'd stuffed my jeans through the wringer for the third time in my effort to turn them into a denim pancake. "It sure would be a big help."

Muttering, I struggled with the basket of wet clothes as I made my way down the narrow first-floor hallway of our tenement building and then down the five wooden steps that led out to the back yard; a small fenced-in patch of grass with a big oak tree on the right and a row of tulips and daffodils on the left.

My parents owned the three-story building, so the yard was a combination of beauty and practicality. Mom loved anything that bloomed, so she wanted to transform every inch of the area into a replica of the Botanical Gardens. My father, however, believed the yard should be more functional than eye-catching. That's why most of the grass was consumed by a Gulliver-sized clothesline – eight lines strung between two large wooden frames he'd painted gray to match the building. He said he'd built the clothesline big so all of the tenants in the building could hang out their laundry at the same time, if ever the need arose. Short of a giant mudslide hitting our block, I honestly couldn't see it ever happening.

As I hung up a pink towel, my mother opened the kitchen window and called out to me, "Remember what I taught you...be sure to hide the unmentionables behind sheets or towels so they won't attract perverts."

I nodded, even though I had no idea what perverts were. I reached into the laundry basket and pulled out a pair of my size-nine cotton panties that had "Thursday" embroidered in blue on them, and held them up. They were so wide, they blocked out the sun. I figured that unless a pervert was a guy who was looking for a new sail for his boat, my unmentionables probably were safe.

"Whatcha doing?" My friend Janet, who lived across the street, opened the wooden gate that led out to the back alley. She walked into the yard. Janet and I had been pals since kindergarten, although we made an odd-looking pair. Janet's goal in life was to finally reach a body weight that was three digits, while mine was to be able to wear clothes that didn't say "Chubbette" on the label. When we stood next to each other, we looked like the number 10.

"You got a haircut!" I greeted her. Her brown hair was so short, it looked as if she'd gone to the barbershop with her father for the two-for-one special.

"Yeah, it was getting too long and hot. My neck was always sweaty. Maybe *you* like wearing ponytails, but I don't."

I flung my panties over one of the lines and jammed a clothespin onto the waistband. "Do you know what a pervert is?" I asked her.

She shrugged. "I think it's a guy who waves his weenie at people."

I giggled. "You're making that up!"

"No, I heard it somewhere! Honest!"

I wasn't sure whether to believe Janet or not. After all, she was the one who'd once come crying to me and insisted she was pregnant because her neighbor, Rusty, had kissed her on the cheek. Heck, even I knew it took more than that to get pregnant. Rusty would've had to have been lying on top of her when he kissed her.

"I'm so bored," Janet said. "What do you want to do?"

"We could walk downtown and get an ice-cream soda."

"Nah, it's too hot. Besides that, I don't have any money." Her gaze suddenly locked on something behind me. "You're about to have company." She pointed at the clothesline.

My eyes followed the direction of her finger and I spotted a black spider, about the size of a dime, doing its best tightrope-walker impersonation as it inched along the line. I screamed, flung a handful of wooden clothespins into the air and then bolted out of the yard and into the alley.

"You're such a sissy about spiders!" Janet said, laughing. "You're a hundred times bigger than that spider!" She followed me out to the alley.

"God! I hate those things!" I said, shuddering. "If a comet landed here tomorrow and gave off a poisonous gas that killed every spider within a hundred miles of here, I would be one happy girl."

"I heard that some lady was shopping down at the A&P and she was looking through some bananas that came from South America or somewhere," Janet said. "A big, hairy tarantula crawled out of the bananas and right up her sleeve! And it bit her like a hundred times! Her arm turned all black and fell off...and then she died!"

She pronounced tarantula as "tare-an-toola," but I knew what she meant. In fact, I made a mental note never to eat bananas again.

"I heard a scream." My mother had come out to the yard to investigate. "Is everything okay?" As she spoke, she glanced at the clothespins scattered on the grass and the still-full laundry basket. Planting her hands on her hips, which never was a good

3

sign, she frowned at Janet and me as we walked back into the yard.

"A huge spider tried to attack us!" I said. "No kidding, it was the size of a dinner plate!"

Mom, who was all too familiar with my tendency to overreact whenever I saw a spider, rolled her eyes and shook her head. "Gee, maybe I should go back in the house and get your father's shotgun, then."

She bent to pick up the clothespins I'd dropped and then methodically began to hang the rest of the clothes. When she lifted my training bra, I felt my cheeks grow warm.

"You don't have to bother hiding that from perverts," I said. "They'll think it's just a white headband anyway. I sure wish I looked like Pam Coulter or Suzanne Tanner. They're really stacked. Well, at least that's what the boys at school say."

"Oh, don't worry," my mother said. "You'll grow breasts someday. After all, your grandmother has extra-large ones."

Actually, my grandmother (on my father's side) had three breasts. She had two that were about the size of basketballs, which she squeezed into a much-too-snug bra that pushed all of the excess flesh together in the middle to form another bulge about the size of a cantaloupe. Sure, I wanted breasts, but only two, and not so large that I'd have trouble seeing my feet.

The problem was, I'd already taken after my grandmother in too many ways. She loved sweets, especially chocolate, which she ate by the pound. I spent all of my pop-bottle refund money on penny candy. She was overweight. I was only twelve and barely could squeeze into a size fourteen. She enjoyed reading and doing crossword puzzles. I enjoyed writing stories and making up my own puzzles. She had a big problem with tooth decay. My teeth had so many fillings, my dentist told me not to go swimming because I'd sink.

Yep, I thought, I was doomed to have three breasts.

I stared at my mom, a perfect size nine with perfect teeth, who often was told she looked like our First Lady, Jackie Kennedy. One of my uncles always said that if a guy wanted to know what his girlfriend would look like when she got older, all he had to do was look at her mother. But frankly, I couldn't picture myself ever looking like my mom, not without the help of a good plastic surgeon. Even our hair was nothing alike. Hers was dark and wavy, while mine was auburn and straight. The only things she and I physically had in common were our green eyes.

Mom suddenly stopped hanging clothes and smiled at me. "I was going to wait until Dad got home tonight to tell you this, but I just can't wait until then. I have a big surprise for you!"

She immediately had Janet's and my full attention.

"We are going to spend the next two weeks at the camp!" Her excited tone indicated she thought she'd actually said something good.

My heart momentarily stopped beating and the three pancakes drenched in melted butter and maple syrup I'd eaten for breakfast rose up to somewhere around my tonsils. Had my mother told me I was going to be spending the next two weeks working as a toilet scrubber in a public restroom, I couldn't have been less thrilled.

The camp actually was a two-room cabin out in the wilds of Arrowwood, New Hampshire (population approximately 950) that my parents had bought a couple years earlier as their getaway from city life. It sat along the banks of the Abenaki River, where my dad planned to do some serious fishing. The cabin had no electricity, no telephone, and worst of all…no indoor plumbing. A day, perhaps two, was all I could stand of the place. After all, I was a city slicker through and through. And I was perfectly content to remain that way.

I shot a "please, help me!" look at Janet, then turned to my mother, "You and Dad can go stay at the camp. I'll stay at Janet's house, okay?"

Janet's eyes widened and her mouth fell open. I could read her mind. She was thinking there was no way her parents ever would allow me to spend two weeks in their already cramped four-room apartment. In fact, because they had only two bedrooms and it wasn't proper for Janet and her younger brother to sleep in the same room, Janet shared a room with her mother, and her brother shared one with her father. Still, I didn't care if I had to sleep on their bare linoleum if it meant I'd have access to a flush toilet and a television.

"I have a better idea," my mother said. "Janet, why don't you ask your parents if you can stay at the camp with us! Sally will have someone to hang around with up there, and the two of you can have a lot of fun together."

For a moment, Janet looked as if she might throw up. I wasn't about to give her the chance to say no, however. If I had to suffer, I wanted her to suffer, too. After all, what were friends for?

"That would be fantastic!" I gushed. "We could go swimming and then we could pick wild blueberries! And think of all the great barbecues we can have! And we can toast marshmallows every night!"

Janet may have been pencil-thin, but she loved to eat. So I knew that using food as ammunition was my only hope of convincing her to share my two weeks of what I knew were going to be nothing short of torture.

"The fresh air and sunshine will do you good, Janet," my mother continued. "Why stay here in the hot city when you could be nice and cool out in the country? Do you have anything better to do, other than sitting around here being bored?"

Janet looked thoughtful for a moment and then shrugged. "Okay...I guess. Let's go ask my parents if I can go."

We ran out of the yard and into the alley, then out to the street and across it to Janet's house. Janet's mother, a thin, dark-haired woman with dark-framed glasses that pointed up at the corners, was sitting on the sofa and watching *Search for Tomorrow*. A package of cookies lay on her lap and she was eating one of them as her eyes remained glued to the television. She tossed a "hello" at us when we entered, but didn't turn to look at us.

"Hey, Crisco!" Janet's dad, who was in the kitchen, greeted me. He always called me Crisco because he claimed I had too much lard in my can. "So, tell me, do you prefer smart fellas or fart smellers?" He paused to laugh at his own joke. "I'm making my famous rabbit-dabbit sandwich. Want one?"

I had no clue what a rabbit-dabbit sandwich was, but as I watched him drop about a pound of raw ground-beef into a metal bowl, then add chopped onions and mayonnaise and mix it all together and spread it onto bread, I figured that unless I wanted a bad case of tapeworms, I'd be wise to pass. The thought crossed my mind that maybe Janet's dad's rabbit-dabbit sandwich was the reason why everyone in her family was so thin.

Just as Janet opened her mouth to ask her dad about going to the camp with me, her mother made a noise that sounded something like a bear's growl. She darted past us and into the bathroom, which was right off the kitchen, where the thin walls did little to conceal the sounds of explosive vomiting.

Several minutes later, Janet's mom emerged, flushed and teary-eyed. The only words she uttered were, "the cookies." Janet's dad went into the living room and picked up the package of peanut-butter cookies.

"Aw, they're just little sugar bugs," he said. He brought the package out to the kitchen and thrust it under my nose. The cookies were covered with tiny black bugs. "They won't hurt you. You might even get a little extra protein from them!"

Janet's mom dashed back into the bathroom.

Janet shot a look at me that clearly told me she thought it might not be such a hot time to ask her parents about going to the camp. But I wasn't about to allow any time to pass that might give her the opportunity to change her mind. "My mother wants to know if Janet can spend the next two weeks with us at our camp in Arrowwood," I blurted out.

Janet's dad was silent for a moment, then a strange expression came over his face. It was the kind of expression a dying explorer might have if he suddenly spotted a lemonade stand in the middle of the desert. When Janet's mom, clutching her stomach and groaning, walked out of the bathroom, he grabbed her around the waist and pulled her toward him. "Guess what?" he said. "You and I are finally going to share a bedroom!"

And so the deal was settled. Janet and I were on our way to spend the next two weeks in a poison-ivy, bug-infested hell…complete with an outhouse.

CHAPTER TWO

Janet and I frowned at each other in the back seat of my dad's old Buick as the last remnants of city life zipped past the car's windows.

"Good-bye, bowling alley," Janet said as the weathered brick building that housed our favorite twenty-four lanes came into view and then disappeared.

"Good-bye, civilization," I said, sighing.

My mother shook her head and laughed. "You'll be less than forty-five minutes from home. You two make it sound like we're going to be stranded on some deserted island thousands of miles away."

"We may as well be," I said. "There's nothing at the camp but trees and bugs...and more trees and more bugs."

"Oh, stop complaining," my mother said. "You'll have fun, you just wait and see. We're all going to have a great time!"

I suspected she was trying to convince herself just as much as she was trying to convince us. After all, my mother was the type who wore high-heels when she vacuumed, and would rather be rolled in grape jelly and staked to an anthill than be seen in public with even one hair out of place. Somehow, I just couldn't picture her sitting in an outhouse or washing her armpits in a river.

I wanted to tell her that unless we arrived at the camp to discover that all of the surrounding woods had been chopped down to make room for an amusement park or a drive-in theater, there wasn't a chance in Hades the next two weeks were going to be great, but the soft voice of Ricky Nelson singing *Young World* made me momentarily forget about the camp.

"Oooh, quick! Turn up the radio!" I squealed.

My dad reached for the knob and cranked it up a few notches. Janet and I leaned back, our heads resting against the cool leather of the seat. We closed our eyes and allowed ourselves to imagine that Ricky was singing solely to us.

"I don't know how I'm going to survive without seeing him on TV," Janet said after the song ended. "I never miss his show. His eyes are the dreamiest, the way he always half-closes them when he sings!"

"His eyes look that way because he's on drugs!" my mother said. "You mark my words, he's taking them!"

I groaned. "Mom, a nice family like the Nelsons would never have drugs! Ozzie and Harriet wouldn't allow it!"

I turned my attention back to Janet. "I'll sure miss seeing Ricky, too. And Johnny Crawford on *The Rifleman*."

"And Paul Petersen and Tony Dow," Janet added.

"Heck, I'm just going to miss TV, period!"

I gazed at the clusters of pine trees that now lined our route. Gone were the tenements and concrete of the city. Gone were the ice-cream trucks and public swimming pools of summers past. I had spent seventeen days living a life of luxury at my cousin Ricky's and now I was going to be living like a hobo. I wondered if my body and brain would be able to adjust to such an abrupt change.

Janet interrupted my thoughts. "I have the feeling that the only thing cute and male we'll be seeing this summer probably will be covered with fur and have four legs."

I didn't laugh.

Twenty minutes later, the car swerved onto Harmon Road, the old dirt road that merged with Shepherdess Road—an even older and dirtier road—on which our camp was located. Clouds of dust surrounded the car as it bounced over rocks, ruts and bumps.

We passed the Harmons' sprawling yellow farmhouse. The only reason I knew it belonged to the Harmons was because the mailbox out front had their name on it. I also figured the town had named the road in their honor. Either that, or the Harmons had lived there for so long, they'd probably just gone ahead and named the road after themselves. I didn't know much about the Harmons, other than they had a shaggy-haired son who looked pretty old—at least 19—and a shaggy-haired dog that liked to

9

chase cars; which, on Harmon Road, probably added up to about two a week.

Five minutes of being bounced around the back seat later, I finally spotted the driveway to the camp up ahead. "Well, there it is," I said in the same tone I usually reserved for trips to the dentist's office.

I could tell that Janet was getting nervous because whenever she got nervous, she passed gas, and she was passing so much, I was afraid the car would blow up if my father decided to light a cigarette.

Despite all of the dust, my mother opened her car window and took a deep breath of non-gaseous air.

"Sorry," Janet said.

"Here we are!" my father announced after he'd parked the car and yanked the key out of the ignition. "Help me unload the stuff in the trunk and bring it inside."

I climbed out of the car and stood on the pine-needle-strewn dirt driveway and stared at the camp. The little white shack with red shutters was even smaller than I'd remembered. It sat surrounded by tall pine trees on a hill overlooking the river, which, for some reason, had brown water.

To the right of the camp stood a green picnic table with two matching benches directly in front of a fieldstone barbecue one of my uncles had spent six months building for us. My uncle was a perfectionist, and his penchant for perfection had become obvious during the construction of the barbecue. He'd made my dad spend endless hours searching for perfectly shaped rocks for the perfectly shaped barbecue. "Too round! Too flat! Too bumpy!" my uncle would say as he examined and then flung aside each rock my dad, sweaty and dirty from dawn-until-dusk rock hunting, handed to him. Then came the day when my uncle rejected a rock because he claimed it didn't have enough moss on it. Dad finally lost his temper.

"The damned thing is going to be burning in a fire!" he shouted. "Why the hell does it need moss on it?"

When my uncle went home that night, my father mixed up some cement, grabbed a bunch of rocks and slapped them onto the barbecue. A half-hour later, he tossed down the trowel and said, "There! It's done!"

Behind the camp was a narrow, winding path that led down to a storage shed and to the building I vowed I never would set foot in again…the outhouse. Just the sight of its weathered boards and lopsided doorway, which lacked a door, was enough to instantly induce a week-long case of constipation.

Janet and I each grabbed a bag of groceries and climbed the three stone steps up to the camp's screened-in porch. My father, who was struggling to balance a box of pots and pans on his left arm, unlocked the door and held it open for us as we stepped inside. Musty air immediately attacked us.

Janet and I paused to eye our surroundings. The tiny front room, with its knotty-pine walls, was overstuffed with a chrome table and four matching chairs, a sofa bed, a rocking chair and a woodstove. A braided rug in several shades of gray covered the wooden floor. Kerosene lamps were perched on the table and the windowsills.

I walked into the second room, which was half the size of the front room. To the left was a two-burner propane stove. Next to it was a small sink with an old-fashioned, bright red hand-pump instead of faucets. Straight ahead was a propane refrigerator, and to the right was a set of bunk beds built into the wall. They were wider than regular bunk beds, but not quite full-sized. The floor was covered with blue linoleum.

I was pretty certain the way I was feeling at that moment was the way convicts must feel when they're first introduced to their cells.

"Cool!" Janet's voice came from behind me. "We're going to be sleeping in the kitchen!"

"At least we won't have far to go if we want a midnight snack," I said with more than a touch of sarcasm. "I think we can reach the fridge without even getting out of bed."

I turned to look at my parents. My dad was smiling like a kid who'd just won a lifetime supply of candy. "Isn't this great?" he said. He took a deep breath and slowly exhaled. "Nothing beats fresh country air!"

I was amazed he didn't choke, seeing that the place had been closed up without the benefit of a broom or a dust rag for the past six months.

"I can't wait to try out my new fly-rod!" Dad added. He set down the box of pots and pans on the table. "I paid a mint for it, but it'll be worth it when I start yanking trout out of the river! Imagine eating trout that's so fresh, it was still swimming just 15 minutes before it ended up on your plate?"

I wrinkled my nose. "But the water in the river is brown. The fish probably are all brown and disgusting inside from drinking it!"

"The water is brown because of the plant life at the bottom of it, along with roots and things like that," Dad said. "It's perfectly fresh water."

It was the "things like that" that concerned me. After all, there were a heck of a lot of "things" that could turn water brown; most of which I didn't even want to think about.

"It's going to be great to just step out of the door and cast my line and catch dinner!" Dad said. "You can't do that in the city, no siree! I sure wish I could stay here all week with you guys!"

My eyes widened. "What do you mean you *wish* you could stay here?"

"I still have to go to work every day, sweetheart," he said. "And then there's my part-time job at night. I can't get time off from both of them right now. But I'll spend weekends here with you."

My dad worked days as a mechanic at my mom's brother's auto-repair shop, and nights as a mechanic at his friend's used-car dealership. Mom once told me that the reason why Dad worked two jobs was because on their wedding day he'd promised her she'd never have to work another day in her life.

I should have realized Dad wouldn't be able to spend the two weeks at the camp with us, not only because of his two jobs, but because he also had to hang around our tenement building just in case someone's pipes broke or a toilet backed up. It seemed as if our phone was always ringing late at night because Mrs. Sikes, the elderly widow on the third floor, had a stopped-up toilet or a clogged bathtub drain. Dad said he suspected she was stuffing things down them on purpose because she had a crush on him. Mom had laughed at his suspicions, but on more than one occasion I'd noticed Mrs. Sikes looking at his backside and smiling when he bent over to fix something in her place. And whenever she called him to do a chore for her, it always seemed to be a job that required Dad to bend over...a lot.

But Mrs. Sikes wasn't the only one in the tenement who bugged my dad to do things. Tenants had been driving him crazy for as far back as I could remember and, according to my mother, even before I was born.

In fact, my mother loved to tell the story about one particularly bad night when it seemed as if every pipe in the building decided to malfunction at the same time. My dad, exhausted after hours of battling plumbing problems, had crawled into bed at three o'clock in the morning and collapsed next to my then-pregnant mother.

About an hour later, my mother abruptly awoke. "Lou!" she said, grabbing his shoulder and shaking him. "Wake up! My water just broke!"

His response was a loud snore.

"Lou!" her voice grew louder and more shrill. "My water just broke!"

A few seconds later, my father, his eyes still closed, got out of bed, walked over to the closet and pulled out a big pipe wrench. "Which floor is it this time?" he'd muttered.

My mom told me she'd laughed so hard, she nearly gave birth to me on the spot.

Anyway, despite all of my dad's chores and duties back in the city, I still hadn't imagined we three women would be left alone, even for a few hours, to fend for ourselves in the wild. Visions of a giant, drooling grizzly bear tearing the camp apart and turning us into hors d'oeuvres popped into my mind. I was positive that my dad, who was the bravest man I knew, could battle a grizzly with his bare hands, if necessary. After all, he was just like my TV hero, Cheyenne Bodie, a man who could wrestle a bear before breakfast, beat up stagecoach robbers in the afternoon, and still have the energy to go square dancing in the evening.

Left alone with my mother, however, I figured Janet and I were certain to become bear chow. Heck, if my mother saw a bear, she'd probably just stand there and scream, "Don't tear my new dress or mess my hair!"

"Nooooo!" my mother's high-pitched wail made me snap back to the present...and my grim surroundings. The three of us

13

turned to look at her. She had lifted the bench-type seat on the sofa bed, which concealed a compartment for blankets and linens. "We have mice in here!" She pulled out a red plaid blanket and held it up. It looked as if it had been blasted with buckshot.

"Are the mice still in there?" Dad asked. He walked over to the sofa and bent to look into the compartment. As Janet and I stepped back, just in case something leaped out, he reached in and lifted out what looked like a fuzzy ball of multicolored cotton. "Here's the nest, but it looks empty. I guess they've moved on."

A nest in the sofa didn't concern me half as much as how the mice had managed to get inside and build it in the first place. If there were gaps in the camp big enough for mice to fit through, then so could spiders, snakes and bees, my three least favorite things in the whole world...other than the outhouse.

"Well, even though there are a few holes in them, we can still use the blankets," Mom said. "We can wash them in the river and hang them out, and they should be dry by tonight."

"And brown," I added.

"Let's go exploring!" Janet suddenly said, probably because she was afraid Mom would send us down to the river to beat the blankets against the rocks. "We have the whole day to find out what's around here."

It was Saturday morning, just after nine o'clock. I thought longingly of my Saturday mornings back home. I, and a big bowl of Kellogg's Sugar Pops, would be parked in front of the TV for a full morning of cartoons, of which *Top Cat* was my favorite.

"I already miss my cartoons." I said.

"Yeah, but just think," Dad said, "out here you just might meet up with the *real* Rocky and Bullwinkle!"

Well, I thought, if I ever did come face to face with a live moose, at least it would be a sure cure for my impending constipation.

"Let's go check out the river," Janet said, heading toward the door.

"You be careful now," my mom said.

"And be sure to stay away from the poison ivy," Dad added.

14

If anyone knew about poison ivy, it was my dad. Back when he was a teenager, he'd bragged to a bunch of his friends that poison ivy had no effect whatsoever on him. To prove his point, he'd actually eaten a couple leaves of it. Two days later, he resembled a giant pink balloon as he lay in a hospital bed and begged for intravenous calamine lotion. I'd never seen poison ivy back in the city, but thanks to Dad and his constant recitation of the poem, "leaves of three, leave them be," I was pretty sure I knew what to avoid.

Janet and I bolted out of the camp and down to the river. I had to admit that the sky seemed more blue and air more breathable than in the city. At the edge of the river, I paused to examine a tree that had pure white bark. It was one of the cleanest looking trees I'd ever seen.

"White birch," Janet said. "She walked over and peeled off a piece of the thin bark. "My dad said the Indians used to use this for paper."

I took the bark from her and ran it between my fingers. It felt exactly like paper. "Cool! I'm going to write a letter on it and mail it to someone!"

"Well, you'll have to find a carrier pigeon to deliver it for you out in this place," Janet said. I dropped the bark.

We walked over to the very edge of the riverbank and stood there. The section of the river that ran past the camp looked pretty shallow and not very wide, probably 20 feet across. In fact, I was certain that I, who'd always been told I threw "just like a girl," easily could toss a rock from one side of the river to the other. To prove it to myself, I picked up a rock and flung it. It landed with a loud plop in the water about five feet from where I stood.

Janet and I, who were wearing shorts, took off our sneakers and socks, and waded into the water. It was so cold, my toes immediately went numb. I also noticed the water didn't smell anything like the water in the city. There, the drinking water and the water in the public pools always smelled like bleach. This water smelled kind of like the mud pies I used to make back in my kindergarten days.

There was a large, flat-topped rock sticking up about two feet out of the water in the middle of the river. It was big enough for us to sit on, even lie on. We waded toward it. The bottom of the river was covered with rocks and mud. As I carefully made my way toward the rock, I felt something cold and slimy squishing between my toes.

"I think I just stepped in whatever's turning the water brown," I said to Janet.

Just as we reached the big rock, the river's bottom suddenly dropped off. Janet and I sank up to our waists in icy brown water.

"Great," Janet said. "Now my underpants are soaked. I should have put on my bathing suit."

We hoisted ourselves up onto the big rock and sat there, our feet dangling in the water.

"It's so quiet here," Janet said.

I eyed our surroundings. I saw nothing but trees and more trees. I felt as if we were the last two kids on earth. "Too quiet," I said. "My transistor radio is in my suitcase. I should have brought it out here with us."

Janet giggled. "Probably the only station it'll pick up out here in the wilderness is Radio Mosquito."

"Yeah, music to hum by! Hmmmmm!" We both dissolved into laughter.

The river's current was slow and lazy as it moved past the rock, and the sun hit the water and made it sparkle as if someone had sprinkled gold glitter into it. I hated to admit it, but I was beginning to enjoy myself.

"Hey!" Janet said. "Look at those weird little fish coming toward my toes. Aren't they cool?"

I peered into the water and saw what looked like flat black worms swimming toward us. They moved by rippling their bodies, sort of like a paper streamer rippled when someone ran while holding it high in the air. I caught a glimpse of the underside of one of the fish. It was a pinkish color.

"They're attacking my toes!" Janet said, giggling. "They sure are friendly!"

"Maybe they're not afraid of people because they've never seen any," I said.

I wasn't quite as brave as Janet, however. I yanked my feet out of the water and tucked them underneath me on the rock. I didn't want any creepy weird fish nibbling on my toes.

Janet lifted her legs out of the water and two of the fish clung to them. One was on top of her foot and the other was just below her ankle. "Look at that!" she said. "They like me so much, they want to stay with me!"

"Well, you'd better put them back in the water, or they'll die."

Janet tried to brush them off her legs, but they didn't budge, so she grabbed one and yanked it off. When she did, a trickle of blood ran down the top of her foot.

I'm pretty sure the people in the next county heard us screaming.

My parents made it down to the river in Olympic-worthy time. By then, Janet and I were standing on the rock, clutching each other in a bear hug and screaming into each other's ears.

"What on earth is wrong?" Dad shouted from the riverbank, his eyes making a quick sweep over us, probably to make certain all of our body parts still were intact.

Janet and I both pointed at her ankle, where the other killer fish still remained.

"Oh, God," Dad said. "Leeches."

"You mean bloodsuckers?" my mom asked. Her shudder did little to put Janet and me at ease.

"Well, jump off the rock and get over here," Dad told us.

"Nooooooo!" Janet and I both screamed in unison, clutching each other even more tightly. There was no way I ever was going to set foot in that water again. My mind flashed back to an image from a horror movie, *Mr. Sardonicus*, that Janet and I had seen at the Rand Theater just a few months earlier. A pretty woman, hanging from chains in a dungeon-like room, had been covered with leeches by her evil torturer, and I'd had nightmares about it for weeks. Under the circumstances, I felt I should have recognized the leeches in the river right away. But they looked different swimming in water than they'd looked when they were clinging to the lady's skin in the movie. Maybe, I figured, it was because the ones in the movie had been fake rubber ones.

"Jump off the rock and run to shore!" my dad again shouted to us. "I'll go light a cigarette!"

"You stay right here and help them, Lou!" my mom said to him. "This is no time to go running off to have a smoke!"

My father shook his head and sighed. "If you touch the leeches with a lit cigarette, they'll drop off. If you try to yank them off, they could leave a scar."

"How did those disgusting things get into our river anyway?" Mom asked. "The guy who sold us this place never mentioned that the water was infested with leeches!"

"Would you have let me buy it if he had?" Dad turned his attention back to us. "Come on, girls, just jump off and run! They can't swim fast enough to catch you!"

"But the bottom is slippery!" I whined. "What if I trip and fall?" I pictured myself covered from head to toe with leeches, my head looking like Medusa's, my body riddled with holes and pale and anemic after being drained of all its blood.

I could tell that my dad was getting impatient. "Well, if you keep standing out there," he said, "the leeches will catch your scent and crawl right up out of the water and onto the rock to get you!"

That did it. Janet and I jumped off the rock and, screaming all the way, headed for dry land.

Dad told Janet to sit on a nearby stump. She plunked down on it and sat there stiffly, her bottom lip quivering as she held back tears. Dad then touched a lit cigarette to the leech and if dropped off, writhing, into the leaves. It left a small, bloody hole on Janet's foot, just below her ankle. I closed my eyes, positive that the next words out of her mouth were going to be, "Take me home!"

"Wow, what a creepy looking thing," she said, leaning over to get a better look at the slimy little vampire. "I hope the mark on my foot will stay there at least until we go back to school so I can show it to everyone! I bet the boys will think it's really cool!"

If a few leech holes were all it would take for boys to pay attention to me, I thought, I'd go jump back into the river.

"God, they look just like worms!" My mother said, just before my dad stomped on the leech. "You know how much I hate worms...and snakes!"

Dad and I knew all right. In fact, we'd shared quite a few secret laughs while watching my mom trying to bait her hook whenever she and I went with Dad on one of his fishing trips. Mom, surprisingly, enjoyed fishing...but not the baiting part, because of her worm phobia. So she'd usually search for a flat rock, dump a few worms out of the bait can onto it and then try to stab one with the hook before it crawled away. To me, watching my mom stabbing everything but the worms was more entertaining than catching fish. But as much as she disliked worms, she hated snakes even more. There was a grass snake back home that liked to hide out in her tulip patch. Every time Mom spotted it, she'd scream and run so fast, the neighbors probably thought she was practicing for a track meet.

"I think you've turned into a city slicker, living in the city all these years," Dad said to my mom. "You grew up out in the country, just like I did, and you used to catch frogs and tadpoles."

"Frogs and tadpoles aren't snakes!" she said.

"So where are we supposed to swim now?" I asked. "And how about taking a bath? I'm not about to put any of my naked body parts in that water!"

Unconsciously, my father's hand moved protectively over the zipper on his jeans as he glanced down at the squished, dead leech. "That makes two of us."

CHAPTER THREE

By noon that same day, I felt as if I'd already been at the camp for two months. With the leech disaster behind us and our bellies full of Franco-American spaghetti, Janet and I headed up Shepherdess Road to do some exploring. I'd wanted to head north, but Janet said we'd come in that way, so we already knew what was down there. So we headed south on the dusty old road.

I already knew, from my past visits to the camp on an occasional Sunday afternoon, that there was nothing south of the place other than a narrow bridge and a gazillion trees. There also was a big boulder near the side of the road. Dad said it probably had been deposited there sometime during the Ice Age, but I didn't know whether it was true or not. I decided to keep silent and allow Janet to discover all of the "excitement" of the place on her own.

"Maybe we'll find some kids our age down here," Janet said. "Wouldn't it be cool if we even met some cute guys and had a summer romance?"

"You've been reading too many of your mother's *True Confessions* magazines," I said. I kicked at some of the thousands of small rocks lying in the road as we walked along. "Guys don't just appear in the middle of nowhere riding on white horses!"

"Maybe not white horses, but they could be riding bicycles. Anything can happen, you know."

Before I could respond, Janet spotted the boulder up ahead and shouted, "Wow! Look at that huge rock! Let's go climb it!"

I rolled my eyes. Climbing anything, even the front steps of the tenement building where I lived, made me grunt like a big sow, so the thought of climbing a boulder definitely wasn't tops on my list of fun things to do.

20

But this boulder was deceiving. It was resting against the side of a small hill, so the front of it was like a cliff, while the back was level with the ground. We climbed the hill and stepped out onto the top of the boulder. Suddenly, we were queens of the universe, perched high on our thrones overlooking Shepherdess Road. We even could see the black roof of the camp in the distance. The boulder was only about 10 feet tall, but to us, it was Mount Everest.

"This will be our special place, when we want to have some privacy." Janet said. "Let's give it a name!"

We sat in silent thought for a moment. "Let's call it Big Rock!" I finally said.

"Great!" Janet's enthusiasm made me feel as if I'd actually thought of something unique.

I pulled my pink transistor radio out of my shorts pocket and fiddled with the tuning dial. After a lengthy concert of static in several octaves, the soft voice of Shelley Fabares singing *Johnny Angel* came through clearly. Janet and I stretched out on our backs on top of Big Rock and sang along with the radio for a while. We also swatted about 11,000 mosquitoes.

"My dad said that mosquitoes come out mostly at dusk and dawn," Janet said.

I smacked one on my arm. It was full of blood, which splattered all over my palm. "I guess these mosquitoes can't tell time."

"If they're worse at dusk and dawn," Janet said, "then I think we'd better make sure we're locked inside the camp before sunset. I don't want to be their blue-plate special."

"God, what if we have to use the outhouse? We could end up with big itchy lumps in some really embarrassing places!"

Janet started to laugh. "Maybe I should sit outside naked from the waist up and let a bunch of mosquitoes bite my chest so it'll swell up and I can wear a bra!"

I laughed so hard, I nearly fell off Big Rock.

"Well, come on," Janet said. She stood up, stretched and then bent down to brush off the back of her tan shorts. "We have some exploring to do."

We headed back up the road. As we walked, dragonflies seemed to fly at us from every direction. I recalled the first time I'd ever seen one in my mother's flower garden back in the city.

21

She'd told me it was called a "darning needle" and that if I said any dirty words in front of it, it would sew up my mouth.

"Don't swear," I said to Janet. "Those darning needles will sew up your mouth!"

"Aw, I don't believe that! That's just something that parents tell little kids to scare them so they won't swear."

"Then I dare you to swear!" I said.

Janet hesitated for a moment then lifted her chin defiantly, took a deep breath and shouted, *"Shit!"*

Two dragonflies immediately darted at her. "You and your bright ideas!" she cried, waving her arms over her head as we ran off.

When we slowed down to a normal pace I again, I couldn't help but notice that the woods seemed to be getting thicker and darker with each step we took. By the time we reached the small steel-railed bridge that crossed over what looked like either a narrow section of the river or a wide brook, I thought the area had become downright spooky looking.

Janet picked up a rock and tossed it over the bridge. It made a loud splash when it hit the black water.

"Let's turn back now," I said. My eyes made a quick sweep of the area. "There's nothing down this way."

"But we're not even at the end of the road yet. Don't you want to see where it comes out?"

I shook my head. "This road could go on for miles for all we know, and end up in some big old swamp. And for some reason, I suddenly feel like Little Red Riding Hood on her way to Grandma's house."

Janet's eyes widened. "You mean, you think there might be wolves watching us?"

"Maybe. And I wouldn't be surprised to see a human hand or foot hanging out of their mouths!" No sooner did I utter the words did a loud, very clear sound come from somewhere deep in the woods: *Ca-coo-coo-coo! Ca-coo-coo-coo!"*

Janet and I ran so fast back to the camp, all we left in our wake was a cloud of dust. I was beginning to think that if nothing else, I was going to end up physically fit by the end of the summer. I was amazed at how fast my plump body could move when I really wanted it to. I also was surprised at how well Janet kept up with me, especially since I was wearing my

Keds sneakers and she was wearing rubber flip-flops. They made a loud flapping noise with every step she took.

"Those flip-flops make you sound like a galloping horse," I said between gasps as we ran.

"Good! I hope whatever is out there is afraid of horses!"

We rounded the bend into the yard and nearly crashed into my dad, who was carrying a bucket of water from the river. "Whoa!" he said. "You two look as if you've seen a ghost!"

"There was something in the woods making loud ca-coo-coo-coo sounds." Janet's impersonation sounded exactly like whatever had made the sound. She crossed her arms against her stomach and bent over in an attempt to catch her breath.

"Oh, that's nothing but a bird…a mourning dove," Dad said.

"But it's afternoon," I said.

"They probably can't tell time, either," Janet added. "Just like the dumb mosquitoes."

"Not *morning*," Dad said. "Mourning, as in what you do when somebody dies."

If Dad was trying to make us feel less threatened, mentioning dead people certainly wasn't helping much.

"What are you doing with the bucket of water?" I asked. I used the back of my hand to wipe the sweat from my forehead. I silently prayed he wasn't going to boil the river water and use it for our drinking water. I didn't care if he boiled it at a thousand degrees, there was no way anything that contained leeches and brown stuff ever was going to touch my lips.

"I'm going to prime the pump in the kitchen sink," Dad said. "That way, we'll have nice cold water from the well to drink and cook with."

Right about then, a glass of cold water sounded pretty good to me. I craned my neck to look at the camp door. "Is Mom inside?"

"No, she went down around the bend to do a little fishing," Dad said. "After you left, we got into a discussion about fishing and I said it's a common fact men are much better fishermen than women. She told me I was wrong and then bet me a dollar she could catch a fish within the next twenty minutes. So I gave her my fishing rod and told her the bet was on!"

My eyebrows arched. "You actually let her use your precious new rod and reel?"

"She'll be careful with it," he said. "I trust her."

Janet climbed the porch steps and held the door open for my dad and his bucket. I suspected she was as eager as I was to get that pump primed so we could guzzle some cool water. All of the running we'd done would have been enough to work up a thirst, but running on a dusty road had made my mouth so dry, my tongue was sticking to the roof of it.

Just as Dad took a step toward the door, a high-pitched scream pierced the air. Dad stopped dead, turned, dropped the bucket and ran toward the scream. Janet and I followed him.

My mother, wearing a green-and-pink-plaid sleeveless housedress and dainty black shoes, came running up over the hill that led down to the portion of the river at the far end of the property. She still was screaming. The minute she spotted my dad, she ran over to him and threw her arms around him. "I caught a big, black ugly snake!" she cried. "Ohmigod! It was horrible!"

Dad, knowing how much she feared snakes, wrapped his big arms around her and patted her on the back in an effort to calm her. "There, there, now," he said, "everything is okay. You're safe now. I'm pretty sure you caught a freshwater eel, though, not a snake."

"It looked like a huge, slimy snake!" she said, choking back tears. "I got so scared when I saw it, I just dropped everything and ran!"

My dad stopped patting her back and pulled away from her so he could look at her face. "Uh…where is my rod and reel?"

"You should have seen that snake!" Mom turned to look at Janet and me. "It was big and fat and shiny black! And it wiggled so hard, it was like someone cracking a bullwhip!"

My dad put his hands on her shoulders and turned her back toward him. "Where is my new rod and reel?" He carefully enunciated every word.

Mom looked down at her feet and cleared her throat. "I, um, flung everything as far out into the river as I could and ran."

Dad looked as if he might be on the verge of having a heart attack. His right hand flew up to his chest and he slowly repeated, "You threw my new fishing rod into the river…with a big eel still attached to it?"

Still looking at her feet, Mom nodded.

Dad dashed off and disappeared over the hill. Within seconds, we could hear a lot splashing, followed by a stream of words that Mom often had preached to me never to use because only vile and vulgar people used them.

"I guess that losing his fishing rod has turned Dad into a vile and vulgar person, huh?" I said to my mother. She was so busy staring in the direction where Dad had gone, she didn't even hear me.

Several minutes later, Dad came back up over the hill. His pants were soaked up to his hips, and his shirtsleeves up to his armpits, apparently from reaching into the water in search of his rod and reel. The expression on his face warned us not ask him if he'd found anything – not unless we wanted to wind up treading water with the leeches.

As he stomped past us, his shoes squished with each step, and he left a trail of water behind him. He retrieved the bucket he'd dropped and went back down to the river to refill it.

"Do you think he's mad at me?" my mother asked me as her eyes followed him.

"Nah, he's just mad at the dumb eel for swimming off with his fishing pole." Even as I said it, I didn't believe a word of it, but I wanted to make my mom feel better.

"Maybe it wasn't an eel or a snake," Janet, who up until that point had been silent, said. "Maybe it was a giant killer leech!"

That did it. I'd had just about enough of rustic, country living. Mom and Dad could keep their brown water, their leeches, snakes, fishing-rod-stealing eels, blanket-eating mice, mosquitoes and birds that made ca-coo-coo-coo sounds. I was ready to pack my bags and hitchhike back to the city. I wanted concrete, sidewalks, traffic, noisy neighbors and corner stores that sold penny candy and ice cream. But the main reason why I wanted to leave at that very moment was because my bladder was about to burst. I couldn't stall a minute longer. I had to use the outhouse.

"I'll be back in a minute," I said. "I gotta *go*."

I followed the narrow, winding path through the bushes to the outhouse. It wasn't one of those tall, skinny outhouses with a crescent moon on the door, like the ones I'd seen in cartoons. This one was short and wide and didn't even have a door to put a crescent moon on. I guess my dad thought the bushes would

25

hide everything. That was fine while the bushes still had leaves on them, but come autumn, I figured the squirrels were going to be treated to a free show.

The outhouse was old and weathered and the boards, gray and rotting. Inside, there was a long bench-type seat with a hole cut in the middle of it. The board easily could have fit one, maybe even two more holes, but frankly, I thought it would be a waste of holes. I mean, I couldn't picture myself sitting next to my mom and Janet and engaging in friendly conversation while we did our duties.

Next to the hole sat a roll of toilet paper and a bucket of sand. The sand was supposed to be used to bury the evidence and smother the smell so it wouldn't attract swarms of flies. Dad referred to it as "the dry flush." Feeling more than slightly apprehensive, I peered down into the hole before I sat on it. I didn't want anything crawling up out of there and biting me on the butt cheek.

I shouldn't have peeked. In the deep hole was a pile of sand with toilet paper sticking out of it. The paper was stained and there already were a few flies sitting on it. I grabbed the bucket and dumped half of the sand down into the hole, hoping to smother anything that might be living.

Finally, I dropped my shorts and panties and sat down. Sitting on a hard, flat board not only was uncomfortable, I was worried about slivers. At the very least, I thought, Mom should have bought a toilet seat to put on the hole so it would have been more comfortable. Still, as Janet's dad would have said, I had enough lard on my butt to cushion the board, unlike poor, bony Janet who didn't even have butt cheeks. In fact, she was so thin, I was worried she might fall right through the hole when she sat on it.

I wanted to break a record for the world's fastest pee and get the heck out of there, but I experienced something I usually experienced only in public restrooms when I knew someone was standing there listening – pee freeze. No matter how hard I tried, nothing came out.

As I sat there, praying for relief, I noticed a hornets' nest in the upper right corner of the outhouse, and a big spider web in the left. The web had a dead hornet in the center of it. Actually, it appeared to be just the shell of a dead hornet, as if its insides had been sucked out. I imagined the spider had to be a pretty big one to do that kind of damage to a wasp.

The pee flowed like a river after that. My shorts still were down around my ankles when I bolted out of the outhouse.

I nearly ran into Janet, who was heading down the path. "I gotta go, too," she said.

"Be sure to hang on tight to the sides when you sit down!" I said.

My dad spent most of the afternoon searching for his fishing rod. He'd once told me that the river emptied into Great Bay near Portsmouth, so my guess was my mother's screams had scared the poor eel so badly, it probably was making a beeline for the ocean.

Janet and I tried to help my dad with his search. We walked along the banks of the river and looked for any signs of a rod or tangled fishing line, but we didn't find anything.

"Look!" Janet suddenly exclaimed. She bent over and picked up something from the water's edge. I prayed it was a clue that would lead us to solve the case of the missing fishing rod. "It's a cute frog!"

She opened her cupped hands to show me the plump, brownish frog with black spots. It didn't seem the least bit frightened of us.

"I'm going to keep him as a pet," Janet said. "Let's find something to put him in!"

"You can't keep a frog as a pet," I said. "They eat live flies…still-flying flies. You want to have to catch a bunch of dirty old flies every day for him? You want to have to hang out in the outhouse to catch them?"

Janet stroked the frog's shiny head with her index finger and frowned. "No, I guess not. But I don't want to let him go, either. I mean, I'll probably never see him again if I do. I think I'm going to call him Butchy!"

"Butchy will be better off in the river. He likes it there."

"He likes me, too!" Janet said. It was more of a whine than a statement. Suddenly, her face brightened. "I've got it! I'll tie his leg to a long piece of string and then tie the other end to a tree right along the riverbank. Then he can still swim and catch flies, and when I want him, all I'll have to do is pull in the string! That way, he can still be my pet!"

27

It sounded like a good idea to me. We tracked down a spool of twine in the storage shed. Janet cut off about a fifteen-foot length of it and tied one end around Butchy's leg. She tied the other end around the base of a pine tree near the edge of the river. When she set Butchy on the ground, he hopped into the river and disappeared beneath the water. As a test, Janet pulled on the twine and Butchy's little head surfaced.

"Cool!" she said. "Now he can have everything he needs and I can still play with him every day. I can untie him and carry him around with me, then put him back on his leash at night."

"Did you find my fishing rod?" Dad's hopeful voice came from behind us. He probably thought Janet had discovered some of his fishing line when he saw her yanking on the twine.

"Nope. Just catching frogs," I said.

He sighed. "Well, if you catch enough of them, we can have frogs' legs for supper. They taste just like chicken, you know. And it sure looks like we won't be having any trout for a while!" I knew he was teasing, but the look on Janet's face told me she wasn't at all amused at the prospect of someone de-legging her pet frog for dinner. It was apparent she already had developed a strong bond with Butchy. I had a feeling that the frog, especially now that he was on a leash, was taking the place of the dog Janet's parents never allowed her to have, despite her endless begging. I was willing to bet she was going to try to teach Butchy how to sit up and roll over.

"Well, I guess I'll give up the search for now and go start a fire in the barbecue," Dad said. "If you guys aren't going to catch enough frogs for supper, we'll have to settle for hot-dogs and burgers." He glanced up at the sky. "Hard to believe, but it'll be getting dark pretty soon. Where'd the day go?"

I hadn't really thought much about the darkness until Dad mentioned it. My bedroom back home was right underneath a streetlight, so when I woke up in the middle of the night, I usually could see everything in the room, like my doll collection and my pin-ups of Bobby Rydell, Ricky Nelson and the Everly Brothers. But the bedroom here (a.k.a. the kitchen) was underneath a bunch of trees. I realized I was about to learn the true meaning of the words "pitch dark."

28

"I wish we could leave at least one light on tonight when we go to bed," I said to Janet as I watched her put Butchy back into the river. "I think it's going to be creepy here at night."

"The only lights you have here are candles and kerosene lamps," Janet said. "I don't think I'd trust leaving one of those burning while I'm asleep. Plus that, the flickering would drive me nuts. Even when your eyes are closed, you can still tell when stuff is flickering."

She had a point.

An hour later, after we'd stuffed ourselves with hot dogs and hamburgers and had toasted about a hundred marshmallows on sharpened branches we'd held over the fire in the barbecue, Janet and I went inside for the night. We sat at the kitchen table and played card games like Old Maid and solitaire by kerosene lamplight until nine o'clock. Never in a million years did I think such words ever would come out of my mouth, but I heard myself saying, "I'm tired. I'm going to bed."

My parents' expressions did little to conceal their shock. Ever since the day I was born, I had been nocturnal. As a baby, I'd slept all day and screamed all night, which often caused my sleep-deprived parents to walk around looking as if they'd been embalmed. When I started school and had to be in bed by eight o'clock, I never fell asleep before midnight. I'd just lie there, wide awake, until I got so bored, I'd get up for a drink of water or to go to the bathroom. And the more water I drank, the more I had to go to the bathroom. One night, I got up twelve times. Only when my mother threatened to take me to a kidney specialist did I finally stay in bed.

But there was something about this place that made me sleepy. Maybe it was the fresh air, or all of the exercise. Maybe it was the hypnotic flicker of the lamps. Whatever it was, it was making my eyelids feel as if they had anchors attached to them.

I washed my face and brushed my teeth with water from the hand pump. As I pumped a glass of the clear, ice-cold water so I could rinse my mouth, I was tempted to chug it right down. I'd made a point of drinking very little liquid with my supper, so I was feeling pretty parched at that moment. Still, I vowed to stay thirsty until sunrise. There was no way I was going to let my bladder get full if it meant I'd have to get up in the middle of the night and walk down to that vermin -infested outhouse.

CHAPTER FOUR

"Pull!" *Blam!* "Pull!" *Blam!*

I sat up in bed, my head nearly hitting the low-hanging eave above the top bunk. "What the heck was that?"

"Somebody across the river must be skeet shooting," Dad's voice came from the bottom bunk. "The Rod and Gun Club is over there, and I've heard that the members like to shoot on Sundays, so it's probably them."

I tried to move to peer over the edge of the bed, but something was blocking me. It was Janet, sound asleep next to me and against the railing. When we'd gone to bed the night before, Janet had been on the bottom bunk. "How'd Janet get up here?"

Dad crawled out from the bottom bunk, stood up, stretched and yawned. "Your mom and I tried to sleep on that sofa bed, but it's hard as a brick and has a raised seam across the middle that dug into us. So we woke up Janet, asked her to move up to the top bunk with you, and we slept down here. You were dead to the world – didn't even budge. Believe me, this mattress sure is a lot more comfortable than that sofa!"

Maybe for them it was a lot more comfortable, I thought, but I had to sleep with Janet, who, at that moment was taking up a lot of room for a skinny kid. And being an only child, I wasn't used to sharing my bed with anyone.

"Are you and Mom going to be sleeping down there from now on?" I asked my father.

"'Fraid so," he said.

I shook Janet awake. We both climbed down from the bunk and, still in our pajamas, dashed outside. The morning air was humid and the sun already was promising to get hot enough to turn my Casper-like city skin into something that resembled red leather.

"Pull!" *Blam!* "Pull!" *Blam!*

I cast a look of disgust at the woods across the river. "I wish they'd finish shooting those skeet things, whatever they are, and get it over with."

"I think my dad once said that skeet are some kinda pigeons," Janet said.

I gasped. "They're shooting at pigeons?"

"I think he said they're fake pigeons that people toss up into the air."

As I stood there trying to picture what a bunch of bullet-ridden fake pigeons would look like, Janet turned her attention toward the water. "I sure hope all that noise doesn't scare Butchy," she said. "Let's go find him!"

We ran down to the tree where Butchy was tied. Janet grabbed the twine and pulled it, hand over hand, until the end of it finally emerged from a clump of bushes. Instead of Butchy, a big striped snake with a golf-ball sized lump in its middle lay at the end of the twine.

Our screams were so loud, the skeet shooters actually stopped shooting – probably because they thought they'd accidentally winged one of us with a stray bullet.

The camp door swung open and my parents came running out. My dad's face was covered with shaving cream and my mom was holding a spatula. I wasn't certain if she'd been cooking breakfast with it or if she intended to use it as a weapon.

Dad rushed over to us to see what was wrong. We pointed at the ground where the twine lay with the bulge-bellied snake attached to the end of it. "You caught a snake?" he asked.

The minute my dad uttered the word *snake*, my mom broke a speed record for the 100-yard dash in the opposite direction.

Janet vigorously shook her head. Tears sprang to her eyes. The only thing she managed to squeak out was, "B-Butchy."

"Butchy?" Dad repeated, his eyes making a quick sweep of the woods, as if he expected some ax murderer named Butchy to pop out.

"Butchy was her pet frog," I explained. "She tied him to a tree last night so he wouldn't get away. But when we went to get him just now, there was this big snake on the end of the line instead of Butchy! I think it's going to have a baby, too, because it's got a really fat belly!"

A look of realization crossed Dad's lather-covered face and for a moment, he looked as if he might laugh. He seemed to be struggling to keep a somber expression when he said, "You shouldn't have tied him to a tree. How could he hop away from a snake or any other predator? See what happened? The snake ate him. That big lump in his stomach isn't a baby...it's Butchy."

My dad was a firm believer in telling the truth, but in this particular instance, I had the feeling he probably shouldn't have been quite so blunt. Janet's complexion paled a few shades and her eyes grew to the size of dinner plates. "We have to get him out!" she cried. "Someone hold the snake so I can yank Butchy out of there!"

My dad looked up at the sky, as if he were praying for strength. "I think Butchy is dead, honey. There's no air in the snake's stomach for him to breathe. Why don't you two go on inside for breakfast and I'll get Butchy out of the snake ...and then the snake can be free to go back into the woods."

"Wahhhhhh!" was Janet's response. "It's my fault that Butchy is dead! I'm a frog murderer!"

* * * * *

Breakfast turned out to be a somber occasion that morning. Janet, who usually ate like a 300-pound trucker at every meal, sat with her left elbow propped on the table and her chin resting on her palm as she picked at her scrambled eggs. And even worse, she didn't even touch her four strips of crisp bacon. Every now and then she emitted a long, pitiful sigh, but other than that, she was silent. I knew I had to find some way to get her mind out of the "frog killer" mode, otherwise, this summer vacation was going to be worse torture than being back in school. I hadn't seen her this upset over the demise of a pet since the time her parakeet, Ty-Boy, had turned up dead in a pot of spaghetti on her kitchen stove. The poor bird apparently had flown head first into the wall behind the stove and then spiraled like a downed airplane...right into the bubbling pot of spaghetti. Janet had been inconsolable for weeks afterwards.

Well, I decided, I wasn't about to allow the Butchy incident to turn into a repeat of the Ty-Boy blues.

"Let's go explore the other end of the road today!" I said, displaying way too many teeth.

Janet didn't respond.

"Maybe we can find a new place to swim," I continued.

Still nothing.

"Or a store that sells ice cream!"

I finally had her attention. She shrugged. "I guess so."

We put on our bathing suits, shoved on shorts and T-shirts over them, grabbed our beach towels (just in case we happened to run across a kid with a built-in, leech-free swimming pool) and headed off to explore.

"Do you think Butchy suffered?" Janet asked as we slowly walked down the dirt road. Her posture – her shoulders slumped and her head hanging – reminded me of a condemned prisoner's as he was being led to the electric chair.

Visions of Butchy being swallowed whole and slowly digested by the snake's stomach acid made me feel like upchucking my breakfast. I wanted to tell Janet that yes, the poor frog on her dumb piece of twine had suffered a slow and agonizingly painful death, but instead I said, "Nah. I think the snake that swallowed him is the kind that bites its victims first to paralyze them so they don't feel a thing.'"

Actually, I was pretty sure the snake I'd just described lived only in the jungles of Borneo somewhere, but I prayed that Janet didn't know that.

"Well, as long as he didn't feel any pain, I guess that's not so bad," she said.

"You know what? I think Butchy already was sick when you caught him. I mean, he was too easy to catch. The snake probably would have caught him anyway, whether he was tied to the tree or not."

Janet's head finally rose and her face brightened. "I think you're right! He didn't put up a fight at all when I caught him!"

I suppressed a smile of satisfaction. Maybe the day wasn't going to be a total loss after all.

By the time we walked a half-mile to nearly the end of the road, I began to worry we were the last two kids on the planet. We'd seen a squirrel and two chipmunks during our trek, but other than that, only trees, dirt and rocks. When we finally reached the Harmons' farmhouse, I prayed someone would be outside, just so I could see humans again. I was desperate to say hello to or wave at some living thing that didn't have four legs. But the Harmons' house showed no signs of life. I was pretty sure everyone inside, including the dog, probably was suffering from boredom-induced comas.

When Janet and I came to Willow Ridge Road, an actual two-lane asphalt road, and we saw cars going by, we acted as if we'd been lost at sea for a few months and finally had returned to civilization.

"Look! A motorcycle!" Janet squealed as a shiny Harley roared past us.

"Should we go left or right?" I asked.

We stood on the side of the road and gazed right. Trees. We gazed left. Houses.

"Left!" we said in unison.

Janet and I walked in a single file along the side of the road because there wasn't room for us to walk two abreast; not unless we wanted to get picked off by a speeding car. I enjoyed the sounds of the cars and even the smell of diesel fuel when a truck passed us. And I especially enjoyed looking at the houses, even though no people were outside.

When a couple of the cars' horns beeped as they sped past, I told myself it was because we were sexy looking and the drivers were flirting, not because we were walking too close to the traffic.

Finally, as we rounded a curve, I spotted something moving on the lawn in front of a Colonial-looking white house on the other side of the road. It was a big black dog. In fact, it was so big, it resembled a bear. The dog was running loose in the yard, and the moment it spotted us, it launched into a series of barks and growls so vicious, it sounded just like Lon Chaney, Jr. when he'd transformed into a werewolf.

"Look straight ahead and keep walking," I said over my shoulder to Janet. "Don't make eye contact with him. He probably won't run across the road anyway. There's too much traffic."

No sooner did I utter the words, did the traffic disappear. Janet seized the vehicle-free opportunity to move up next to me and together, our shoulders touching, we walked quickly and stiffly. I heard the dog's barking growing louder and more frenzied. It also got closer. Soon, the barking was directly behind us.

"Walk a little faster," I said to Janet out of the corner of my mouth.

"I-I can't." Her voice barely was a whisper.

"Why not?"

"Because the dog is attached to the seat of my shorts."

I stopped to look. Sure enough, there was a big black dog with its teeth sunk into the back of Janet's shorts, which, luckily, were so baggy (because she was too thin to even come close to filling them), the dog hadn't been able to grab any of her flesh. He was doing a pretty mean job of tugging on the shorts, though.

I prayed that the dog wouldn't decide Janet was such slim pickings, he'd switch over to my shorts. Mine were so tight, the beast would be all but guaranteed to taste a big chunk of butt meat.

A sharp whistle, apparently from the dog's owner, made the mutt release its grip on Janet and dart back home. I made a quick check of the back of her shorts. There were two holes in the tan cloth, but to my relief, no blood was gushing out of them. The minute the dog was out of sight, we ran as fast as our legs would carry us. We didn't stop running until our lungs threatened to burst.

"How are we going to get back to the camp?" Janet asked through gasps. "I don't want to walk by that dog again! I bet he has rabies!"

"You're not the only one," I said, wheezing.

In the past two days, I'd done more running than I'd done in my entire life. The last time I'd run this fast in the city was the day I'd bolted two blocks to catch up with the ice-cream truck. I could feel the sweat running down my back and forming a pool in the bottom of my swimsuit.

"Maybe we can hitchhike back," Janet said. "I'll bet someone would give us a ride."

"Yeah, and with our luck, it would be Jack the Ripper's great-grandson."

We were too exhausted to move so we just stood in a shallow gully on the side of the road, neither one of us speaking as we tried to catch our breaths. That's when we heard a sound that made both of us stop gasping and lift our heads.

It was the sound of kids laughing and shouting.

We stared wide-eyed at each other. The laughter grew louder. Somewhere, someone was having fun…without us.

"Up ahead!" Janet said. "Let's go!"

We followed the sounds to a dirt driveway in the woods on the other side of the road.

"You think we should follow it?" Janet asked. "What if it leads to someone's front lawn and they're having a private party?"

"Then I hope they have some extra food!" I said. "Let's go!"

We followed the path for about 75 yards and came to a clearing. In the middle of it sat a small variety store. There were pictures of Popsicles and Fudgesicles in the window, and a Coca-Cola sign out front with an image of a frosty-looking bottle of Coke on it. We stood motionless, just staring at the pictures.

"I think I've had too much sun," I said to Janet. "I'm hallucinating."

"I think I'm having the same hallucination," she said.

I felt saliva – what little was left of it, my mouth was so dry – oozing from the corner of my mouth.

"You have any money on you?" Janet asked.

I shook my head. "What the heck is a store doing out here in the middle of nowhere anyway?"

Squeals and a chorus of laughter, followed by a series of splashing sounds, came from the woods behind the store, as if to answer my question. Janet and I moved closer to the sounds. There, through a gap in the trees, we spotted something that caused our mouths to fall open. It was a pond. And in that pond, groups of people were playing and swimming and obviously having a great time.

I suddenly felt as if we had stumbled upon Arrowwood's equivalent of Disneyland.

There was a path to the right of the store that looked as if it led down to the pond. With renewed energy, spurred by our

36

desire to cool our sweaty bodies, Janet and I raced each other down to the pond.

A hill covered with pine trees sloped into the section of the water where everyone was swimming. Beneath the trees, people had spread out an assortment of towels, blankets, coolers and picnic baskets. From what I could tell, there probably were about twenty people there. Janet and I found a shady spot between two pines, laid our beach towels on a bed of pine needles and plunked down.

"What if this is someone's private property and all of these people are the owner's relatives?" Janet asked me.

"Then they'll probably throw us out," I said. "But maybe if we act like we belong here, we'll blend in and can at least get in a swim before they call the cops on us."

Janet and I stared at the people who were swimming. There were several young kids floating around on inflated inner tubes, an older man stretched out on an air mattress, and a group of four kids – three boys and a girl – who looked about our age, standing in waist-deep water and playing catch with a striped beach ball. One of the guys in the beach-ball group instantly caught my eye. He was tall, deeply tanned, slim – but solidly built, and had short black hair.

"That dark-haired guy is kinda cute," I said to Janet.

Her eyes also were riveted on the group. "I think the guy with the long, dirty-blond hair is cuter," she said.

As if they had ESP, or super-sensitive hearing, the group of beach-ball tossers stopped tossing and turned to look at us.

"Uh oh," Janet whispered. "We've been spotted."

"Smile at them." I flashed my warmest smile at the group. "They can't be too mean to us if we act friendly."

Janet smiled, too, but her smile was aimed directly at the blondish guy she thought was cute. The group, the three guys and the girl, gathered closer together in the water and, in a football-huddle sort of way, engaged in a discussion. Every few seconds, one of them would turn to look at us and then rejoin the conversation.

"No doubt about it," I said. "They're talking about us."

"Not anymore." Janet nodded in their direction. "They're heading this way."

I sucked in my breath as the quartet emerged from the water. The girl, who was wearing a white T-shirt and cut-off jeans that were so short, the pockets hung down below the raveled leg edges, set down the beach ball by a tree and then rushed ahead of the three guys. I couldn't help but notice that although she looked as if she might be younger than we were, she already had apple-sized breasts, which clearly were visible – too visible – through her dripping T-shirt.

The girl was the first to reach us. "Hi," she said, smiling. "I'm Tweaky."

The three guys had stopped walking.

"I'm Janet, and that's Sally," Janet said. "Does your family own this place?"

Tweaky laughed. "This is Cutter's, the public swimming hole. Everyone hangs out here in the summer. I take it you guys aren't from around here?"

"We're from the city," I said. "But we're staying at my parents' camp over on Shepherdess Road."

"That little red and white place?" she asked. When I nodded, she said, "I always thought it was abandoned. Never saw anyone there before."

"Well, there's someone there now," I said. "Unfortunately."

Tweaky sat down on the ground in front of us. The way she sat, with her knees bent and her legs spread apart, made me think she was more guy-like than girl-like. She rested her arms on her knees and stared at us for a moment. "See those guys behind me?" she said. "The fat one is my brother, Jake. The dark one is Conrad and the other one is Scott."

"Is one of them your boyfriend?" Janet asked. I could tell she was trying to sound casual, but there was an air of desperation in her voice.

Tweaky's nose crinkled. "Heck, no." She shook her head and a shower of water flew off her shoulder-length brown hair. "But I happen to know that Scott and Conrad think you're both pretty cute."

She had our full attention.

"In fact, they sent me over here," she said, "to see if you might want to meet them."

I looked past her and at Conrad. He was wearing a very tight black swimsuit that clung to him like a second skin. My eyes

38

lingered so long on that swimsuit, when I finally raised them to look up at Conrad's face, there was an unmistakable look of amusement on it. I thought for sure my face was going to burst into flames.

"Sure! We'd love to meet them!" I heard Janet saying.

I froze. I had no idea what to say to a cool guy, especially one who actually thought I was cute when I was all sweaty and sticky and could afford to lose about 20 pounds. I found myself wishing I'd at least brought a mirror and a comb with me so I could spruce up a bit, particularly after having just run the dog-attack marathon.

"Scott, Conrad," Tweaky said when the two approached, "this is Janet and that's Sally. They're here from the city, staying at that little camp on Shepherdess Road."

Scott flashed a big smile at Janet. He had a broken front tooth, which, combined with his round face, gave him a jack-o-lantern sort of look. The way Janet blushed and giggled, however, led me to suspect she barely even noticed.

I said hi to Conrad, and he nodded at me, his dark eyes looking directly into mine. I had to remind myself to breathe.

"Want to go for a swim?" Scott asked us. "The water's great!"

"Any leeches in there?" Janet asked. She pointed to the scab on her foot. "I was attacked by a giant leech in the river yesterday."

"There's probably some in there," Scott said. "But don't worry, I'll protect you."

Janet was out of her shorts and shirt and down to her black-and-white striped swimsuit so fast, she probably wouldn't have cared if anacondas were lurking at the bottom of the pond, just so long as she could be in it with Scott.

I slipped out of my clothes to reveal my navy-blue woolen swimsuit with red and white stripes across the top and along the criss-crossed straps. There even was a padded bra concealed inside that gave me a couple extra curves. From the corner of my eye, I caught a glimpse of Conrad staring at me...from head to toe.

"All set?" he asked me, extending his hand.

"I'm a lousy swimmer," I warned him, hesitating before I allowed my hand to slip into his. I thought his hand felt pretty hot and clammy for a guy who'd just come out of the water. "I can barely do the dog paddle."

"Well, I'm a great swimmer," he said. "When I was a kid, they used to call me Tadpole, because I was in the water so much. So you have nothing to worry about." He flashed me a broad smile.

That's when I saw it...the most hideous, shocking sight I'd ever had the misfortune of seeing. Conrad's front teeth were so decayed, they looked like a row of black-eyed peas. I, who, ever since I was old enough to grow teeth, had been forced, kicking and screaming, to visit the dentist every six months, couldn't hide my revulsion.

Conrad noticed. "I got hit in the mouth with a Coke bottle when I was younger," he explained. "Really messed up my teeth."

Coke bottle or not, it still didn't change the way he looked or the way I felt about his smile. As far as I was concerned, all of his previous cuteness had vanished. And unfortunately, at age twelve, going on thirteen, cuteness was very important to me.

Conrad tightened his grasp on my hand. "Come on! Let's go swimming!"

I opened my mouth to protest, but he and Scott began to run down the hill, dragging Janet and me behind them. I stubbed my bare toe on a tree root and stumbled forward, but Conrad jerked me to my feet just before I landed on my face. I couldn't help but think that if I had fallen, I might have banged my front teeth and ended up with a smile that matched Conrad's – or at the very least, Scott's.

Janet and I hit the water simultaneously with a resounding splash. We both let out screams that were loud enough to waken poor, departed Butchy back at the camp. Janet's scream, however, was more like a squeal of delight. There was nothing delightful about mine.

The water, which also had the same brown tint as the water back at the camp, felt as if it had been siphoned from glaciers. I could have sworn I saw a cloud of steam rise from my overheated body the second it hit the water. My feet sank into mud up to my ankles.

"This mud feels so disgusting squishing between my toes," I said to Conrad. "It's like standing in a giant bowl of chocolate pudding!"

He laughed, his mouth wide open, which made me wish I hadn't said anything funny.

I glanced over at Scott and Janet, who already were involved in a dunking match. If Conrad tried to dunk me, I thought, I'd yank my foot out of the mud and give him a kick right in his tight swimsuit. But he turned out to be a perfect gentleman. He gave me swimming lessons, his hand at my waist, guiding me. He taught me how to hold my breath and swim under the water, which he said was the easiest way to swim.

"Open your eyes while you're under there," he said, as I was about to submerge again. "It looks really cool."

I waited until my body sank to the bottom of the pond before I opened my eyes. I saw mud and rocks and a scum-covered beer bottle. I clamped my eyes shut again.

I didn't get out of the water until my skin began to look like cheesecloth and my teeth were chattering. I ran up to my towel, grabbed it and wrapped it around my shoulders, then sat down on a tree root. My eyes scanned the water for Janet, but I didn't see her. I silently prayed that Scott hadn't accidentally drowned her.

Conrad, wiping his face with a towel, walked up to me.

"When I find Janet, I guess we'd better head back to the camp," I said to him. "My parents have no idea where we are and I'm getting hungry. Plus that, it's a long walk back."

"Two miles, to be exact," he said. "And I live another couple miles from there, on Red Oak Road."

"You walk eight miles round-trip just to come swimming here?"

He shrugged. "The only way to get around out here if you're not old enough to drive is to walk or ride a bike...or a horse, if you have one."

"During your travels, have you ever met up with a big black dog that likes to bite the seats of pants?" I asked.

He laughed. "I've seen lots of dogs that do that around here."

"Well, there's this big one that chased us when we walked over here, so now we're scared to walk back."

"Don't worry," he said. "I'll walk you home. I'm not afraid of dogs."

Immediately I realized I shouldn't have opened my big mouth about the dog. The thought of Conrad walking me to my door and maybe wanting a kiss as his reward was even worse than the thought of losing a piece of butt cheek to the attack dog.

"All done swimming?" Janet's voice came from somewhere behind me.

I turned around. She and Scott were standing close together, drinking Cokes. "Want a sip?" she asked me.

I shook my head. Coke always made me belch, and when I belched, it was louder than any man's. In fact, one time when I'd belched at home while standing behind my mother as she was washing the dishes, I startled her so much, she'd dropped a dish and snapped at me, "Will you please go erupt someplace else!"

The thought did cross my mind that a well-aimed belch might turn off Conrad, but I didn't want the other people around me to think I was a pig.

"I'm starving!" I said to Janet. "Are you ready to head back to the camp?"

I could tell by her expression that she wasn't. But when Scott added, "Yeah, I'm going to be heading home, too. I still have chores to do," she instantly picked up her clothes from the ground and started shoving them on.

Tweaky, Conrad, Scott, Janet and I headed back toward the camp. Tweaky's brother, Jake, decided to take another route – a much shorter one, he said – up some road called Wyatt Road.

I tried to walk next to Tweaky, but every time I got near her, Conrad wedged between us and she'd fall behind, probably because she thought I wanted to be next to him. When we passed the killer dog's house, there wasn't any sign of the beast anywhere. I frowned. Janet and I hadn't needed protection after all, which meant I was stuck walking another mile with Conrad for nothing. Judging from Janet's animated chatter as she and Scott walked behind us, however, she actually was enjoying being escorted back to the camp.

At least that made one of us.

CHAPTER FIVE

"Tweaky should wear a bra," my mother said at supper that night. She, my dad, Janet and I were gathered around the picnic table, which was heaped with plates of hot dogs, baked beans and potato salad. I silently questioned my mother's choice of serving beans, especially since I had to share a bunk with Janet, the queen of gaseousness.

"I don't even think she knows what a bra is," I said. "And she probably doesn't care."

"Well, if she's going to hang around with boys all the time," my mother said, "her chest shouldn't be bouncing all over the place like that. And what kind of name is Tweaky anyway? Doesn't she have a real name?"

"I have no clue," I said.

"It's Eleanor," Janet said. "Scott told me."

"Well, never mind bras," my dad added. "Don't they have any dentists around here?" He held the ketchup bottle upside down over his beans and pounded the bottom of it with the heel of his hand. "Those two guys who walked you home today sure could use one."

"I think Conrad said he has something like twelve brothers and sisters," I said. "They probably can't afford a dentist."

"Well, I think Scott would be cute even if he had no teeth at all," Janet stopped chewing long enough to say. "And I think the four of us are going to have lots of fun while we're here."

"*Four* of us?" I repeated.

"Yeah, you and Conrad and me and Scott. It's going to be a blast!"

I nearly choked on my hot dog. "Whoa – wait just a second! I don't plan on ever seeing Conrad again! He seems like a nice enough guy and all, but he's not my type, so I certainly don't need him hanging around with us for the next two weeks."

Janet looked as if I'd just slapped her. "You *have* to like Conrad! If you treat him mean and he gets mad and doesn't come back, then Scott won't come back, either! You wouldn't do that to me, your best friend, would you? Besides that, it's only a couple weeks, not six months!"

"Well, if you were my friend, you wouldn't make me suffer with some guy I don't even like!"

"Just give him a chance," Janet said. "For all you know, he may end up being your future husband! Lots of people who can't stand each other when they first meet end up falling in love."

I rolled my eyes. "Fat chance of that ever happening. The only person Conrad should marry is the tooth fairy."

"Now, now, be nice," my mother said. "If you can't say something nice about someone, then you shouldn't say anything at all."

I stuck my fork into a chunk of mayonnaise-covered potato. "Then I guess I'm going to be quiet a lot."

Nine o'clock that evening, after playing about 45 rip-roaring games of solitaire, the numbers on the cards on the table began to blur. My mom was out in the kitchen, rearranging the dishes, pots and pans for the umpteenth time. Dad was sitting in the rocking chair near the woodstove and had his nose buried in a book. I figured it was another Western because those were his favorites. Actually, Dad was so hooked on reading, he would read anything you put in front of him. He'd practically memorized every word on the backs of the cereal boxes, and he never went to the bathroom unless he was armed with a stack of reading material. Even the outhouse now had a pile of *Popular Mechanics* magazines lying on the board next to the hole. I couldn't imagine anyone wanting to sit down there long enough to read anything. In fact when I'd first spotted the stack of magazines, I was horror-stricken, thinking my parents had gone completely primitive and wanted us to use the pages for toilet paper.

"I'm exhausted," I said to Janet. "I think I'm going to go to bed. All of the running and swimming we did today was more exercise than I've had in my entire life. My legs are sore."

45

"I guess I'll go to bed, too, then," Janet said. She hesitated before she added, "After all, Conrad and Scott will be here to get us at nine sharp."

Immediately, I was wide awake. "What are you talking about?"

"Scott said they want to give us a tour of where everyone lives and their favorite places to hang out and stuff, so I said okay."

I cast her my very best I-want-to-leap-across-the-table-and-strangle-you look before I whined, "I don't want to be stuck with them all day! Especially from early in the morning! We'll never get rid of them!"

Janet threw down the cards in her hand and shot me a look of unmistakable defiance. "Well, I'm *glad* to be stuck with them! At least it's better than staring at a bunch of trees and squirrels all day, or sitting around swatting mosquitoes!"

I couldn't argue with that. Maybe Conrad and Scott weren't Ricky Nelson and Johnny Crawford, but, and I hated to admit it, being with them at least would be more exciting than counting bug bites.

"Well, next time, ask me before you start making plans, okay?"

Janet nodded.

"Oh!" I said, "I nearly forgot to write in my diary! I can't go to bed until I do that!" I reached into my big black handbag, which was sitting on the edge of the table, and pulled out a small pink book with a padlock on it. I retrieved the key and a pen from a zippered compartment inside the purse, then opened the diary and began to write in it.

"You're always writing in that thing," Janet said. "Why?"

"Because fifty years from now, I want to be able to read what I did on this exact day back when I was twelve. Think of how cool that will be! It'll be like having a time machine!"

Janet looked deep in thought for a moment. "That does sound pretty cool. I mean, when it's the year 2000 and we're sitting in a restaurant on the moon, eating our meals of little dried-up cubes of stuff instead of real food, we can look back at your diary and remember the day we ate Franco-American spaghetti! I think maybe I'll start keeping a diary, too." A lovesick sort of smile slowly spread across her face. "And now that I've met Scott, I'll actually have something interesting to write about!"

I finished writing a sentence about my first impression of Conrad and how it had changed when he'd smiled. I frowned at the page. "On second thought, maybe I won't want to read this again fifty years from now."

I dug into my handbag and pulled out a small, spiral-bound yellow notebook and a pencil and handed them to Janet. "Here, start writing."

Janet grabbed the notebook and pencil and immediately began to scribble something on the first page. Her lovesick expression grew worse with each word she wrote. My expression grew more nauseated.

* * * * *

I sat up in bed and opened my eyes. I thought it was morning, but the total blackness that greeted me told me it wasn't. I groaned. My stomach was making gurgling sounds that made it impossible for me to deny the inevitable. I had to go to the bathroom. I silently cursed myself for eating those darned beans.

"Janet!" I whispered, giving the body lying next to me a gentle shake. "Wake up! I have to go to the outhouse!"

Janet muttered something unintelligible and rolled over, still asleep. I shook her again, this time more frantically. "Janet! Come down to the outhouse with me!"

Still, she didn't budge. I gave up and climbed down from the bunk.

"Dad!" My voice was soft but urgent as I leaned into the bottom bunk. I poked him on the shoulder. "I have to go to the bathroom!"

It was so dark, I couldn't tell if his eyes were open or closed. "Take my flashlight. It's on top of the fridge," his froggy voice finally said.

"No! You have to come with me! I'm scared!"

He sighed. "Honey, you're a big girl now and there's nothing to be afraid of. Any animal out there is much more afraid of you than you are of it, believe me."

I very much doubted that statement.

I would have continued to whine until someone escorted me down to the outhouse, but my stomach had other ideas. There was no time to waste, not unless I wanted to spend the rest of the night cleaning up an accident on the middle of the kitchen floor.

I felt my way over to the refrigerator, reached up for the flashlight, and then turned it on so I could find my slippers. I shoved my feet into them, grabbed my bathrobe and headed out the door.

The woods were black and silent…too silent, I thought. I stood on the top step for a moment, trying to gather the courage to walk down the narrow path. A familiar high-pitched hum in my ear told me the mosquitoes were hungry and probably had rung the dinner bell the moment I set foot outside. I decided I'd better get moving, and the faster the better.

My slippered feet flew down the winding path to the building of doom. I aimed the flashlight at the ground so I wouldn't trip over a rock or tree root. I didn't dare shine it into the woods because I was certain the light would make all of the beady little eyes I just knew were watching me, glow in the dark.

By the time I reached the doorway of the rickety, dark building, my breath was coming in gasps, not because I was out of breath, but because I was so scared, I'd forgotten to breathe. I used the flashlight to make a quick sweep across the hole to make sure nothing was sticking up out of it before I dropped my pajama bottoms and sat down. Not wanting to illuminate myself just in case there were any starving animals or those pervert guys Mom was always warning me about, lurking in the bushes, I turned off the flashlight.

As I sat there, a feeling I wasn't alone in the outhouse suddenly swept over me. Although I didn't hear any distinct sounds like footsteps or breathing, I felt a sense of something moving…but I couldn't pinpoint exactly where. I considered turning on the flashlight and searching the nooks and crannies of the outhouse as I sat there, but quickly dismissed the thought. I was pretty sure I'd be better off not knowing what, if anything, was sharing the building with me.

"It's just your dumb imagination," I said out loud. "There's nothing in here." I didn't want to think logically at that point, because I knew if I did, logic would tell me that an outhouse without a door was like a four-star hotel for crawly and hairy things.

I felt around for the toilet paper and for a moment, thought I felt something like cold vinyl brush up against my hand. I wadded up a big ball of the paper and in my haste, wiped myself so hard, I was pretty sure I'd removed some of my skin. Then I leapt to my feet and yanked up my pajama bottoms with such force, I nearly sliced myself in half. I'd just stepped out of the door when I remembered I hadn't buried the evidence that now was lying at the bottom of the hole. The last thing I wanted was for my dad or Janet to come down to the outhouse in the morning and see the souvenir I'd left behind. Muttering, I grabbed the bucket of sand, dumped most of it into the hole – or at least what I hoped was the hole, it was so dark in there – and then slammed the bucket back down on the seat's board.

I didn't even bother to turn on the flashlight as I bolted out the door and back up to the camp.

When I entered the front room, I was so relieved, I nearly knelt down and kissed the braided rug. I stood with my back against the door and took several deep, calming breaths. *I did it!* I managed a tight smile. I'd gone to the outhouse by myself in the middle of the night and had lived to tell about it!

I walked into the kitchen. Now that I'd gone to the bathroom and was comfortable, I figured I could get at least a few good hours of sleep before I had to face Conrad. A hard-boiled egg odor greeted me. The beans must have taken their toll on the whole family, I thought, wrinkling my nose as I removed my robe.

When I reached up to put the flashlight back on top of the refrigerator, I realized the smell was stronger in that particular spot. It also started to become more familiar to me. I gasped. I recognized it from the time the pilot light had gone out on our stove back home. It was gas...and not the kind Janet passed.

"Dad!" I reached into the bottom bunk and shook him.

He groaned. "I told you...go down to the outhouse by yourself." His voice barely was audible.

"No, Dad! I think we have a gas leak!"

I felt him move to sit up. "Yeah, I can smell it. Get me the flashlight."

49

Dad took the flashlight from me, turned it on and then got out of bed to check the refrigerator. "The pilot light's out," he said. "You probably caused a draft and it blew out."

As he dug a book of matches out of the catch-all drawer so he could re-light the pilot light, I stood there wondering if he was right; that I somehow had caused a big enough breeze to blow it out and nearly asphyxiate my family and my friend. I could just see the newspaper headline now: *Family's Death Attributed to Swishing of Daughter's Hindenburg-Sized Butt.*

It was more likely, I thought, that Dad's wall-rattling snoring had blown out the pilot light. In the past, Mom and I had shared some good laughs over the way Dad snored. He would suck in his breath with a loud snort, and then when he let it out again, his lips would form a perfect circle and he'd make a high-pitched "poo-poo-poo" sound. One time, after Dad had dozed off in his chair, Mom had jokingly taken a piece of Cheerios cereal and when he made the "poo-poo-poo" sound, held it in front of his mouth and moved it with each "poo" to simulate someone blowing smoke rings. We'd laughed so hard, our stomachs hurt.

I held my breath as Dad prepared to light a match. I was certain the gas that had leaked out beforehand would ignite and blow the bunk beds right off the wall.

Aside from a quiet "poof," the pilot-lighting ceremony was pretty uneventful.

I climbed back up to my bunk and stretched out next to a still-sleeping, oblivious Janet. I'd had just about enough gas – both my own and the refrigerator's – for one night.

* * * * *

My father woke me the next morning. "Sally, did you finally go down to the outhouse last night?"

I sat up in bed and shook my head in an attempt to clear my fuzzy brain. The first thing I noticed was that Janet wasn't next to me. "Where's Janet?"

"She's already eating her cereal," Dad said.

Janet probably had gotten up with the birds, I thought, she was so anxious to see Scott.

"Did you go down to the outhouse last night?" Dad repeated.

"Yeah, I did, and all by myself, too, just like you told me to. Why?"

"Well, I was just down there and there's something really funny I think you should see!"

Immediately, my mind was filled with thoughts of what chuckle-inducing thing I could have done there last night in the pitch dark. Had I missed the hole? Left my panties on the floor? Did the end of the toilet paper roll get stuck in some crevice of my body and unroll all the way back to the camp?

"Can't you just tell me what's so funny?" I asked.

"No," Dad said. "I really think it's something you should see for yourself!"

My curiosity was piqued. I climbed down from the bunk, put on my slippers and robe and headed toward the door. I was going to invite Janet to join me, but then thought against it. If there was something embarrassing in the outhouse and she saw it, she'd be sure to tell Scott and Conrad about it, and I really didn't feel like being teased by them. Besides that, she seemed too engrossed in reading her *Little Lulu* comic book and shoveling Sugar Smacks into her mouth to care about whatever was down in the outhouse.

I approached the outhouse with caution, not certain what to expect. At least, to my relief, there was no trail of toilet paper leading from it. When I reached the doorway, I poked my head inside for a quick peek at the hole. It seemed fine, as far as stinky old holes went. I stepped inside for a better look. My eyes scanned the board.

"Ohmigod!" my hand flew up to my mouth. "Ohmigod!"

There, pinned underneath the bucket of sand, was a big black snake. Its tail began to whip back and forth as I approached. Apparently it had been on the board when I was down there the night before, and in my haste in the darkness, I'd set down the bucket right on top of it. I couldn't help but wonder what would have happened if I hadn't stood up from the seat when I had. Just the thought of a big old snake slithering across my naked lap sent me dashing back into the camp.

"This place is nothing but a snake pit!" I shouted, slamming the screen door behind me as I stomped inside. "Mom caught a snake while fishing, a snake ate Butchy, and now there's a snake in the outhouse…and I hate to think about what it was doing in there in the first place!"

My mother, who was standing at the stove and scrambling eggs, stopped scrambling. "Did you say there's a snake in the outhouse?"

"Yeah!" Dad said, laughing. "Sally went down there in the dark last night and apparently didn't even realize it was right there on the seat next to her. She ended up putting the bucket of sand down on it and pinning it to the board! When I went down there a few minutes ago, I couldn't believe it!"

My mother's expression did little to conceal the fact she didn't share Dad's amusement. "That does it!" she said. "From now on, we are putting a bucket on the porch at night. That will be our bathroom until daylight!"

"Fine with me," I said. "You're not going to catch me going anywhere near that outhouse again after dark!"

"Speaking of buckets, did you lift the bucket off the poor snake?" Dad asked me.

"Are you kidding? I'm not going near that thing!"

"I'll go let him loose then, before I head to work," Dad said. He glanced at his watch and shook his head. "Boy, I'm beginning to wonder if I should leave you girls here alone or not. Are you sure you're going to be okay without me all week?"

My mouth fell open. I'd completely forgotten that in a few minutes Dad would be leaving us to fend for ourselves in the wilderness. "No! We won't be okay!" I said. "What if another snake shows up inside the camp or something? Who'll get rid of it for us?"

"I'm sure Conrad or Scott could do it, no problem," Janet said with her mouth full of cereal.

"And how do you intend to get them over here to do it?" I snapped. "Send them a smoke signal?"

Mom brought a pan of steaming scrambled eggs to the table and began spooning them onto the blue and white plates she'd gotten as premiums from Grand Union supermarket. "Eat your breakfast now," she said to no one in particular. "And please, let's stop talking about snakes!"

* * * * *

52

Conrad arrived fifteen minutes early…and alone. He'd walked all the way from his house, over two miles, and the armpits on his yellow polo shirt showed it. They were soaked nearly down to his waist.

"Where's Scott?" Janet asked him without even saying hello first. She craned her neck to look past him.

"Well, his house is right next to Tweaky's, so we'll meet him there," Conrad said. "You have your bathing suits on? It's going to be a scorcher, and we can go swimming."

Janet and I had hoped he'd say that. We'd put on our swimsuits right after breakfast and had stuffed some money into the pockets of our shorts so we could buy ourselves a treat at the variety store. My mouth watered every time I thought about eating ice cream. It seemed like ten years since I'd last had any. Back in the city, the ice-cream truck came right by my tenement building every night at 6:30 sharp. And every night at 6:30, Janet and I were out there waiting for it. I was positive I'd sampled every item the truck carried.

The three of us, with Conrad walking between Janet and me, headed south on Shepherdess Road. Conrad and Janet did most of the talking as we walked. I heard bits and pieces of their conversation about Conrad being in the Boy Scouts and entering high school in the fall. But mostly I tuned them out. I wasn't the least bit interested in anything Conrad had to say, mainly because I wasn't the least bit interested in him. Janet was going to owe me one heck of a big favor, I thought, after this vacation.

"Those are the graves of two Minutemen," Conrad said as we passed two graves with small American flags on them. They were on the side of the road on a small hill with nothing but woods surrounding them. A white wooden fence encircled the graves.

"What're they doing out here in the middle of nowhere?" I asked.

Conrad pointed to a large, stone-lined hole in the ground in a weed-covered clearing on the other side of the road. Trees were growing up from the center of it. "That's an old foundation from a house that must have been here years and years ago," he said. "I guess these guys and their family lived there."

To the left of the foundation was a trail, which also was somewhat overgrown.

"Where does that go?" I asked.

"It's an old logging trail," he said. "It comes out on Wyatt Road. It's pretty spooky through there, though. The woods are so thick, it looks like nighttime in there even in broad daylight."

The trail intrigued me. I wanted to explore it, but not with Conrad. The last place I wanted to be with him was in the middle some pitch-dark woods – even though the darkness probably would hide his rotted teeth. Janet and I, I decided, would have to come back at another time and explore the trail on our own.

We continued walking until we reached a paved road. "This is Red Oak Road," Conrad said. He pointed to the left. "I live up that way." He then pointed to the right, "Scott lives down this way."

We set off toward Scott's house. We'd taken only a few steps when Conrad said, "That's my brother Eric's house up ahead on the right." He nodded in the direction of a gray Colonial house with black shutters. The exterior was so badly peeling, it looked as if a strong sneeze could strip off all of the paint.

"Your brother has his own house?" I asked, thinking his brother probably was only sixteen or seventeen.

"Yeah, he's a lot older than I am," Conrad said. "He's nearly thirty, and married."

Another twenty minutes passed before Conrad finally said the words Janet had been longing to hear. "There's Scott's place up on the right."

Up until then, Janet had been walking slowly and dragging her feet, but the second she found out we were near Scott's house, she acted as if someone had given her a booster shot of energy. She quickened her pace and practically left Conrad and me in the dust.

Scott lived in a sprawling farmhouse with a huge barn next to it on a grassy corner lot. There were quite a few young kids playing out in the yard when we approached.

"Scott's family takes in foster kids," Conrad explained.

The object of Janet's desire finally emerged from the house. His hair was tousled and he was wearing a striped T-shirt and jeans that were cuffed up at the ankles. "Hi," he said, with all the enthusiasm of someone who'd just been told he needed an appendectomy. Janet didn't seem fazed, however. The moment she set eyes on Scott, her smile grew so wide, the sunlight bouncing off her teeth nearly blinded me.

Janet happened to notice the name on the mailbox in front of the farmhouse. "Your last name is Wyatt?" she asked Scott.

He nodded.

"Then Wyatt Road was named after you?" she asked.

Again, he nodded. "My family has lived in this farmhouse for generations."

"Cool!" Janet said. "I've never met anyone who has a road named after him before!"

I didn't think it was such a big deal. After all, the Harmons had a road named after them, too. Seemed like a pretty common thing in this town.

The four of us headed around the corner to Tweaky and Jake's house, which appeared to be in various stages of construction...with none of the stages completed. Tweaky, in a gray T-shirt, still was very obviously braless when she came to the door. "Come on inside a minute," she said. "I'm not ready yet."

The first thing I noticed when we entered the house was it had no interior walls, just insulation. There were framed pictures hanging on the insulation, which I thought looked pretty funny. The floors were just sheets of plywood, with not even so much as a scatter rug on them. And aside from a table and four chairs, there wasn't much furniture in the room. Our footsteps made hollow, echoing sounds as we walked across the floor.

"Is Jake coming?" Conrad asked.

"Nah, he's sleeping in," Tweaky said. "He'll be sorry when it's 100 degrees this afternoon and he's wishing he'd gotten up earlier and gone swimming with us."

* * * * *

"How much farther to Cutter's?" I asked. We'd left Tweaky's and were headed up Wyatt Road, an asphalt road with, from what I could tell, quite a few houses on it.

"About a mile," Conrad said.

55

I groaned. The way I figured it, by the time we reached Cutter's, I'd have walked over three miles, and all before lunchtime. Back in the city, I'd just be getting out of bed at lunchtime. "You guys sure do walk a lot," I said. "If I lived out here and walked this far every day, I'd probably end up looking like a stick figure."

"You're too pretty to ever look like one of those," Conrad said. When I turned to look at him, he winked at me. I couldn't help it...I smiled.

After we'd walked about ten minutes, I spotted a guy on a bicycle coming toward us. As he got closer, I could tell he was about our age. I also could tell he was pretty cute. He looked out of place, however, in his crisp, white dress-shirt and what appeared to be brand new dungarees. His sandy hair was long and shiny, and when he flashed a smile at us, all of his teeth were there.

"Hi, Tim!" Tweaky greeted him. "Want to go swimming?"

"Can't today," he said. "But thanks anyway." He then rode off on his bike.

"That's Tim Argent," Conrad said.

"His dad is an officer in the military," Tweaky added. "I think he's some kind of sergeant."

"Sergeant Argent?" I said, giggling. "That's funny!"

"There's Old Lady Wood's place up ahead," Scott said. He pointed at a weathered red farmhouse flanked by two big barns and a silo. "She's a school teacher who weighs about 500 pounds and has these huge plow horses. She gives hayrides all summer. Sometimes she even goes all the way down your road."

My eyes widened. "Really? I've never been on a hayride."

"I'll have to take you on one then," Conrad said.

A vision of him cuddled up next to me in a bunch of hay immediately dimmed my enthusiasm. "Now that I think about it," I said, "my mother once mentioned that when I was little, I nearly died from a bad case of hay fever."

CHAPTER SIX

Supper was a dismal event that night. Not only did I miss having my father at the table, I was suffering from a 9,000-degree sunburn. I'd been too dumb to cover up or even sit in the shade during my five hours at Cutter's. I looked down at my neon-red arms and felt pretty sure that when I got up the next morning, I was going to be a giant, oozing blister. I also had a stomachache. The three ice-cream sandwiches, Milky-Way bar and Almond Joy I'd bought at the convenience store and washed down with a pint of chocolate milk, might have had something to do with it. I sat and stared at the plate of macaroni and cheese growing cold in front of me and wished I had a hungry dog hiding underneath the table.

Janet was even more miserable than I was, but not because she'd eaten too much candy and ice cream or had overdosed on sunlight the way I had. Janet's long face was the result of a love affair gone bad before it even started

"Did you hear the lame excuse Scott gave me when I asked him if we'd see him tomorrow?" Janet asked. She lifted a forkful of the orange-colored macaroni to her mouth, briefly studied it and then set it back down on her plate. "He said he had to do chores all week and couldn't get any time away from the farm. I even offered to go over there and help him, but he said no thanks!"

I wanted to tell her that perhaps the fact she'd clung to Scott like flypaper all day might have scared him off, but I kept silent. Still, Janet's clinginess had been mild compared to Conrad's. The guy was an expert at clinging. In fact, it wouldn't have surprised me if he'd been a leech in his former life. He'd stuck so close to me all day, whenever I stopped short, he crashed into me. And when I finally did manage to slip away with Tweaky to get an ice cream at the convenience store, Conrad had come rushing through the door two minutes later, his expression panicky and his breath coming in gasps. "Thank God!" he said when he saw us. "I thought you'd gone back to the camp without me!"

"You're so lucky that Conrad likes you," Janet said as she pushed her supper plate aside. "I sure wish Scott acted with me the way Conrad does with you."

I rolled my eyes. "Tell you what. You can have him. He's all yours!"

"But I want Scott!" Her voice came out as a whine.

"Oh, don't go getting all depressed over him," I said. "You should know by now that boys are all *so* juvenile."

Janet took a deep breath and slowly shook her head. "But what does that say about me if a guy would rather shovel manure all week than be with me?"

"It says he's not worthy of you," my mother, who'd been eating in silence until then, cut in. "Scott doesn't know what he's missing."

"On the bright side," I added, "now that you and Scott are through, I don't ever have to see Conrad again! It'll be just you and me. Tomorrow, we can go explore that trail Conrad showed us today."

"Good luck getting rid of him," Janet said. "I think you're stuck with him for life. If you told him to get lost, he'd probably climb up Big Rock and threaten to jump off if you didn't take him back."

" I'd let him jump," I said. "Big Rock's not high enough to kill him anyway."

* * * * *

After all of the swimming and walking I'd done, I slept like the dead that night…that is, until my mother's screams made me jump up and whack my head on one of the eaves.

For once, Janet (a.k.a., She Who Could Sleep Through a Tornado) also woke up.

"What's wrong?" I cried out, trying to open my eyes. When I finally succeeded, all I saw was blackness.

"Something just ran across my stomach!" my mother's voice came from the bunk below.

I was fully awake. "Define *something*!" I said. I wondered if she'd meant *something* like a spider or *something* like a snake, which, considering all of the snakes that already had slithered into our lives since we'd been at the camp, wouldn't have surprised me at all.

"An animal," my mother said. "It was something furry."

I hadn't expected that answer. And I hadn't expected that an animal actually could squeeze into the camp. I lay back down, curled up into a fetal position and pulled the blankets over my head.

"Cool! What kind of animal?" Janet said. She leaned over the railing to look down at the kitchen floor, which wasn't visible in the pitch darkness. "You think it might be a rat?"

"Find it and get rid of it!" my voice was muffled under the blankets. "I'm not getting down from here until you do!"

I heard my mother climb out of bed and pad over to the fridge to get the flashlight. Only after I heard her strike a match did I dare peek out from underneath the covers.

The glow of the gas lamp on the wall illuminated the kitchen in a golden, flickering light. Mom, holding the flashlight, inched her way backwards, toward the sink. Her stiff posture and darting eyes told me she expected to be pounced on by some creature of the wild at any second. Slowly, she got down on her knees, leaned forward and aimed the flashlight underneath the bottom bunk.

Her body snapped to an upright position. "It's under there!"

"*It?*" I managed to squeak. "Exactly what is *it*?"

"I don't know! I just saw two beady little eyes glowing under there when the light hit them."

"Cool!" Janet repeated. "I'm coming down to see what it is!"

"Stay right where you are!" Mom said. She slowly rose to her feet and took a few steps sideways, her eyes never leaving the bottom bunk. She then reached to the left and felt for the broom, which was leaning up against the side of the fridge. Once she had the broom in her hand, she announced, "Whatever it is, I'm going to flush it out of there!"

Mom moved closer to the bed, bent down and began to poke underneath it with the broom. After about thirty seconds or so, our mystery guest, probably fed up with being poked, decided to make a dash for it. It came running out, straight at Mom. She screamed, dropped the broom and took a dive – actually a belly flop – onto the bottom bunk.

"It's a chipmunk!" Janet announced. "A cute little chipmunk! You scared the poor little thing!"

"Not as much as it scared me," my mother said.

"It's probably been in here all along," Janet said. "We just never knew it because it hid all day and only came out at night."

"Well, it's going to go live outside where it belongs," Mom said. She climbed off the bed, grabbed the broom and walked out to the front room. I heard her open both the front door and the screen door on the porch. Then she apparently went on a chipmunk hunt. I didn't actually witness any of the battle because I didn't venture down from the safety of the top bunk, but I could hear sounds coming from the front room that pretty much told me Mom was using the broom to whack everything within the general vicinity of the creature. I fell back to sleep before I found out who won the battle of the chipmunk.

And I didn't crawl out of bed until ten o'clock the next morning.

I shuffled out to the front room where Janet was playing solitaire at the table. "Where's Mom?" I asked her. "Did the chipmunk gnaw off her big toe or something last night?"

"No, she got rid of the chipmunk just fine," she said. "She told me she was going out to pick some wild blueberries so she can make a batch of blueberry muffins." She glanced up from her cards. "You look like an Indian."

I held out my bare arm. My sunburn had darkened a few shades overnight. At least, I was pleased to see, I wasn't the giant ball of ooze I'd expected to be.

I went back out to the kitchen and grabbed a bottle of milk and a bunch of single-serving boxes of assorted cereals.

"I already ate the Sugar Pops," Janet said as I took a seat at the table. She knew that Sugar Pops were my favorites, so I had the feeling she'd taken them on purpose, just because she was in a bad mood about Scott. Any other day, I would have said something about it, but seeing she was suffering from an apparent broken heart, I decided to let the subject slide. I tore open a box of bran cereal, which conveniently made its own little foil-lined square bowl, and poured milk into it. I knew I was asking for trouble as soon as I shoveled the first spoonful of cereal into my mouth. Bran pretty much guaranteed I'd be trotting down to the outhouse at some point within the next twenty-four hours.

The front door suddenly burst open and my mother, breathless and with leaves sticking out of her dark hair, ran inside.

"I was bending over picking blueberries," she said, "and I heard a snorting noise behind me. I turned around and you'll never guess what was standing right there looking at me!"

"A giant snake," I said in a monotone.

"No, a big buck! A huge deer! I dropped the blueberries and ran!"

"You dropped the blueberries?" I repeated, frowning. Visions of warm blueberry muffins with blobs of butter melting on them had been filling my mind ever since Janet mentioned the blueberries. Mom, I decided, had to get out of the habit of flinging stuff when something scared her.

My mother seemed offended by our lack of interest in her story. "Don't you even care that some big old deer probably wanted to attack me?"

Janet giggled. "Why, was he one of those perverts you're always warning us about?"

"Yeah, did he wave his weenie at you?" I added with a snort of laughter. When I did, cereal milk squirted out of my nose. Janet laughed so hard, she couldn't catch her breath.

My mother shook her head. "You two are impossible!"

After breakfast, I shoved on shorts and a T-shirt and ran a comb through my hair. "If anyone needs me," I announced, "I'll be down at the outhouse."

My mother glanced at my feet. "Where are your sneakers? You can't go running around outside barefooted."

"Tweaky never wears shoes," I said. "And she gets around just fine."

"Well, when you end up slicing open your foot on a sharp rock," Mom said, "get *Tweaky* to stitch it up for you!"

I ignored my mother's words and headed for the door. "When I get back," I said to Janet, who was sitting on the top step of the porch, "we'll go see if we can find the container of blueberries Mom dropped, then we'll go explore that trail down by the Minutemen's graves, okay?"

61

She shrugged. "Okay."

I spent all of one minute in the outhouse, then, still yanking up my shorts, got out of there as fast as I could. "I'm sure glad I only had to pee," I shouted to Janet as I walked back up the path toward the camp. "I'd hate to be constipated and have to sit there straining for a half-hour! My butt cheeks would be covered with mosquito bites! Or even worse, I might get a bee up my crack!"

I rounded the corner of the camp and came face to face with Conrad.

"Look who dropped by!" Janet said, giggling, probably because of the expression on my face. I said a silent prayer of thanks that my sunburn concealed the crimson I could feel creeping up my neck and into my cheeks.

"So what brings you here?" I asked Conrad, as if I didn't already know.

"Oh, I thought I'd hang out with you guys for a while," he said. "I just got back from Jake's and no one was around."

The armpits on his shirt weren't nearly wet enough yet for him to have walked all the way to Jake's and back. I knew he was lying. He'd come straight to the camp from his house.

"So what are you guys up to?" he asked.

"We were just going to go down to explore the tra…" Janet began, but clamped her mouth shut when I cast her my most threatening shut-up-or-die look.

"Uh, we were just about to do our chores," I said. "You know, boring stuff like laundry and scraping the crud off the barbecue grill."

"I'll help!" Conrad said.

Janet giggled again. For a person who was supposed to be mourning the demise of her short-lived romance, she sure seemed to be doing a lot of giggling.

"I was just picturing Conrad helping us with the laundry," she said. "Can you see him down at the river, beating your underpants against the rocks?"

Conrad burst out laughing. I glared at him.

"And just imagine if a big leech swam into the underpants!" Janet added.

I decided to change the subject, mainly because my underpants were not something I thought Conrad should be picturing.

"Mom left some rope on the porch so she could hang it up for a clothesline later, around those two trees over there." I pointed at two tall pines spaced about ten feet apart. "Let's hang it up for her."

As I passed by Janet on my way to the porch, I spoke to her in carnival Latin, a code language my dad had taught us. Janet and I often used it, especially at school. It involved adding an "iz" between each syllable of a word. When Janet and I spoke the language fast, no one knew what the heck we were talking about, which, of course, was the reason why we used it. *"Lizet's tizie Cizonrizad tizo thize trizee,"* I said to her out of the corner of my mouth. Janet smiled and nodded.

I found the rope, handed one end of it to Janet and then took the other end. We walked over to the fatter of the two pine trees and stood holding the rope in front of it.

"Conrad," I said, smiling at him, "can you come stand against the tree and grab the rope in the middle while Janet and I each hold an end? I want to make sure we find the center of it." He nearly tripped over himself rushing toward the tree. He grabbed the rope in the middle.

In an instant, Janet and I were running in opposite directions around the tree, winding the rope around Conrad until he was pinned against the tree and unable to move. I disappeared behind him and tied the rope in three tight knots.

"What are you doing?" Conrad's voice sounded higher pitched than usual.

"Playing a game!" Janet said. "We're part of a secret village of alien warrior women and we've captured you because we caught you spying on us!"

"Yeah, and now we're going to have to burn you at the stake!" I added with a sinister cackle.

Of course, I was joking. Still, the more I thought about it, the more I thought it might be fun to make Conrad believe we actually were going to torch him. I was enjoying the sense of power I was feeling, and I wanted to use it to make Conrad squirm.

"Come on, Janet," I said. "Help me gather some leaves and twigs for the execution fire."

She stared at me for a moment, then followed my lead and began to stack branches and dead leaves around Conrad's sneaker-clad feet. After we'd constructed a neat little pile, Janet, who, since we'd arrived at the camp, had made a habit of carrying a book of matches in her pocket just in case we ever got lost and needed to survive in the wilderness, reached into her shorts and withdrew the matches.

Seeing her holding them made me feel a little uneasy, even though I knew she just wanted to scare Conrad...not charcoal broil him.

Beads of perspiration began to pop out on Conrad's forehead as he struggled to free himself from the rope. I turned to look at Janet. The smirk on her face told me exactly what she intended to do next. She was going to light a match.

Sure enough, she tore one from the matchbook and struck it against the strip on the cover. A small yellow flame burst from the tip.

"Okay, okay, I surrender!" Conrad said. His voice sounded a lot like a woman's by then. "The game is over. You guys win! I promise I won't ever spy on your secret warrior village again! Now untie me!"

Janet winked at me. "Think we should untie him? Or do you think he's lying and will reveal our secret civilization to the human race?"

That's when something completely unplanned happened. Janet hadn't been paying attention to the match she'd lit, and was holding it much too close to the matchbook. The entire book of matches suddenly went up in flames.

"Ow!" she cried, and dropped the fireball. It landed in the pile of dead leaves surrounding Conrad's feet.

Within seconds, several of the leaves were on fire.

"Stomp it out!" I shouted at Janet. "I'm barefooted, I can't!"

"I can't either!" she cried. "Not in my flip-flops!"

The fire rapidly grew in height and width and inched closer to Conrad's feet. "Untie me!" he yelled. He tried to move, but the rope, visibly digging into him, was too tight to allow him even a quarter of an inch of slack. "Go get a knife and cut me loose!"

My brain was screaming at me to run over and untie him, but for some reason, my body wasn't receiving the message. Janet and I just stood there, unmoving, unblinking. I resigned myself to the fact we were going to rot in jail for shish-kabobbing Conrad. Visions of myself sharing a cell with some heavily tattooed woman flashed through my mind.

"Oh, my God!" my mother's voice came from behind us. "What on earth are you two doing?"

Before we could answer, she ran up onto the porch, grabbed the nighttime pee bucket, dashed back to the tree and flung pee on the fire…and all over Conrad. No signs of the fire remained.

I rushed over to untie him before anything else happened that we could be blamed – or arrested – for.

"We were just playing a game," Janet explained. "But the matchbook accidentally caught fire and I dropped it!"

"Why on earth would you be lighting matches in the first place?" my mother asked. Her perfectly arched eyebrows met in a deep crease at the bridge of her nose, a sure sign she wasn't pleased. "Certainly you're old enough to know that playing with fire is dangerous! You're not three years old, you know!"

Janet and I hung our heads. I really did feel sorry that we'd nearly barbecued Conrad, yet all I wanted to do was giggle. In fact, I had to bite my bottom lip to keep from laughing. I couldn't help it. The thought of Conrad being doused with pee really struck me funny.

* * * * *

Guilt forced me to be nice to Conrad for the rest of the day. My mom made us a lunch of tuna-salad sandwiches, potato chips and ginger ale, and then we spent a lazy afternoon playing card games like Go Fish and Old Maid, and looking at my *Little Dot* and *Richie Rich* comic books. I still wanted to go exploring, but not with Conrad around.

Conrad seemed to be staring at one page in a comic book for an unusually long time. Finally he handed the book to me and pointed to an advertisement that showed pictures of a bunch of sterling-silver rings that cost a couple dollars each. "Which one of these rings do you like the best?"

A wide band with a circle of roses engraved all around it and a little loop on the front with a silver heart hanging from it caught my eye. "That one is pretty," I said, pointing.

He studied my fingers for a moment, then went back to reading the comic book.

"You know something?" I said to no one in particular. "I'm the only one here who's not a teenager yet. You two are thirteen already and I'm still only twelve. Twelve makes me feel like a little kid."

"You sure don't *look* like a little kid." Conrad's black-eyed-peas smile bordered on fiendish.

Janet shrugged. "You'll be thirteen in a couple of months."

"Yeah, but I'll still always be the baby of the bunch."

Conrad winked at me. "You'll always be *my* baby."

That did it. The conversation was getting far too personal to suit me. I had to find a way to get rid of Conrad…and fast…before he started to drool all over himself. Plus that, he smelled like pee.

I grabbed my stomach and groaned. "I don't feel so good all of a sudden. I think my lunch might come up." If there was one thing I figured would be guaranteed to put an abrupt end to Conrad's romantic notions, it was puke.

"Can I get you something?" he asked. "A glass of water? A Rolaid?"

"No, I think I'll just go lie down for a while and see if that helps." I stood up and headed toward the kitchen. Conrad leapt to his feet and began to follow me. I really hated to do it, but I figured he gave me no choice. I gulped some air, turned to face him and then let loose with a loud belch—a real window rattler. If Conrad's hair had been longer, I'm pretty sure it would have parted. He stopped dead.

"Sorry," I said, rubbing my stomach and moaning. "I'm not sure the next one will be only air."

"I think I'd better get going," he said, his smile tight. "My mother doesn't even know where I am, and I don't want her to worry. I'll drop by tomorrow to see if you're feeling any better. Maybe we can go swimming or something."

I belched even more loudly and groaned. "I don't think I'll live to see tomorrow."

As soon as Conrad had disappeared down the road, Janet looked at me. "You really sick?" she asked.

"Sick of *him,* that's all." I looked at my watch. It was nearly three o'clock. "Want to go exploring now?"

"Sure. I'm getting tired of comic books and cards. I could do that back home…only while sitting in front of the TV, which would make things a heck of a lot more interesting."

Janet and I waited about twenty minutes, to make sure Conrad was far enough down the road, then headed off to explore the trail. My mother, wearing a flowered turquoise bathing suit with a built-in privacy panel across the crotch, was stretched out on a lounge chair in the sun.

"Bye, Mom," I called to her. "Janet and I are going exploring."

"Don't get lost," she said. "And be back in time for supper."

"What are we having?" I asked.

"Hummingbirds' eyebrows on toast."

Janet and I laughed. That was my dad's favorite delicacy, or so he always claimed. In fact, he liked to tease waitresses by ordering it whenever we went to a restaurant. I suspected he'd made up the whole hummingbird thing, but he insisted it actually was a real dish in some obscure country like Wingtopia or someplace.

"We'll be back in a couple hours," I said to my mother as we walked past her. I paused, turned and added, "Are you sure you'll be okay here all alone with the outhouse snake, snorting deer and savage chipmunk?"

"I'll be just fine," she said.

CHAPTER SEVEN

As Janet and I walked down the road toward the mystery trail, we started singing the "Junior Birdman" song we'd learned during our singing class at the Girls' Club back home.

"Up in the air, Junior Birdman, up in the air, upside down. Up in the air, Junior Birdman, keep your nose up off the ground. And when you hear the big announcement that your wings are made of tin, come on, Junior Birdman, send your box tops in!"

Janet and I had enjoyed our classes at the Girls' Club, especially the good-grooming class, which taught proper etiquette and grooming techniques to impressionable young ladies. One Saturday morning as we were sitting in grooming class, learning about the proper way to brush our teeth (up and down, never side to side) and clean our fingernails (with a fingernail brush and soap, not digging underneath them with the tip of a paring knife), a big bug with antennae on its head crawled across Janet's foot.

It seemed ironic that our first introduction to the cockroach would be in a class about proper etiquette. Janet had stomped the innards out of the bug – not nearly daintily enough to be classified as ladylike, in my opinion. In fact, she'd probably had a few grade points deducted for not discreetly picking it up in a tissue and disposing of it in a wastebasket instead of squishing it into something that needed to be scraped off the floor with a putty knife.

Our mothers had not been the least bit amused with our tales of roach stomping. In fact, that Saturday morning was the last time we ever saw the interior of the Girls' Club.

My thoughts turned back to the present as Janet and I reached the trail. The moment we started down it, I realized

Conrad had spoken the truth. The tall evergreen, pine and maple trees lining the trail were so thick with so many overhanging branches, we instantly were thrust into near darkness. I felt a shiver go up my spine.

We walked in silence for about ten minutes. I couldn't help but notice that everything around us seemed silent, too. No birds were singing, no squirrels were chattering and no crows were squawking the way they usually did back at the camp.

"This place is creepy," Janet said, as if reading my thoughts. Her eyes darted left and right as we quickened our pace. "I sure wish Scott was here to protect us."

I couldn't believe the next words that came out of my mouth. "Yeah, I'm kind of regretting I didn't let Conrad tag along."

The woods got deeper and darker as we walked. Conrad had said the trail came out somewhere on Wyatt Road, so as long as we kept walking, I knew we'd reach civilization at some point…unless something like the Creature from the Black Lagoon found us first.

No sooner had I thought about a lagoon did Janet stop and point to her left. "Look over there – it looks like a big swamp! Maybe we can find a turtle!"

If there was one thing Janet and I both loved, it was turtles. Countless allowances had been spent at Woolworth's, buying quarter-sized, green-shelled turtles, complete with a spiffy plastic bowl with a built-in plastic palm tree sticking up from the center. And countless times we had gathered around the toilet bowl to mourn the passing of those poor turtles…with a tearful send-off…and a flush.

I couldn't keep up with Janet as she dashed down the fern-covered slope toward the swamp. The closer I got to it, however, the less I wanted to explore it. The water was black with green-colored slime floating on top. The remains of dead, rotted trees poked up out of the water, where the darkness made them look like silhouettes of multi-armed monsters.

Janet arrived at the edge of the swamp before I did. "Eeeeyewwww!" she cried and jumped back a couple feet.

An odor that reminded me of the time a package of ground beef had fallen out of Mom's grocery bag and remained under the front seat of the car for about a week during a heat wave, drifted up from the swamp. I moved to stand behind Janet, using her for a shield (even though her body covered an area only about the width of my spine), and then finally dared to peer over her shoulder. I gasped. Decaying bones of all shapes and sizes were lying in the water at the edge of the swamp.

"Do you think they're human?" My voice barely was audible. Immediately, I felt as if every tree near the swamp had a pair of glowing yellow eyeballs peering out from behind it.

"Well, that skull right there has antlers on it," Janet said. "So that's definitely not a human…unless it's some kind of weird mutant. Maybe this is where the animals around here come to die. Or maybe this is where hunters dump the remains of what they can't carry out of the woods."

"Or maybe the swamp is poisonous or has a curse on it!" I said. "Or maybe it's like that movie, *The Blob*, and something is lurking in the water that oozes out and grabs you by the ankle and pulls you in when you get too close, then sucks all of the flesh off your bones!"

Janet and I stared into the slime-covered water and then turned to look at each other. Without a word, we bolted back up the hill.

"I really have the creeps now," Janet said once our feet were back on the pine-needle covered trail. "Let's head back to the camp! I've had enough exploring for one day. And I'm starving!"

"But we've already come this far!" I said. "Let's just keep going. I'd rather walk back to the camp on Wyatt Road than have to go back the way we came, through the woods."

"This whole trail is like something out of a horror movie," Janet said. "And is it just me, or have you also had the feeling something's been following us during our whole walk?"

"It's just you," I said. "I haven't had that feeling at all. If something was following us, we'd have heard it rustling in the bushes by now." That is, I thought, swallowing the lump of fear in my throat, unless it was a really sneaky monster that had perfected the art of silently slithering through the woods as it stalked its prey.

"I sure wish I'd have been brave and kissed Scott," Janet said. "At least then I could die with a smile on my face!"

I rolled my eyes. "Come on, let's just keep going. Wyatt Road is probably right around the next bend and we'll still be very much alive for supper."

"That's if something doesn't eat us for supper first!" she said.

I headed off at a fast clip, causing Janet to run after me. With each step we took, the bugs seemed to get worse, lining up in attack formation and dive- bombing at us. I wanted to smack the guts out of each and every one that dared to land on me, but there was my sunburn to consider. After I swatted the first two mosquitoes and ended up screaming like a wounded animal, I settled for gently brushing them away. They, however, apparently were determined to enjoy some tasty city blood, so they just kept coming back.

"Look!" Janet's voice interrupted my thoughts of the best way to capture, torture, and decapitate a mosquito. "I see some light up ahead…on the right!"

I could see it, too – an area of bright daylight in the midst of the dark forest. "You think that's Wyatt Road over there?" I asked.

"There's only one way to find out!" Janet said. "Let's go!"

We ran toward the light, our feet flying over the rooted path. When we reached the source of the light, our mouths collectively fell open.

"I think I've just died and gone to heaven!" Janet whispered.

For a moment, I was afraid she was right – that maybe our bodies, with all of the flesh sucked off them, were lying back in Bone Swamp, and our spirits now were at the Pearly Gates.

To the right of the trail was a short path that opened into a sun-bathed clearing. A small pond, edged with wildflowers and green grass, sat in the middle of the clearing. From the pond exited a stream that formed a small waterfall as it spilled over a slope of rocks beneath a wooden footbridge. Two ducks, an all-brown one and one with a green head and a white ring around its neck, were swimming in the pond.

Janet and I stared at the clearing and then back each other – and then back at the clearing. We couldn't believe our eyes. The scene was worthy of the finest picture postcard.

I grabbed Janet's hand because if we really were dead, I didn't want to risk being separated from her. We walked, one careful step at a time, toward the footbridge and then began to make our way across it. When we were about halfway across, we sat on the edge of the thick, wooden planks and allowed our legs to dangle. Our feet didn't reach the water, but we still enjoyed swinging them back and forth as we watched the ducks.

"I'm going to call this place 'Little Paradise'," Janet said.

"And it will be our secret place," I added. "We discovered it and we'll come here and enjoy it without anyone else bugging us...especially Conrad."

Janet looked thoughtful for a moment. "Well, I'd sure like to take Scott here. This place is really romantic. We could sit on the bridge or even in the grass next to the water and maybe have a picnic."

If nothing else, poor Janet was a dreamer. There was no way I could picture Scott ever sharing a picnic with her unless maybe she served all of his favorite foods and invited his favorite professional baseball player to join them. After all, from what I'd witnessed, he was about as romantic as the statues in Petrosky Park back home.

"I can picture myself here with Ricky Nelson," I said. "This would be the perfect place to bring a dreamboat like him."

"Mmmmm," was Janet's response. She'd moved to lie on her back with her arms folded under her head and was staring up at the sky. "Isn't it amazing how such a beautiful place can be hidden by such a dark, creepy forest?"

"Well, speaking of that dark, creepy forest, I think we'd better give up on finding Wyatt Road and just head back to the camp. It's getting late and I don't want to have to deal with anything darker than what's in there right now."

Janet sat up and shuddered. "If it gets any darker in those woods we'll be like Hansel and Gretel and wander around lost until an old witch finds us. I wish we could just stay here forever and never have to set foot on that trail again."

"That trail is the only way we know how to get to and from Little Paradise. So we'd better get used to walking on it if we ever want to come back here!"

With one last lingering look at the pond, we headed back out to the trail and toward Bone Swamp. After being in the bright, sunlit clearing, the woods seemed even darker and spookier…and the mosquitoes even more ravenous. Sunburn or no sunburn, I smacked the little buggers.

* * * * *

"You girls are eating like you haven't seen food in years," my mother said at suppertime that night.

"We must have walked twenty miles through the woods today," I said, my words muffled beneath the mound of mashed potatoes I'd just stuffed into my mouth. "I never thought we'd see food or water again."

"Yeah, we saw plenty of water, but I sure as heck wouldn't have dared to drink any of it," Janet added, slathering butter on a slice of bread so she could use it to mop up the gravy on her plate. "We found Bone Swamp and then there was Little Paradise, with a really beautiful pond with a waterfall and a wooden bridge. But there were ducks swimming in the water there, and I wouldn't want to drink anything that has ducks' butts in it!"

"Bone Swamp?" my mom repeated. "That doesn't sound like someplace I want you girls hanging around."

"Don't worry," I said. "I don't intend to go back there. I might run past it on my way to Little Paradise, but I'm not going to stop there again."

"And why do you call it Bone Swamp?" Mom seemed almost hesitant to ask.

Janet shrugged. "Because it's full of rotten old animal bones."

"Dear Lord," Mom said mostly to herself. She moved her chair away from the table, stood up and walked over to the door, where she latched the hook-and-eye lock, something she hadn't previously done so early in the evening. When she sat back down at the table, she glanced at the corner of the room behind the sofa bed, where Dad's .22 rifle was propped against the wall.

"Is it loaded?" I asked her.

Her eyes remained fixed on the rifle. "No, but it will be."

I suspected Dad had brought the rifle to make Mom feel more secure about being alone when he had to return to the city. I hadn't even realized it was there in the corner until Mom looked at it. My mom actually was a pretty good shot, which

73

made me feel less frightened about the possibility of a flesh-eating monster roaming around searching for more bones to add to its swamp. She and Dad often had enjoyed target practicing and hunting together before I was born. Mom had quit hunting, however, after she experienced what she described as the most humiliating incident of her life.

She and Dad had gone deer hunting one morning in a popular hunting area and decided, once they were in the middle of the snow-covered woods, to separate and walk in opposite directions in a circular pattern, then meet up again at the top of the hill.

A half-hour later, Mom arrived at the designated meeting spot, where she spotted my father, his back toward her, sitting on a big rock.

He didn't hear her approach, so she crept up behind him, playfully whacked him on the back of the head and shouted, "Don't sit on that cold rock! You'll get hemorrhoids!"

A total stranger, some bearded man wearing the same hunting outfit as my Dad's, turned around and narrowed his eyes at her. Mom said she was surprised he didn't shoot her.

My father appeared over the hill shortly thereafter, and when Mom explained what had happened, he nearly wet his pants laughing. That ended their couples' hunting expeditions. Mom never donned her woolen red-and-black-plaid hunting outfit again.

When Mom and Dad first told me that story back when I was about nine, I'd immediately asked them what hemorrhoids were. Dad said, "Piles."

"Piles of what?" I'd asked.

"It's kind of like when your guts hang out of your rear end," Mom had said, her tone matter-of-fact.

The hideous, blindness-inducing vision that had popped into my mind made me vow to never sit on anything cold again.

"Are you daydreaming about Conrad?" Janet's voice cut into my thoughts of hemorrhoids. "You have a faraway look on your face!"

"No," I said. "But I suppose you could say I was thinking about something that reminded me of him."

"He'll be over tomorrow for sure," Janet said. "So how are you planning to get rid of him?"

I'd been so busy all afternoon, I hadn't even thought about how I was going to deal with him. "Maybe we should get up at the crack of dawn and head over to Cutter's swimming hole so we won't be here when he gets here."

"I don't know what you've got against that poor boy," my mother said. "What has he ever done to you other than be nice?"

"He smiled at me," I said. "With those black-eyed peas teeth of his."

"And that makes him a bad person?" Mom asked.

"No, just a creepy-looking one."

"Well, you'll be sorry when he gets older and gets his teeth fixed and turns into a real hunk!" Janet had to add her two cents' worth. "Then you'll wish you'd been nicer to him."

Her words made me wonder how Conrad would look with a nice white smile. Not bad at all, I concluded, especially against his deeply tanned skin. But the way I figured it, he wouldn't get a new smile until years in the future, after he got a job and could save up the money for some new teeth or caps, or whatever he needed. And at the present time, he still looked...well, totally unkissable. I wanted my first kiss to be from a guy who had all of his teeth, not a bunch of yucky little brown stumps.

Suddenly, I lost my appetite. I pushed away my plate, which still had some potatoes and chicken on it. "What's for dessert?"

I could be nauseated, suffering from knife-like stomach pains and have heartburn that felt like molten lava rising in my throat ...but still I'd never pass up dessert.

I expected the usual, "Clean your plate or no dessert!" lecture from Mom, but instead she said, "Table Talk pie – lemon!"

Table Talk lemon pie was my favorite, followed by Table Talk chocolate-cream pie. My mom and dad preferred strawberry-rhubarb, but it wasn't nearly sweet enough for me.

Janet, my mom and I polished off the entire lemon pie. I glared at the two of them as I licked the final remnants of lemon pie-filling off my fingers. They could consume a billion calories a day and still not gain weight, but I was doomed to yet another year of wearing Chubbette dresses for my back-to-school wardrobe.

* * * * *

I rolled over in bed and looked at the wind-up clock on the shelf over the stove. It was 10:18! I could hear Janet and my mom's muffled voices coming from the front room. I climbed down from the bunk and stomped out there.

"Why didn't anyone wake me?" I shouted. "You knew I wanted to get out of here early, before Conrad showed up!"

"My mother always says that if you sleep late it's because your body needs it," Janet said. "So if you really need it, you should sleep."

"Your mother never had to deal with Conrad!" I said. "Now I'm going to have to rush and gulp down some cereal so we can head off to Cutter's. For all I know, Conrad could already be standing out in the driveway!"

"I don't feel like going swimming today," Janet said.

I narrowed my eyes at her. "What do you mean you don't feel like going swimming?"

She shrugged. "It's just that Cutter's was where I first met Scott and had so much fun with him and…well, it brings back too many memories of what could have been."

I wanted to groan and tell her she was being just a wee bit too dramatic about the whole Scott thing, but instead I said, "But we can go to the variety store over there and get candy and ice cream and stuff!" I once again tried to appeal to her insatiable appetite.

"Nah, I don't want to go." It was the first time I'd ever seen Janet turn down food. Her expression suddenly brightened as she added, "Let's take a walk over to Tweaky's instead and see if she's around!"

She wasn't fooling me. Tweaky lived right around the corner from Scott, so we'd have to pass by his place to get to hers. I wasn't about to walk a couple miles and work up a sweat just to hang around some smelly old farm while Janet looked for Scott. I wanted to walk somewhere where ice-cold, blue-raspberry Popsicles or a Creamsicle would be waiting for me. Just the thought of them made the saliva pool in my mouth.

I didn't give an immediate answer to Janet's suggestion. I ate my cereal, visited the outhouse, washed up with glacier-cold water from the pump and got dressed. By then, it was nearly noon. I sat on the rocker on the front porch so I could think...mostly about all of the Popsicles with my name on them at Cutter's store.

The sound of a car coming up the road made me stand up and crane my neck. After all, cars on Shepherdess Road were about as common as udders on a bull, so actually seeing one pass by the camp was as exciting as watching the Macy's Thanksgiving Day parade. When the car finally came into sight, I blinked my eyes, certain they were deceiving me.

"Mom!" I shouted. "Get out here, quick!"

My mother and Janet appeared on the porch in a flash, just in time to see the car pull into the driveway.

"Lou!" my mom cried, running toward the car.

The old Buick came to a halt and out stepped my dad, grinning. "I decided to take the day off and treat you girls to a night out," he said. "I work my butt off every day, so I figured I'm entitled to a few hours off now and then! And I'm pretty sure that by now you're craving some civilization!"

Janet and I both rushed over to hug him, nearly knocking him over as we did. I didn't know what I was happier about – the fact my dad was there with us again, or that we'd actually be going somewhere in the car, away from the wilderness.

I happened to glance over my dad's shoulder, and what I saw made me want to run and hide. There was Conrad, walking up the driveway. I broke away from Dad and backed up a few feet.

"Conrad, isn't it?" my dad greeted him as he approached.

"Hello, sir," Conrad said, extending his hand for a handshake. "Nice to see you again."

"Anyway," Dad continued, looking back at Janet and me. "How would you girls like to go to the drive-in movies tonight? There's a Rock Hudson and Doris Day comedy playing that's supposed to be good. And I think the other feature has Connie Stevens in it."

Janet and I let out simultaneous squeals. We were going to a drive-in movie theater – one that had a snack bar with pizza and ice cream! And a restroom with flush toilets! I felt as if Santa Claus had arrived a few months early.

Even my mother was smiling with obvious pleasure. My dad slipped his arm around her waist and drew her to him. "So does that sound like a plan?" he asked.

Janet and I nodded and shouted, "Yeah!" at the same time.

Conrad was the only one not smiling. "I've never been to a drive-in movie," he said. "I've always wanted to, but I never have."

I felt my heart stop beating as I silently prayed that my dad wouldn't say what I had an overwhelming fear he might say.

"Then why don't you come with us?" Dad said.

At that moment, I promised God I'd go to church every Sunday and drop my entire allowance in the collection plate if He would have mercy on me and make Conrad say he wouldn't be able to go.

"Really?" Conrad answered, his wide smile revealing the teeth (or lack thereof) from Hell. "Cool! I'll have to run home and tell my parents! What time are you leaving?"

"Be back here at 6:30," Dad said. "Oh, and if you'd like, you can invite that friend of yours, too."

Janet's head snapped in Dad's direction. "You mean Scott?"

"Sure," Dad said, "if that's his name. Why not?"

"Okay, I'll call Scott from my house when I get back there," Conrad said as he jogged out of the driveway. "I'll be back later!"

Never have I wanted to see my father boiled in oil more than I wanted to at that moment. The mere thought of spending an evening watching a double feature with Conrad sitting next to me in a crowded back seat and even possibly trying to put his arm around me or, heaven forbid, kiss me, made me want to go jump into the leech-filled river and offer myself as a sacrifice.

Janet, however, acted as if she'd just been told a rich uncle had died and left her a couple million dollars.

"Do you really think Scott might come with us?" she breathlessly asked me. "Just think! Over four hours of sitting in the back seat next to him at the drive-in, and another hour-and-a-half in the car for traveling time! I would be in heaven!"

Her words made me realize just how long I was going to be stuck in close quarters with Conrad. My expression must have revealed my thoughts because my dad said, "Did I do something wrong by inviting Conrad? I felt bad for the poor kid, never having been to a drive-in."

My mother's smile did little to hide her amusement. "Um, you might say the budding romance between Conrad and Sally is pretty much one-sided.

"Yeah," Janet said. "All *his* side!"

I had the feeling I was about to face the longest, most torturous night of my life.

CHAPTER EIGHT

At 6:15, I checked my watch for the 500th time. Only fifteen more minutes and we could leave for the drive-in. I was certain if Conrad's parents had given him permission to go with us, he'd have been back at the camp hours ago. I actually allowed myself to become optimistic about not having to suffer through the double feature after all. With every Conrad-less minute that ticked by, I grew one step closer to being able to enjoy the movies without any sweaty armpits next to me.

Janet, on the other hand, was pacing like a dad-to-be in a maternity ward. I was afraid she was going to wear a rut in the braided rug.

"Do you think Conrad is coming?" she asked. "Do you think he asked Scott if he wants to go? Do you think Scott will still go if Conrad doesn't?"

Before I could open my mouth to answer, my mother, who'd been outside, probably coming back from the outhouse, ran up onto the porch and whispered through the screen door, "Sally, quick! You *have* to see this!"

Janet and I headed outside just in time to see Conrad coming up the road. He was wearing a brown woolen sports jacket, a green polo-shirt, plaid necktie, black slacks, and on his feet, white bucks. I stared at his feet. The only people on earth I'd ever seen wear white bucks were members of a marching band…and Pat Boone. And a woolen sports jacket? It was 90 degrees outside, for crying out loud!

Just as Conrad was about to round the corner into our driveway, a pickup truck zoomed up behind him, screeched to a halt, and a gray-haired man jumped out. The man was holding a pair of beat-up black and white high-top sneakers.

"You take off my good church shoes and wear these!" he shouted, flinging the sneakers at Conrad. "You didn't even ask me if you could wear them!"

"But Dad, it's a special night!" Conrad said. "Mom didn't think you'd mind." I could see the color creeping up his neck, even from where I stood.

"Give them back to me!" his father repeated.

Conrad slipped out of the precious white bucks and handed them to his father. Then he sat on a log on the side of the road and put on the high-top sneakers. His father slammed back into the truck and sped off.

My mom, unable to control her laughter, disappeared into the camp. For some reason even I didn't understand, I felt sorry for Conrad.

Janet practically knocked me over as she ran over to him. "Did you call Scott? Is he coming?"

"Yes, I called him," Conrad said. "And he wasn't home."

I honestly thought Janet was going to burst into tears that would have rivaled the ones she'd shed over Butchy the frog.

"So I waited a couple hours and called him again," Conrad added. "And he's coming with us!"

Janet broke into a smile so wide, I was afraid she might pull a muscle in her face. "Then what are we waiting for? Let's get going!"

She ran back into the camp to gather her things, like her sweater and some snack money, leaving me alone with Conrad out in the driveway. As he moved closer to me, I could see beads of sweat all over his forehead and a trickle of sweat running down his temple. The thought of sitting next to him all night when he was going to end up soaked and probably smelling like B.O., made me blurt out, "You know, no one wears a sports jacket and tie to a drive-in movie. A lot of people even wear their pajamas. You're supposed to sit in comfort all night. I mean, that's why they invented drive-ins."

A look of relief crossed his face as he practically ripped off the necktie and then slipped out of his jacket. He walked over to the camp, opened the screen door on the porch and flung the jacket and tie onto the rocking chair.

When he returned to me he said, "My mom told me I should look good for my first date, no matter where I was going. She said girls like that sort of thing."

I was too busy staring at his already soaked armpits to register the fact he'd said *date*. When his words finally sank in, my head snapped up and I glared at him. "This isn't a date!"

He smiled. "I'm going to be sitting in the back seat next to you all night at a movie. If that's not a date, I don't know what is."

"Well, if I make you sit against the door and then put Scott next to you, Janet next to him and I sit against the other door, what would you call that?"

His smug smile faded. "I'd call that torture."

The camp door slammed and my parents and Janet exited in a single file and headed toward the car.

"Time to go," Dad said. He turned to Conrad. "Janet told me your friend is coming with us, so we'd better hustle."

Conrad took a deep breath, as if to calm his nerves. "Ready?" he asked me.

I didn't answer. I walked past him and climbed into the back seat of the car. Janet already was sitting there, and from the odor that greeted me, she obviously was full of nervous gaseousness. Poor Scott, I thought. If he dared to put his arm around her or try to kiss her, he'd probably end up needing a gas mask. On the other hand, I reasoned, if he'd spent the past few days shoveling manure, he just might be desensitized to anything that was smelly.

I ended up sitting between Janet and Conrad. I realized that no matter which door Scott used when he got into the car, I'd still be stuck sitting next to Conrad and his armpits. All I needed was for Scott to show up with manure-covered boots and my night would be complete.

When we pulled up at Scott's house, he was waiting outside at the end of his driveway and actually looked pretty good. He was wearing jeans, a clean T-shirt and sneakers, and his shaggy corn-colored hair was shiny. Before the car barely had come to a halt, Janet flung open the door and patted the portion of the seat next to her.

"Hi, Scott!" she said. "Get in!"

82

Scott's rear end barely made it onto the seat before Janet reached across him and slammed the door and locked it. I figured it was more because she was afraid he might jump out rather than for safety reasons.

* * * * *

The Skylight Drive-in was located only eight miles from our house in the city. When I saw the familiar sights again – streetlights, for example – a pang of homesickness struck me and I found myself wishing I could fling open the door, leap out and hitchhike back to our tenement building. If Conrad hadn't been blocking the car door and I hadn't been afraid of injuring some essential body part when I jumped, I'd seriously have considered it.

A line of cars snaked down the winding dirt drive leading into the drive-in. When we reached the booth, Dad handed a $5 bill to the attendant for the $5-per-carload admission price, and then found a parking spot in the center of the sixth row.

There was a playground down front, at the bottom of the towering screen, and I could see dozens of little kids in their pajamas, sliding down the slide and swinging on the swings.

"Remember when you used to wear your pajamas to the drive-in?" My mom had to turn around and ask me.

Conrad smiled at me.

"We took her to a lot of Disney movies," Mom continued, "but she always fell asleep before the first movie was even half through. Dad used to have to carry her into the house when we got home."

"But I'm wide awake tonight!" I said. I wanted to make certain Conrad didn't think I'd be dozing off and letting my guard down. I planned to stay fully awake all night, even if it meant I had to go to the snack bar and buy a cup of coffee. I'd never had coffee before, except in the form of coffee-flavored ice cream, but I was willing to drink a gallon of it if it meant it would keep me awake so I could keep an eye on Conrad.

Dad rolled down the car window and reached out to remove the speaker from the pole, then hung it over the top edge of the glass on the car window. He fiddled with the knob on it and some staticky music filled the car.

83

"So this is a drive-in theater, eh?" Conrad said. His eyes made a wide sweep of his surroundings. "Boy, I'll bet it gets really dark here once the sun goes down."

"Darker than a regular indoor movie theater," Janet said. "That's why so many teenagers come here to make out! Nobody can see them!"

I wanted to give her an elbow in the ribs for even mentioning the words "make out" in Conrad's presence. After all, if he thought the car was going to get dark enough so my parents couldn't see anything, his lips might get ideas.

It seemed like twenty years before the cartoon finally started. My parents sat as far apart as possible so we kids could see between their heads. That meant we had to squish closer together, which I knew Janet must be enjoying. I, however, felt as if I were a blob of peanut butter stuck between two slices of bread…one of which was sweaty.

The first movie was called *Parrish* and I soon found myself completely lost in it. It wasn't the plot that captured my attention. It was the most gorgeous blond-haired, blue-eyed hunk I'd ever seen in my life – Troy Donahue. Just looking at him made my heart feel as if it were being jolted with electricity.

When Troy kissed Connie Stevens and I saw his lips in all of their big-screen lusciousness, I wasn't certain, but I think I actually sighed out loud. And then I unconsciously did something I would come to regret for the rest of my life. I leaned my head on Conrad's shoulder.

In a split second, his arm was around me, pulling me closer to him…and his perspiration-soaked shirt. Common sense told me to pull away, but I still was feeling sorry for him because of the white-bucks incident, so I didn't budge. Out of the corner of my eye, I could see Janet snuggled up against Scott but I couldn't tell if his arm was around her or not. Still, I figured I'd stay where I was for at least a few more minutes so I wouldn't humiliate Conrad even more than he'd already been humiliated that day.

I once again lost myself in the movie and Troy's blue eyes. There was no one else in the world at that moment, just Troy and me. I wanted the moment never to end. I wanted the movie never to end. I wanted Troy Donahue wrapped up in red ribbon and shipped to my doorstep. Just watching him speak, especially when the camera zoomed in on his perfect face, made me feel like...well, kind of like my insides had been removed and replaced with twenty pounds of quivering Jell-O.

Unfortunately, something happened to jolt me back to reality and remind me I still was in drive-in hell. I felt Conrad's hot breath against my hair. Then I heard him gulp. A couple seconds later, he gulped again...and again. It sounded like nervous gulping, the kind of gulping I usually did when I knew I had to get a shot at the doctor's office and I sat waiting for him to come into the room and jab me. It also sounded like the kind of gulping my now-deceased cat used to do just before it threw up.

So, I wondered, why was Conrad gulping? What was he so nervous about? Having his arm around me? He gulped again and I felt his breath even closer to my ear. It suddenly dawned on me he might be trying to get up the courage to sneak a kiss. That did it. I pulled away from him.

Conrad took the hint and removed his arm from around me. He stared out the side window for a moment, then said, "I'm really thirsty."

Before I could stop myself, I blurted out, "Well, if you weren't breathing in my ear all night and gulping so much air, your throat wouldn't be so darned dry!"

So much for sparing him from humiliation.

I heard my parents trying to muffle their chuckles and realized I'd probably ruined Conrad's evening. I felt guilty, but not guilty enough to lean against him again. I wanted to be able to watch the second movie – the Doris Day, Rock Hudson movie – without having to listen to the sounds of a cat hacking up a fur ball in my ear through the whole thing.

"I'm going to the snack bar to get a cold drink," Conrad announced.

"I'll go with you," Scott volunteered almost too quickly.

"But you'll both miss the end of the movie!" Janet protested.

I wanted to say that Conrad hadn't watched any of it anyway, so it wouldn't matter, but I held my tongue.

"Can I get anybody anything?" Conrad asked.

I reached into the pocket of my shorts and pulled out a dime. "I'd like a Drumstick if they have one."

Conrad and Scott disappeared into the darkness.

The minute the guys were out of sight, my mother turned around to scold me. "Sally, you embarrassed the heck out of poor Conrad!"

I shrugged. "How would you like to try to watch a movie with someone's hot breath in your ear all night? And the gulping! He sounds like the kitchen drain when it gets backed up!"

My father burst out laughing.

"And his sweaty armpit was resting on my shoulder! I think he took the color out of my blouse!"

My mother also laughed, even though I could tell she was trying hard not to. "Be nice, now! He can't help it if he has a crush on you and you make him gulp and sweat!"

"Scott had his arm around me and I liked it!" Janet cut in. "And his armpits are nice and dry!"

"Well, la-di-dah!" I shot back. "Maybe his family can afford deodorant!"

Much too soon, the guys returned. Conrad had a frown on his face and remained silent as he handed the Drumstick to me. At that moment I didn't care about anything other than the creamy vanilla ice cream layered in thick chocolate, sprinkled with chopped nuts and wrapped in a chewy sugar cone. I took a big bite of the Drumstick.

Conrad downed an entire large cola in seconds, which didn't surprise me. I figured his throat must have been as dry as the Sahara. Scott slurped his drink, which he said was 7-Up, through a straw. To my surprise, he turned and offered Janet a sip. She grabbed the cup and used his straw, which I thought was pretty disgusting. But I had the feeling she probably thought it was symbolic of something meaningful, kind of like a kiss without actually involving any lips.

"Here," Conrad said. He handed my dime back to me. "My treat. I hope your Drumstick is good."

"Thank you, it's great!"

His eyes lingered on my ice cream as I took another bite of the chocolate layer. I hoped he wasn't waiting for me to offer him a bite because even if he were on the verge of dying of starvation, there still would be no way I'd ever allow his rotted stumpy teeth to come in contact with any portion of my ice cream.

At intermission, Dad headed to the snack bar and returned with enough food to feed a family of ten. There were hot dogs and burgers in foil packages, candy bars, pizza, popcorn and French fries. We spent the entire intermission stuffing our faces. I especially enjoyed the pizza, which seemed like a delicacy, I hadn't had it for so long. It also had a lot of garlic in the sauce. I hoped, as I gulped down my third slice, that I'd get a severe case of bad breath from it so I could breathe in Conrad's face and make him back off a few inches.

I was happy to see that the Doris Day and Rock Hudson movie was a comedy. I thought the Troy Donahue movie had been much too serious, so I was more than ready for a good laugh.

Halfway through the movie, Conrad yawned, stretched, and slipped his arm around me. I decided I'd let him keep it there as long as no gulping or ear breathing came with it.

By the time the happily-ever-after ending of the movie arrived, I was so tired, even the thought of the squeaky old bunk bed at the camp seemed appealing. Dad quickly revved up the car's engine and hung up the speaker on the pole.

"Let's get out of here and beat the crowd!" he said.

"No!" I shouted. "I have to use the restroom first!"

Dad groaned. "Well, make it snappy, okay?"

I would have asked Janet if she wanted to go with me, but she was still snuggled up against Scott, so I knew she wasn't about to do anything to jeopardize her position, even if her bladder was on the verge of exploding.

Conrad stepped out of the car to let me out. "Want me to walk you over there?" he asked.

I shook my head. "I'll be fine. All the lights are on now. Those two big spotlights on the top of the screen really shed a lot of light."

I dashed toward the restroom. Once in there, I took my time, mainly because I wanted to pamper myself, first by using an actual flush toilet and then the running water – both hot and cold. I washed my face and hands with warm water and then washed them again, just because the non-icy water felt so good.

Even though the restroom was littered with crumpled paper towels lying in puddles of heaven only knew what all over the floor, and it smelled like the monkey cage at the zoo, it still seemed like the bathroom at the Ritz Carlton to me. After all, anything was better than the bug-infested, stinky-holed outhouse at the camp. Just the thought of the place made me dart back into the stall and try to pee again.

All four of us in the back seat must have fallen asleep during the ride back to the camp because when my father's voice announced, "Okay, Scott, you're home!" our heads snapped up at the same time and we stared squinty-eyed at our surroundings.

"Thank you for taking me, and for the refreshments," Scott said as he moved to open the door. Janet, who still was leaning against him, didn't budge.

"Um, maybe I'll see you guys around again before your vacation is over," Scott said.

"Tomorrow?" Janet sat up straight.

"I don't know," Scott said. "I have a lot of chores to do."

"But I was hoping you could go to Little Paradise with me," Janet said.

I cringed.

"Little Paradise?" Scott and Conrad repeated in unison.

"Yeah, Sally and I followed that old logging trail near the Minutemen's graves and came to this beautiful pond with a bridge and waterfall. We named it Little Paradise!"

Again, I cringed.

Scott chuckled and cast an amused look at Conrad. "That's the Pendletons' pond! It's in their back yard. If you'd gone around to the front of the pond, right through that row of trees, you'd have seen their house! It's right on Wyatt Road!"

"You're lucky they didn't throw you out of there," Conrad said. "It's private property."

I rolled my eyes. Our wonderful discovery had turned out to be someone's private pond where we could have been arrested for trespassing. Just great. So much for ever taking Ricky Nelson there for a dream picnic. Although I had to admit Ricky was beginning to pale in comparison to my newest crush, Troy Donahue.

"And to think we had to go by creepy Bone Swamp to get there, too," Janet said.

"Bone swamp?" Conrad asked.

"There's a swamp on that trail with all kinds of animal bones in it," Janet explained.

"We call that Quicksand Swamp," Scott said. "The mud is so deep in it, animals get stuck in there when they go to drink."

"Nice of you to tell us that now!" I said. "We could have been two of the skeletons lying in it if we'd have stepped too close to the mud!"

"Well, if you'd have waited to go exploring when I could have gone with you," Conrad said, his lips tightening, "then you wouldn't have had anything to worry about."

Dad waited until Scott was safely inside the farmhouse before he drove off. "So, where do you live, Conrad?" he asked.

"Oh, no problem," he said. "I can walk home from your place."

"It's after midnight and pitch dark out," my mother said. "Don't be silly! Just tell us how to get to your house. I won't sleep tonight unless I know you're safely on your doorstep!"

Conrad directed my dad to keep going straight for a couple miles. When we came to a big white Colonial house with a crooked picket fence in front of it, he told Dad to stop. The house and front yard were bathed in light from a spotlight type of porch light, which Conrad's parents apparently had left on for him.

"Well, thank you for a great night," he said to my parents.

"So, did you enjoy your first drive-in movie?" my mom asked him.

"Not as much as I enjoyed having my arm around your daughter," he answered, much too honestly, in my opinion.

Conrad opened the car door and put one foot on the ground. "Oh, before I forget!" he said. "This Saturday my school is sponsoring a donkey ballgame in the baseball field behind the school. I have some free tickets if you'd all like to go."

"Donkey ballgame?" my dad repeated.

"The players have to play baseball while riding on donkeys," Conrad explained.

"You're joking, right?" Dad said.

"No, I'm serious. It's a riot to watch. The school sponsors it every year and everyone has a blast!"

"Sounds like fun!" Dad said. "Sure, we'll go!"

"Great!" Conrad said, smiling. He climbed all the way out of the car, turned and blew a kiss at me, then shut the door and walked toward his house. He paused to wave at us from his porch before he went inside.

Finally, for the first time all night, I was free. I felt as if I'd just been paroled after being in prison for six hours and 23 minutes.

"I wonder if Scott is going to the donkey ballgame?" Janet said.

I was too upset to care. My father, in my eyes, was becoming a traitor, a Conrad lover. It almost seemed as if he'd concocted some evil plan to shove the two of us closer together instead of trying to help me get rid of the guy. There I was, relieved to have made it through the drive-in without suffering any permanent emotional scars, and now my dad was making me go to some dumb ballgame where I'd have to spend hours with Conrad again, this time watching a bunch of donkeys running around a field and probably pooping everywhere. It wasn't fair at all.

I seriously considered stowing away in the trunk of the car when my dad headed back to work in the city in the morning. I'd had just about all I could take of Arrowwood and its wacky residents...especially one in particular.

CHAPTER NINE

At 7 a.m. I stood in the driveway and waved goodbye to my dad as he drove off down Shepherdess Road. I knew he'd be back again on Friday night, only two days away, to stay for the whole weekend, but I still felt as if I were bidding farewell to someone going off to war. When dad's car disappeared behind a cloud of road dust, I stomped back into the camp and sulked.

Janet was still asleep and my mom was clearing the breakfast dishes from the table. She'd made Dad his favorite – bacon, sunnyside-up eggs and toast with strawberry jam – real strawberry jam, not the artificially flavored one. Dad always said if there was one thing that was an insult to his palate, it was fake strawberry anything. I'd missed breakfast because I hadn't crawled out of bed until Dad was about to leave. Plus that, I'd thought maybe he and my mom wanted some time alone in the other room before he had to leave so they could sneak some kisses or do whatever it was parents did before one of them went away.

One of the good things about Dad's surprise visit was he'd brought a couple bags of groceries with him, so there was an entire new array of snacks and goodies to munch on. I tore a banana from a bunch lying on the table, then peeled it and broke off a piece, which I shoved into my mouth. As I chewed, I debated whether I should stay up or go back to bed. After all, by the time I'd finally crawled into the bunk after getting back from the drive-in, it was after one o'clock in the morning. That meant I'd had only about five hours of sleep.

"Going to be another hot one today," Mom said. "Are you going to go swimming?"

"I'm too tired to walk that far," I said, still chewing. "Why can't this dumb river be full of nice clear water with no bloodsuckers in it? Then we could just go swimming right outside our door."

"That would be nice," Mom said. "Believe me, I'd be in there myself, cooling off. But not with that eel or snake still in there!" Her own words made her shudder.

She started talking about something else, but I stopped listening. That was because I was thinking about something that had happened during the night – something so disturbing, so hideously shocking, I still was having trouble believing it really had occurred.

I'd had a dream about Conrad...and he was naked.

In the dream, which was more like a nightmare, Conrad and I were alone in the camp. When I walked out of the kitchen and into the front room, I caught him putting on his bathing trunks. He froze when he saw me and just stood there, his trunks around his ankles. I'd never seen a naked male before, other than when I'd watched my aunt change my baby cousin's diaper, so in my dream, Conrad had a baby's weenie. And it was really, really white compared to the rest of his deeply tanned skin. If I lived to be 100, I knew I'd never be able to get that image out of my mind. And how, I wondered, would I ever be able to face Conrad again after a dream like that?

"I guess I'll go pick some more blueberries," I heard Mom saying. I stopped thinking about my nightmare long enough to look at her as she continued, "I still want to make some blueberry muffins with fresh, wild blueberries before the birds eat them all. Have you noticed all of the purple bird-droppings around here? That means the birds are eating the blueberries!"

"Did someone mention blueberry muffins?" Janet's hoarse voice came from behind me. Before anyone could answer, she added, "I'm really thirsty. Sleeping way up near the ceiling sure gets hot!"

She went to the fridge, poured herself a glass of orange juice and took a seat at the table.

"You know what I want to do today?" she asked.

I rolled my eyes. "Walk by Scott's house a half-dozen times?"

She shook her head. "I saw part of an old wooden fence lying on the ground behind the outhouse. I think we should bring it up here and use it to build a raft with. Then we can float down the river on it, like Huckleberry Finn did!"

First of all, I wondered what she'd been doing behind the outhouse. I mean, it wasn't exactly a place where anyone would go on purpose. Maybe she'd finally fallen through the hole and had to crawl out through the back of the place.

I did think her idea about the raft wasn't a bad one, though. On a raft, we could explore the river without having to worry about the leeches or eels. And if we saw an interesting place along the shore, we could pull over and check it out. But best of all, floating down the river would keep me away from Conrad…and having to face him after my embarrassing dream.

Janet and I gulped down our cereal and got dressed in our swimsuits and shorts. We then headed down to the outhouse and, after we both used it, went behind it and dragged the six-foot section of wooden fence up to the camp. In the storage shed, we found a hammer, nails, rope, some wrinkled-up sheets of plastic, an old air mattress and a zillion spiders. I came out of there feeling itchy all over.

"We can patch the holes in the air mattress with Band-Aids from the first-aid kit in the kitchen," Janet said, "then blow it up and use it to help float the raft."

We spent the next two hours building our raft. We used the fence for the base, nailed a bunch of sticks and branches across the top of it and then nailed the plastic over the top of that. We patched the air mattress and took turns blowing it up. When it was so full of air, one more puff would have turned it into the Hindenburg, we tied it to the underside of the raft. Janet found two big tree limbs that we de-branched to use as poles to push the raft down the river.

"Looks good," Janet said. She stood with her hands on her hips and admired our handiwork.

I wiped my dirt-covered hands on my denim shorts. "But will it float?"

"Only one way to find out," she said. "Let's get some stuff together and prepare for our maiden voyage."

We shoved some fruit into a waxed-paper bread wrapper, then filled a jar with drinking water and headed for the river. We each grabbed a section of the pull-rope we'd attached to the front of the raft and started to drag it down the hill. But after only a few feet, the bottom of the raft snagged on a twig and it nearly tore a hole in the air mattress, so we decided to carry the raft the rest of the way. I picked up the front of it and Janet grabbed the back, and together, we made our way toward the water. The raft felt as if it weighed a ton. I thought about the hernias my dad always complained about getting whenever he lifted something heavy. I wasn't sure what a hernia was, but I was pretty sure I was about to find out.

Finally, the USS *Jan-Sal* made it into the water.

"It floats!" Janet squealed.

"Don't get excited yet," I said. "My fat rear-end isn't on it."

My mother, wearing a brown-and-orange flowered housedress and carrying a plastic container, apparently for the yet-to-be-picked blueberries, came out of the camp. I looked up when I heard the screen door slam.

"Bye, Mom!" I called out. "Janet and I are going to explore the river now!"

Mom walked over to study our means of transportation. Her expression clearly displayed her concern. "Are you sure that thing is safe? I don't want you two to drown!"

"I don't think you have much to worry about," I said. "The water's not even up to our waists."

"Well, you be careful!" Mom said. "And don't go getting lost!"

As much as Janet and I didn't want to, we had to stand up to our thighs in the water so we could climb onto the raft. I could have sworn that every slimy creature ever created was slithering up my legs as I waited for Janet to climb on board.

"I'm on!" Janet called out to me. "Quick! Get on!"

I slid on my stomach onto the raft. As I did, I felt the branches under the plastic poking into my ribs and nearly impaling my spleen. I curled into a fetal position, just waiting to sink into the murky depths of the river…and be attacked by a gang of bloodthirsty leeches. Nothing happened.

"Here!" Janet handed one of the makeshift poles to me. "Sit up and help me shove the raft away from the shore and out into the current."

I obeyed and took the pole from her. Together, we pushed the raft out to the middle of the river, which was only a few feet from the edge. Within seconds, we were floating with the current. I had no clue where we were going or where we'd end up, but it didn't matter to me as long as we were far away from Conrad and any reminders of my nightmarish dream about his teeny white weenie.

We laid the poles on the raft and then sat stiffly, afraid to move, as we floated downstream. The current moved at a lazy pace, giving us time to scan our surroundings. The woods lining the river were thick and dark, and I noticed the banks were getting steeper as we went along. I began to feel as if we were in a tunnel. The river also got wider, and from what I could tell, deeper. I grabbed the pole and tried to touch the bottom with it. I couldn't.

"The water's over our heads now!" I said, my voice rising. "The banks are too high for us to dock the raft and the water's too deep for us to wade in. We're stuck going wherever the river takes us! My father said it empties into the ocean! We're going to end up being shark bait!"

Janet didn't seem at all fazed by my words. "This is only one part of the river," she said. "We're bound to come to a part where the banks are level with the water and it's shallow again. Besides that, the ocean is probably still 40 miles from here. We're not going to drift that far!"

"We will if we can't get out of the water!" I said. "And have you noticed that the current seems to be getting a little faster?"

"Yeah, I did," Janet said. "Wouldn't it be scary if we came to a waterfall?"

I hadn't even considered the possibility of waterfalls in the crummy old river, but now that Janet had put the idea into my head, visions of the raft plunging over the likes of Niagara Falls and shattering into a million splinters at the bottom, filled my head.

"We should be coming to some houses soon," Janet said. "The river crosses Harmon Road at the tar road. We've been over that bridge in the car and on foot, so I know it's up ahead somewhere!"

"Bridge? We have to go underneath a bridge? How do we know what's living under there?"

"You mean like trolls?" Janet chuckled.

"No, like bats and giant spiders and rats that will leap onto our heads when we disturb them!"

"Will you stop worrying and just relax and enjoy our adventure?" Janet said. "You've been acting jumpy all morning! What's wrong with you anyway?"

She'd be jumpy, too, I thought, if she'd seen what I'd seen in my sleep the night before. "Well...if you must know," I said, "I had a dream about Conrad last night and he was..." The word stuck in my throat.

"He was what?" Janet turned around to look at me.

I hung my head so I wouldn't have to look her in the eye. "He was..."

"He was what?" Janet repeated. "Dead? Angry? Murdering someone?"

I took a deep breath and closed my eyes. "Naked."

The silence that followed caused me to open my eyes. The first thing I saw was Janet – with both hands over her mouth. She looked like one of those "speak no evil" monkey statues I'd seen in a gift shops. She slowly dropped her hands and whispered, "Are you serious? How did he look?"

"Very tan...with a teeny white weenie," I said.

Janet laughed so hard, I was scared she was going to fall off the raft and drown.

"It's not funny!" I said. "It's disgusting – a nightmare!"

"Well, you're the one who dreamt it! So it came from nobody's brain but yours! I think it means you really want to see him naked!"

"I would rather jump into this river right now and be swept away by the current than ever see Conrad naked!"

"I think I'll tell him about your dream," Janet said, giggling. "I'll bet he'd really love to hear all about it!"

"You breathe even one word of it and I'll never speak to you again! Conrad's already too eager to please. If you told him I was picturing him without his clothes on, he might think it's what I want and do a striptease for me!"

"Eeeeyewww!" Janet and I said in unison.

Laughing, I looked past Janet and at the river ahead. My smile faded. "Waterfall!" I shouted.

Janet turned around to face straight ahead. "Grab your pole! Maybe we can turn around!"

Poles not long enough to touch the bottom of the river, we discovered, were about as useful as two toothpicks. I was pretty sure we were doomed. And even if we somehow managed to survive the trip over the waterfall, I was positive we'd end up treading water until we drowned. Our bloated bodies would be found out in the middle of the ocean somewhere – that's if sharks didn't eat us first.

We could hear the sound of the waterfall as the now-strong current pulled us toward it. Janet and I grasped the edges of the raft and braced ourselves for a wild ride. I closed my eyes and held my breath.

The waterfall turned out to be a lot smaller than I'd thought it was. Going over it felt kind of like going down the small kiddies' slide at the playground, but without the hard landing (usually flat on my back with my legs in the air) on the ground at the bottom. The waterfall emptied into a wide, calm area that looked like a big round pool. I could see white beach sand on the bottom. And the bank, also covered with sand, gently sloped into the water.

"I think this is someone's private swimming hole," I said to Janet. "Let's try to get the raft up onto the shore here."

"But we've only been rafting for 15 minutes!" she said. "What kind of adventure is that? We could never do anything like this in the city! Besides that, do you want to go back to the camp and spend the day with Conrad?"

I felt the color rush to my face.

"How are we supposed to get this raft back to the camp anyway?" Janet continued. "We can't go back upstream, not against the current and up over the waterfall. And we can't carry it all the way back on foot."

"We're going to have to leave it wherever we dock it," I said. "And then we'll have to walk back to the camp. So we shouldn't go 100 miles or anything like that. I don't know about you, but I can't walk that far!"

"Well, we can go at least another mile before we ditch it," she said. "We worked too hard building this raft to leave it to rot after only a mile or two. Let's at least get some good use out of it first."

"I wonder if there are leeches in this swimming hole?" I said. The place looked cool and inviting, and the beach sand on the bottom made the water look much less dark and murky than the water back at the camp.

"It's still the same river," Janet said, "so it probably has leeches here, too." She paused before adding, with a chuckle, "Maybe these leeches are more high-class, though. This is like the Hollywood area of the river for leeches!"

"What do they do, wear tuxedoes and use silverware when they feast on our blood?" I joked. "Still, I wouldn't mind coming here to swim." I eyed the thick woods surrounding the area. "I wonder how we'd get here on dry land from the camp?"

Janet shrugged. "I don't know, but I don't think I'm about to go exploring any more woods to find out. Finding Little Paradise was scary enough. And after all we went through, thinking we made such a great discovery, we could have been arrested for trespassing. This beach probably is on private property, too. I mean, someone had to put all of this sand here. I don't think it just fell out of the sky!"

The raft drifted through the pool and back into a narrow part of the river with high banks on each side, giving me that stuck-in-a-tunnel feeling again. When I looked to see what was up ahead, the bridge came into view.

"It's the bridge!" I said, groaning. "I knew we should have docked on the beach back there. I really, really don't want to go underneath the bridge!"

"Oh, don't be such a big chicken!" Janet said. "It's not every day you get to see a bridge from underneath it!"

"I don't want to see a bridge from underneath it!" I wouldn't have minded so much if it had been a big, high bridge, but this one was low and just wide enough for one car to cross it at a time. I was pretty sure I'd have to duck my head when we went under it.

The underside of the bridge, as it turned out, was dark, rusty and loaded with giant spider webs. Even worse, the river under the bridge was shallow and loaded with rocks, many of which were sticking up out of the water. The raft bounced around like a pinball as it hit one rock after the other. On the other side of the bridge was a set of small rapids that emptied into a wide section of the river that curved away from the road and back into the woods.

I didn't know about Janet, but I was getting pretty tired of our Tom Sawyer, Huckleberry Finn or whatever the heck it was, adventure. For one thing, my legs were beginning to cramp from keeping them tucked up on the raft. I wanted to sit spread-eagle, but I didn't dare let even a toe dangle in the water.

The current carried us into a wide area surrounded by thick trees with tangled branches that hung over the water and blocked out the sun. The water was calm – too calm, I thought – and inky black. The whole area made me feel as if we'd drifted onto a movie set. I'd seen plenty of horror movies with similar scenes, where everything always was really calm before some hideous creature jumped up out of the water and shredded innocent people into confetti.

My heartbeat quickened and my throat suddenly felt as if I'd been gargling with dust. Not only was the pool dark, calm and quiet, the odor that rose from it reminded me of the odor at Bone Swamp...or my aunt's septic tank that was constantly backing up and spilling across her driveway. Whenever we went to visit her, Dad always parked out on the road and we walked across the lawn, just to avoid the driveway.

"I-I think something died in here," Janet said, her blue eyes wide as they made a sweep of our surroundings. The black, stagnant water didn't even have so much as a ripple in it. With no current to move us along, we just sat there, surrounded by stinkiness.

"How are we going to get out of here with nothing to paddle with?" I asked. My shaky voice betrayed my determination not to let Janet know I was very close to bursting into tears.

"I wish I knew," she said. "I'd swim for the bank, but it's too high to climb up."

"You'd actually swim in this cesspool? Are you crazy? This water probably would eat off our skin, just like battery acid!"

Janet turned around to look directly at me. "Would you rather still be sitting here on this raft in the pitch dark tonight when all of the bugs and creatures come out? Or would you rather swim for it now in the daylight?"

"Neither!" I no longer could hold back the tears. "I wish I was back at the camp...with Conrad!"

My own words shocked me. I was convinced the fear of dying must have made me temporarily lose what little sanity I had left.

"Stop crying!" Janet said. "You're going to make me cry, too! We have to think of some way to get out of this dumb river!"

A slight breeze came from our right. I prayed it would move the raft a few feet, but all it did was lift the aroma from the water directly to our noses.

"I bet this is where everyone's sewer pipes empty," Janet said. I barely could understand her because her hand was cupped over her nose and mouth. "I'd sure hate to touch bottom! Can you just imagine what's lying in the mud down there?"

I didn't want to imagine anything. I studied our surroundings and tried to see beyond the wall of trees. There were no houses, no signs of life. If people were draining their sewage into this part of the river, they must have had pipes about a mile long.

The breeze grew stronger and so did the odor. But the raft moved a few feet toward the left bank. I'd never seen a real tornado before, but at that moment, I was praying that one like in *The Wizard of Oz* would magically appear and lift us and our crummy raft out of the water and drop us on dry land.

"I suppose we could always use our hands to paddle with," Janet said.

Not only did the thought of thrusting my hands into cesspool water make me want to upchuck, I was afraid I'd probably have to lie on my stomach on the raft to do it. And that meant my nose would be even closer to the foul smell.

"Hissssssssss!"

Janet and I turned to stare at each other.

"Hisssssssss!"

"Is that a snake?" I whispered, not daring to move. I calculated that if the snake's size matched the volume of its hissing, it probably was big enough to swallow the entire raft.

Janet barely moved her lips as she answered, "It's worse than a snake. I think we have a leak in the air mattress. One of those rocks under the bridge probably tore it."

I closed my eyes and took a deep breath. "Are you saying we're going to sink?"

"Maybe not," Janet said. "Maybe we don't need the air mattress. Maybe the raft will float by itself. After all, wood floats."

"That's a lot of maybes! I can already feel the raft getting lower!"

"Stop being so panicky! You're just imagining things. The raft isn't sinking!"

I pointed to the right side of the raft, where the water was beginning to come up over the edge. "If we're not sinking, then the tide is rising."

Janet slid away from the edge of the raft, a move that caused it to tilt to the left. "We have no choice!" she said. "We're going to have to swim for it!"

"Nooooo!" The tears practically squirted out of my eyes. "I can't! I-I won't!"

"We're going to end up in the water either way," Janet said. "So are you going to jump in now and swim or are you going to sit on the raft and go down with it?"

"I'm not good at swimming!" I paused to swallow a sob. "I can only do the dog paddle! Conrad taught me how to swim underwater, but there's no way in Hades I'm going to put my face in there!"

Janet was busy studying the banks that surrounded us. "Over there!" she said, pointing to an area on the left about thirty-five feet ahead. "There's a small clearing and the bank isn't very high. It's our only hope!"

The clearing looked so far away, I felt as if I'd have to swim the equivalent of the English Channel. That, I thought, trembling, was if I *could* swim that far. Paddling around the local swimming hole with Conrad guiding my every move was a lot different than swimming for my life. I had visions of myself jumping off the raft and sinking right down to the bottom where I'd be sucked into a quicksand-like pile of poop, never to be seen again.

Before I could say anything, I heard a splash. My head snapped in the direction of the sound and I saw Janet swimming toward the shore.

"Janet! Wait!" I called out. "Don't leave me!"

She didn't stop swimming, but lifted her head out of the water and shouted, "Hurry up! The raft is going to sink any minute!"

I froze. My body didn't want to move, no matter how much I commanded it to. I couldn't blame it. Taking a dip in the equivalent of my aunt's septic tank wasn't exactly a great incentive.

I sat unmoving on the raft until the water rose up over my thighs. When I felt something slimy touch my bare leg, I stopped thinking about the smelly water or what was on the bottom. I stretched out my arms and hit the water, dog paddling for my life.

By the time I reached the clearing where Janet already was standing, I was gasping for breath. Janet wrapped her right arm around a small tree and extended her left arm toward me. I reached up and grasped her hand and she yanked me onto the shore. I thought that for a skinny girl, she sure was strong, especially when it came to lifting someone who wasn't exactly a featherweight. I collapsed into some weeds and tried to spit the disgusting taste of the water out of my mouth. It reminded me of the sauerkraut juice my dad once had dared me to take a sip of…only worse.

As I lay there, gasping and groaning, I could have sworn I heard Janet laughing. I lifted my head just high enough to see her face. Sure enough, she practically was busting a gut.

"What on earth is so funny?" I asked.

"This whole adventure!" she said. "I mean, it was so cool! We went down a strange river on a piece of fence and an air mattress, then over a waterfall, under a bridge and into some creepy lagoon where we had to swim for our lives! Wait'll we tell the kids back home this one!"

Unlike Janet, I didn't think anything about our little expedition was humorous. "We stink! We smell like the public restrooms downtown."

"Well, if you want Conrad to keep his distance from you, just don't wash up when we get back!" she said.

"You know how fussy my mom is about cleanliness! She'll probably make us sleep out in the outhouse tonight!"

"At least the outhouse will smell better than us for a change!" Janet said, laughing.

All I wanted to do at that moment was figure out where we were and how to get back to the camp, and the sooner the better. I knew the bridge wasn't too far away, but the woods were so thick, I had the feeling we'd end up covered with thorns and poison ivy before we ever found our way back there.

"I need to take a bath in pure bleach to disinfect myself!" I said, sitting up and wrinkling my nose.

"Well, are you ready to start walking back?" Janet asked and rose to her feet. "I'm hungry! My stomach is growling so loud, I'm scared it will attract bears!"

"I'm hungry, too. After all, our provisions went down with the raft. But how do we get out of here and back to civilization?"

"The way I figure it, we just walk through the woods along the edge of the river and follow it back upstream until we reach the bridge on Harmon Road. Then we'll be back at the camp in a snap."

"We'll need a machete to get through these woods," I said. I knew all about machetes because my dad owned one. He'd bought it at a yard sale a few years ago and had used it to hack through some of the thicker brush around the camp.

Janet and I took off through the woods. My sneakers squished with every step and I kept tripping over the maze of tangled tree roots and underbrush. Janet was no help. She walked in front of me and whenever she pushed a branch aside, she'd just let it go, apparently forgetting I was right behind her. I got smacked in the face so many times, I was pretty sure I had permanent leaf prints on my face.

Janet suddenly stopped walking – so abruptly, I nearly crashed into her. She turned to look at me. "I have to pee really bad!"

"You should have gone while you were swimming in the smelly water," I said. "Believe me, you wouldn't have polluted anything."

"Where can I go?" she asked, eyeing our surroundings. "I'm not going to be able to hold it all the way back to the camp!"

"We don't even know where the heck the camp is!" I said. "If we end up getting lost, you'll probably have to pee ten more times before we find it!"

"Look! Over there!" She pointed to her right. "It's perfect!"

103

I followed the direction of her finger and spotted a rotted old stump. It was about knee-high, perfectly round in shape and where the wood had rotted away in the center of it, there was hole about the size of a dinner plate. It kind of resembled a wooden toilet. When I realized it looked like a toilet, I turned back to stare at Janet. "You're not thinking about sitting on that thing and peeing, are you?"

She shrugged. "Why not? It's better than trying to squat down on the ground and peeing on my feet!"

"Well, just hurry up and go!" I snapped. "I don't feel like standing here in the jungle all day!"

"Turn your back. I'm going to go sit on the stump. Make sure no one is coming!"

"Who on earth would be out here in the middle of nowhere? Smokey the Bear? And be careful when you sit on that stump! You might get termites up your rear!"

Two hours later, Janet and I were standing on the porch steps at the camp. My mother immediately came out to greet us.

"Where on earth have you two been?" she asked. She used her right hand to fan the air around her in an obvious attempt to move our stinkiness away from her nose. "You both look…and smell…terrible! And I've been worried sick about you. If I'd have had a car here, I'd have driven down to the police station!"

"What time is it?" I asked. "I'm starving!"

"It's two-and-a-half hours until supper!" Mom said. "You didn't answer my question! What happened to you?"

"Well," Janet said, "we floated down the river on our raft and we went over a waterfall, under a bridge and over some rapids and ended up in this big giant cesspool. Then the raft sprang a leak and sank and we had to swim through the poop water to get to the shore. I guess that's about it!"

My mother's eyebrows rose and her mouth opened, but she took a few seconds to speak. "You had to swim? I thought the river was shallow?"

"Not in the cesspool part!" Janet said. "It must have been 100 feet deep!" She paused for a moment and put the back of her hand up to her forehead. "I really need food…or I'm going to faint!"

She wasn't lying. One Saturday morning when she and I had gone downtown and she'd skipped breakfast, she passed out while in line at the post office. Luckily, she fell forward and landed on the man in front of us, who turned and grabbed her just before she hit the floor. After she gulped down a Snickers bar from the newspaper stand in the corner of the lobby, she was fine.

As Janet headed into the camp, my mother shouted after her, "Just grab something to eat and come right back out! Don't sit on anything until you get out of those smelly shorts and bathing suit and wash up!"

I waited until Janet disappeared before I, in what I hoped was a casual-sounding voice, asked my mother, "So, what time did Conrad show up today looking for me?"

"He didn't come by," she said. "I was surprised after your big 'date' last night." She smiled. "Maybe the drive-in was too emotionally draining for him and he had to recover today."

"Well, it's just fine with me that he didn't show up," I said. "If he never comes over here again, I'll be happy."

But the truth was I felt somewhat let down that Conrad hadn't come around. Had I, I wondered, been such a terrible date? I already knew the answer...yes, I'd been the world's worst date. Not that I'd considered the drive-in to be an official date anyway. But still, I'd been nothing but mean and sarcastic to him all night. Then why, I wondered, had he invited all of us to the donkey ballgame this weekend if he had no intention of ever seeing me again? Maybe he hadn't come over today because he was sick from all of the drive-in food he'd eaten. After all, I reasoned, he'd never been to a drive-in before, so his stomach hadn't previously been introduced to drive-in food. It could have been too much for his intestines to handle.

"Well, I'm going to go get undressed," I said to my mother. "Then I'm going to scrub every inch of my body. What's for supper?"

"Canned beef stew."

It sounded as good to me as T-bone steak.

CHAPTER TEN

I woke up Friday morning to the sound of rain on the roof. Seeing that the top bunk was so close to the ceiling, the rain seemed to be drumming within an inch of my ear, making it impossible for me to sleep. I sighed, rolled over and buried my face in my pillow. Nothing was worse, I thought, than a rainy day at the camp. Back home, I'd be watching TV, listening to my records, talking on the phone, or walking half a block to the bus stop and then hopping a bus downtown. I'd hang out in Reynold's department store all day and ride the elevator to all six floors – from the toy department in the basement to the housewares department on the top floor. I'd also stop in the Gold Bond stamp redemption center and check out what I could get for my two-and-a-half books of stamps. New items arrived weekly, so I liked to see if anything tempted me to cash in my precious stamps. If not, I'd continue to save them until I had enough to get something big, like a TV set. Most of my mother's pots and pans had come from saving Gold Bond stamps or S & H green stamps. But I fully intended to get something a lot more exciting with mine.

Here at the camp, with no electricity, no TV, no telephone, no record player and no buses, the only way to pass the time on a rainy day, other than sleeping, was to read comic books, play cards or listen to my transistor radio. The problem was, I'd already read all of my comic books so many times, I could recite the characters' lines word for word. I was bored before I even got out of bed.

On the bright side, in only a few more hours my dad would be coming up for the weekend, so at least I had that to look forward to.

My thoughts turned to Conrad. Would he, I wondered, show up today? And if he didn't, what about the donkey ballgame on Saturday? Would we be left hanging, wondering if we still were going? Life, I thought, certainly would be a heck of a lot easier if the camp had a telephone...and indoor plumbing.

That was another bad thing about rainy days at the camp. The outhouse roof had a leak in it...directly above the seat. Dad once had commented about it, saying that while he was taking a leak, he'd been getting leaked on. I hadn't gotten the joke, but he and Mom, judging from their outburst of laugher, obviously had thought it was pretty funny.

I didn't climb down from bed until nearly noon. Janet and my mother were sitting at the table and playing separate games of solitaire. I looked out the window, praying I would see the sun peeking out from behind a cloud. All I saw was a gray sky and rain coming down in sheets. Seeing all of that water reminded me that I urgently had to use the outhouse. I'd have just gone out and straddled the pee bucket on the porch if I hadn't feared that Conrad, probably dressed from head to toe in plastic, would come walking up the driveway just as I dropped my underpants.

"Well, hello, sleepyhead!" Mom looked up from her cards. "You missed breakfast. Are you ready for lunch?"

"I'm not very hungry," I said. "I think I accidentally swallowed some of that stinky water yesterday and it poisoned me or something."

"Or maybe you swallowed some leeches and they're in your stomach, sucking all of your blood right now," Janet said, smiling. "If you start to look really pale, you should start worrying!"

I narrowed my eyes at her. "If I die from loss of blood, it'll be all your fault! You're the one who wanted to keep going on that crummy death trap of a raft!"

"Now, girls," Mom interrupted, "no one is going to die from blood loss!" I'm going to go make some grilled-cheese sandwiches." She stood and turned to face me. "Do you want one or not?"

"Yeah, I guess so. I also guess I'll go down to the outhouse while you're cooking. If I'm not back in ten minutes, come looking for me because it'll probably mean I drowned in the hole!"

By the time I made the round trip to the outhouse and then finished my lunch, the rain had stopped and the sun was peeking out from behind the clouds. The brighter the sun grew, the more my gloomy mood lifted.

"So, what do you want to do?" Janet asked me.

"I want to go check out the Rod and Gun Club, where they shoot those fake pigeons," I said. "I saw a trail I think goes to it, just after that stream past Big Rock."

"We can't just go walking into a place where they're shooting guns!" Janet said. "You want to end up full of holes?"

"Dad said they only shoot on Sundays. Today is Friday."

Janet didn't immediately answer. I figured she was trying to think of something more exciting to do, but couldn't come up with anything. "Okay, then," she finally said. "It's not like we've got anything thrilling planned for today. Yesterday was more than enough excitement anyway. Hey, did you write in your diary about our rafting adventure?"

"Of course I did."

"I did, too! In fact, I wrote in it first thing when I got up this morning. Only I added a few more exciting things to it to make it sound like even a bigger adventure! Like I put we lassoed a beaver that was swimming by us in the lagoon and it pulled us to shore!"

My mother laughed. "That's quite an imagination you have there, Janet!"

"Well, when future explorers find my diary, I want them to have something exciting to read," she said.

"Then while you're at it, why don't you go really big and write that Troy Donahue went on the raft with us?" I said.

She shook her head and sighed. "Because I'm more likely to lasso a beaver!"

* * * * *

Janet and I set off up the road in search of the Rod and Gun Club. The air was humid from the rain, and there were puddles scattered all over the dirt road. We had walked only about a quarter of a mile when something coming toward us made us stop in our tracks.

"Is that Conrad?" Janet's voice was barely a whisper.

"I-I think so," I said.

"Do you see what I see?"

I nodded. "He's wearing those big Halloween teeth made out of wax like the ones we used to buy at Hamel's Variety."

As Conrad came closer, his smile widened.

"I don't think they're wax," Janet said out of the corner of her mouth. "I think they're real fake ones, like from a dentist!"

I sucked in my breath. Was the reason why Conrad hadn't been around yesterday, I wondered, because he was having his teeth pulled and getting dentures?

My answer came a few seconds later as Conrad, still smiling, rushed up to me. "Surprise!" he shouted. "Look what I did yesterday!"

He didn't have to tell me to look. I honestly couldn't tear my eyes from his mouth. The teeth were way too big for him, and they had what looked like dried blood on the tops of them. He reminded me of the cartoon character, Charlie – Mr. Magoo's houseboy.

"That was pretty fast." I finally managed to find my voice. "I thought dentures took weeks to make."

"Oh, I had the impressions taken about ten days ago, before I even met you." he said. "I'm going to be in high school this year so I wanted to look good. I'd have mentioned it to you, but I didn't feel comfortable talking about stuff like having my teeth yanked out when I barely knew you. Then as I got to know you better, I decided I wanted it to be a surprise. When I had my teeth pulled yesterday, the dentist put these right in. He told me not to take them out so my gums will mold to them."

That explained the blood on them, I thought. I had trouble understanding him because the huge teeth made him sound as if he'd just stuffed his mouth full of marshmallows. The only explanation I could come up with for the dentures fitting him the way they did was they'd been made for someone else, a much bigger person, but the guy had dropped dead.

"They cost me a whole hundred bucks!" Conrad said. "And I had to have 15 shots to numb me before I had my teeth pulled. I was going to wait until tomorrow to show you, when I felt better, because I'm really sore, but I couldn't wait! I knew how pleasantly surprised you'd be!"

Janet still hadn't uttered a word. When I glanced at her, her mouth was open and her eyes, wide and unblinking, were riveted on Conrad's smile.

"I'm surprised all right!" I said. Shocked was more like it. And there was nothing pleasant about it.

Conrad smiled even wider. When he did, the top part of the denture slipped down a little, revealing a gap between the fake teeth and his gums. The clotted blood along the gum line was a dark, almost black color. I gulped back a wave of nausea.

"Jake dropped over to see me yesterday when I got home from the dentist's," Conrad said, "and he really embarrassed me with something he said about you."

"Jake said something embarrassing about me?"

"Yeah, he said I'd better be careful if I try to kiss you because my teeth might fall out!"

Kiss me? He couldn't even close his lips over those massive teeth! Even worse, when he spoke, they made clicking noises like castanets.

"So?" Conrad said, taking a step closer to me. "What do you think? Am I handsome now? Was all of my suffering worth it?"

I never thought I'd ever want to see his old, black-eyed-peas smile again, but at that moment, I would have given anything to have it back. I figured that anything, even no teeth at all, was better than these Halloween-worthy horse teeth. If I were Conrad's parents, I would have been making a beeline to the nearest lawyer's office and filling out the paperwork to sue the dentist.

"I think it'll take some time for me to get used to them," I said. "I mean, I'm not used to seeing you with such big white teeth."

"I know what you mean," he said. "When the dentist handed me a mirror, the first thing I said was they looked really big. He said that's because I'm still growing and I'll grow into them."

I couldn't help thinking that even if he grew to be the size of Paul Bunyan, he'd still never grow into those teeth.

"So where are you headed?" he asked.

"We were going to just take a walk," I said, "but let's go back to the camp and show my mom your surprise instead!" I couldn't wait to see the expression on my mom's face when Conrad and his teeth came walking in, although I was pretty sure the teeth would beat him into the camp, they stuck out so far. I wished I'd brought a camera with me so I could capture my mother's reaction for eternity.

Janet and I turned around and headed back toward the camp. Conrad fell into step next to me.

"Why don't you ask Sally about the dream she had about you!" Janet finally found her voice. I silently wished she'd have stayed shut-up.

Conrad's head snapped in my direction. His eyebrows arched and his cartoon-like smile widened. "You had a dream about me?"

I shrugged. "It was nothing."

"*Nothing?*" Janet persisted. "It was all she talked about all day yesterday!"

I rammed my elbow into her ribs. When she gasped and turned to look at me, I gave her my very best evil eye.

Conrad, however, wasn't about to let the subject rest. "So, tell me...exactly what was I doing in your dream?"

Janet giggled, for which she received another jab in the ribs.

"Nothing," I said. "It was nothing. You and I were swimming, that's all."

Janet ran a few feet ahead. Then, when she was safely out of rib-jabbing range, turned to face us and said, "Conrad, you had no clothes on!"

He stopped walking and his mouth dropped open. When it did, his teeth nearly landed on the road, but he made a quick catch and salvaged the hundred-dollar masterpieces. He shoved them back into his mouth, then said, "Was I really...naked?"

I stood there wishing I had ten-foot arms so I could give Janet another well-deserved poke. "Janet is just being silly and making things up! Don't believe anything she says."

"If I'm lying, then why is your face so red right now?" Janet asked.

I had to fight a strong urge to take her back to join her sunken raft.

"You really *are* blushing!" Conrad said, his smile revealing his obvious pleasure. "Tell me more! I want to hear all about this dream!"

"The subject is closed," I said. "Not one more word about my dream, understand?"

"Then I'm sure Janet will tell me all about it if you won't!" he said.

"Not unless Janet wants me to tell Scott what she did with a stump yesterday!" I shot back.

Janet's grin faded. If she wanted to tell Conrad about the teeny white weenie, then I wouldn't hesitate to tell Scott about her peeing in a tree stump that looked like a toilet. After all, fair was fair.

"Okay, I'll never mention the dream again." Janet raised her hands in a gesture of surrender. "Conrad, you'll just have to use your imagination to figure out what it was about."

I thought that was the worst thing she could have said. Left to Conrad's imagination, I was willing to bet I'd somehow end up naked in the dream, too.

He scratched his head. "Now I'm not only wondering about the dream about me, I'm wondering what the heck Janet did with a stump! You city girls sure are hard to figure out!"

We rounded the corner into the camp's driveway. My mother was outside, kneeling on the ground to the right of the porch steps and replanting some wildflowers she'd dug up out in the woods. When she heard us, she stood up and smiled. "Back already? You weren't gone very lo..." Her eyes suddenly looked as if they might bulge out of their sockets.

"Conrad had his teeth pulled out and got dentures yesterday!" I, smiling sweetly, said. "He paid a whole hundred dollars for them, too!"

Conrad moved closer to my mother and flashed his new smile at her. I was glad he was in front of me because that way, he wasn't able to see how hard I was biting on my bottom lip to keep from laughing at my mother.

My mother's gaze focused on the giant teeth. She opened her mouth to speak, but instantly clamped it shut.

"Well, what do you think?" I asked her. I couldn't wait to hear her answer.

She looked past Conrad to glare at me, then managed to say, "Um, well, what do *you* think, Conrad? Are you happy with your new teeth?"

"Yeah!" he said. "I always wanted nice white teeth. I cut a lot of lawns and picked a lot of green beans to save up enough money for these. Once I get used to them, I think I'll be real happy with them! And the kids at school won't razz me or call me Stumpy Mouth anymore."

Stumpy Mouth? That was the first I'd heard of that one. I was pretty certain, however, that when the kids at school saw his new teeth, they'd give him a whole new nickname – and it wasn't going to be a flattering one.

Conrad reached into the back pocket of his faded jeans and pulled out four slips of yellow paper. "Here are the tickets to the donkey baseball game tomorrow. It starts at three o'clock. I'll be here at 2:30 and will show you how to get there. I can't wait! You'll love it, you really will!"

"Is Scott going?" Janet asked.

"Yep. He's going with Jake and Tweaky. We'll meet up with them there."

Janet smiled. At least someone was happy, I thought. I, on the other hand, was going to once again be stuck spending hour upon torturous hour with Conrad...and his teeth. I was afraid if he smiled during the ball game, the donkeys would think he was a relative and come stampeding toward us.

"Thank you so much for the tickets," my mother said, taking them from his hand. "Are you sure you don't want us to pay for them?"

"Nah," he said, shaking his head. "You took me to a drive-in movie. It's the least I can do."

"In a couple hours," my mother said, "Sally's father will be coming up for the weekend. Would you like to stay for supper?"

I nearly gasped out loud when she extended the invitation. But after I had a moment to think about it, a knowing smile slowly spread across my face. Mom, I decided, had felt obligated to invite Conrad to eat with us because he'd given us free tickets that probably would have cost us at least a couple dollars each if we'd had to buy them at the event. But she knew he wouldn't accept because he still couldn't chew, so the invitation really wasn't a genuine invitation at all, just a token gesture. Heck, the way I figured it, Conrad probably would be slurping soup for at least another week or two.

"Thank you, I'd love to stay," he said.

I prayed that the total body-consuming panic I suddenly felt didn't show on my face. The thought of watching him trying to

113

chew food while his castanet teeth kept a snappy beat was enough to make me swear off food for life.

"But sorry, I can't," he continued. "My mouth is still real sore and I have to rinse it out every two hours with warm salt water. And the dentist said not to try to eat anything solid until after my stitches come out next Thursday. But thank you for inviting me."

"That's a shame," Mom said. Her tone sounded so sincere, even I nearly believed she meant it. "But maybe we can do it some other time."

Over my dead body, I thought. It seemed to me that a lot of invitations involving Conrad were either being accepted or extended lately without anyone consulting me first. Didn't anyone care that Conrad was driving me crazy or that even if he were the last guy on the planet and the entire future of mankind depended on us being together, the human race would become extinct?

"Well, I'd better get going now," Conrad said. "I think I'll get some rest so I can be up for the ballgame tomorrow."

"You shouldn't be walking all that way home when you're not feeling well," my mom said. "Why don't you wait for Sally's father to get here and he can give you a ride?"

That did it. I was convinced my parents were sadists, out to make my life as miserable as possible. I'd always been a good, obedient kid who got straight A's in school, and this was how they repaid me? By forcing me to spend even *more* time with Conrad? I wondered what they'd do to me if I were a bad kid! Sign papers giving me permission to marry him?

"If you don't think he'd mind," Conrad said. "I could really use a ride. The walk over here made me feel kinda woozy."

I wanted to say it probably was because his head wasn't used to carrying ten extra pounds of porcelain, or whatever his dentures were made of, but I bit my lip. All of this lip biting was beginning to hurt.

So for at least the next two hours I was going to be stuck with Conrad – unless, by some miracle, my dad decided to get out of work early and rush to see us. But with my luck, a truck carrying a thousand dozen eggs would roll over on the main road to the camp and my dad would end up backed up for hours in the world's biggest traffic jam.

"So what do you want to do until your dad gets here?" Janet asked.

The thought had crossed my mind that it might be fun to throw Conrad into the river and see if all of the blood on his teeth would attract leeches. "I don't know," I said.

She turned to look at Conrad. "You want to go check out the Rod and Gun Club with us? Or do you feel too woozy, Conrad?"

"No, I can walk there," he said. "It's not far at all. There's a path through the woods right near where I ran into you girls today. My dad and two of my brothers are members. They have a man-made pond there where they dammed up the brook."

I'd seen enough water the day before to last a lifetime, so the pond didn't intrigue me. But neither did hanging around the camp with Conrad and doing nothing. So the three of us headed up the road.

The Rod and Gun Club wasn't anything like I'd imagined it would be. We emerged from the wooded trail into a huge clearing, most of which was muddy, thanks to the morning's rain. To the left was a pond that looked even muddier, with the remnants of dead trees sticking out of it. Straight ahead was a shack-like building made of some kind of metal, with a rusty-looking roof.

"Come on," Conrad said. "Let's go see if anyone is in the clubhouse."

There was only one problem...an obstacle standing between the clubhouse and us. Leading from the pond and dissecting the property was what looked like a concrete canal. There was no water in it, but I thought maybe when they opened the dam to drain the pond, or to let water in, that's where the water went. Over the canal was a makeshift bridge – two steel girders placed next to each other.

"I hope you don't think I'm going to walk across those things!" I said. "Forget it!"

Falling into a concrete canal and possibly cracking open my skull and having my brains splatter everywhere wasn't my idea of fun.

"Oh, don't be such a chicken!" Janet said. "It'll be fun! Just pretend you're one of those gymnast girls that walk on those balance beams."

"But those girls on the balance beams have something I don't," I said. "A good sense of balance! Do you remember what happened when I tried to walk on that little wall that goes around the Burkes' yard?"

"You fell into their rose bush," she said.

Conrad looked as if he wanted to laugh. "Did my baby get some thorns stuck in some painful places?" he asked, patting my shoulder.

"Look! It's easy!" Janet called out, interrupting my urge to shove Conrad into the canal. She stood with one foot on each girder. Even beneath her light weight, the two slabs of steel wobbled back and forth. I imagined that if I stepped on them, my weight on one end would make the other end pop up like a seesaw.

Before I could say anything, Janet ran across to the other side. "I made it!" she shouted, clapping her hands. "Now you do it!"

"Thanks, I think I'll pass!" I said. "You go explore the place and let me know what's there. I'll wait here!"

Conrad laughed. "I'll help you across. Here, take my hand. I won't let you fall."

I would rather have risked a concussion than to grab Conrad's clammy hand. I took a deep breath, gathered my courage, told myself that if Janet could do it, I could do it, and said to Conrad, "I don't need any help."

"Well, I'll be right behind you, then," he said.

I walked over to the girders and placed one foot on each. Then I shuffled along, taking baby steps. My knees felt a little shaky and my heart was pounding in my chest, but I was determined to make it across. I looked ahead. The Golden Gate Bridge looked shorter.

Then I looked down. I felt as if I were standing on top of the Empire State Building. The cement canal began to swirl beneath me and my feet suddenly felt as if they were powerful magnets, holding me to the steel. I couldn't move.

Conrad, who'd been walking right behind me, bumped into me. "Keep going," he said. "You're almost there. Why'd you stop?"

"I-I can't move!" I said. "I'm too scared!"

"I'll hang on to you," he said. "I won't let you fall."

116

I felt his arms slide around my waist and pull me back against him. "Okay, I've got you now," he said. "Just start walking."

My legs still refused to move, even though I wanted to bolt across those girders, just to get away from Conrad. I could feel his hot breath on the back of my neck as he pulled me even closer to him. I was worried that if he got any closer, his teeth would scrape the hair off the back of my head.

I sucked in my breath, closed my eyes and took one careful step after another until my feet touched something that felt softer than the steel. Never had I been so happy to step in mud.

"Yay! You made it!" Janet cheered.

I finally exhaled. "And I never want to do it again!"

"Hate to say it," Conrad's voice came from the back of my neck, "but it's the only way back to the camp...unless you want to walk three miles out of your way."

I broke away from his grasp and turned to face him. "Why didn't you tell me that before I went across the dumb girders?"

"I thought a smart girl like you would have figured that out," he said, smiling. The sun hit his teeth and nearly blinded me.

"What are you guys doing here?" a young man's voice came from somewhere behind Janet, whose back was toward the clubhouse shack.

"Hey, Tom!" Conrad called back to him. "Just showing the girls around the place."

Tom looked about 17. He also looked as if he hadn't taken a bath since Eisenhower was president. His baseball cap had so much dirt on it, I couldn't even read the logo on the front. And his jeans were covered with everything from grease stains to paint...and I hated to even imagine what else.

"Hey, Connie!" Tom greeted Conrad. He walked over to us. My nostrils instantly wished he hadn't. "Long time no see!"

Connie? I stifled a groan. I thought even "Stumpy Mouth" was better than calling a guy Connie.

"I've been busy," Conrad said. "Mowing lawns, picking beans at Ramsey's farm, hanging around with these city girls here." He winked at me.

"I'm Tom." He extended a dirt-encrusted hand to me.

117

I shook it with just the tips of my fingers. "Sally. And that's Janet."

He nodded a silent greeting at Janet, then said, "Hey! You guys want to see something cool? Come over here and I'll show you!"

The three of us followed him as he headed toward a weed-covered area at the edge of the pond. There, curled up on a flat rock, was a huge black snake. When I spotted it, I jumped back a good three feet and almost knocked down Conrad who, as usual, was walking with his nose practically piercing the back of my head.

"It's a water mossican!" Tom said.

"Water mossican?" I repeated.

"I think he means water *moccasin*," Conrad said. "But to me, it looks more like just a regular black snake...maybe a milk snake."

Tom vigorously shook his head. "Uh, uh! That's a poisonous water mossican! Just one bite and you'll be dead in ten minutes!"

"And we're standing within striking distance of it for what reason?" Janet asked.

"Because it's so cool!" Tom said.

Even if the snake had been a 25-foot anaconda that knew how to sing show tunes and tap dance, I wouldn't have been impressed at that point. I'd seen so many snakes since being at the camp, I was sick of looking at them.

I glanced at my watch. We'd killed nearly an hour-and-a-half. By the time we walked back to the camp, my dad probably would be there. I suddenly felt as if new life had been breathed into me.

"We'd better head back now," I said to no one in particular. "My dad will be getting to the camp soon."

"Yeah, that's probably a good idea," Conrad said. "I wouldn't want to disturb him for a ride after he's all comfortable and getting ready to eat."

Tom, his eyebrows drawn together, kept staring at Conrad. "Hey, Connie," he finally said, "you do something to your teeth?"

I couldn't believe he'd ask such a dumb question. What did he think? That Conrad's teeth miraculously had grown to their huge proportions all on their own?

"Yeah, I had the old ones pulled out and got new ones yesterday." Conrad said.

I held my breath, just waiting for the rude comment.

"They look great!" Tom said. "You're gonna have all the girls chasing after you now!"

"Aw, I already have the only girl I want right here," Conrad said, tossing another wink in my direction. "No other girls matter to me."

I ran back across those steel girders in record time.

CHAPTER ELEVEN

Eating breakfast across the table from Dad on Saturday morning was a real treat. For one thing, he updated us on everything that was going on back in the city. Janet and I stared wide-eyed at him, absorbing every morsel he threw at us, no matter how small, about the life we'd left behind two hundred years ago – or so it seemed. Even his description of the neighbor's tomatoes in the postage-stamp-sized plot in his yard was worthy of our rapt attention.

"So what time is Conrad coming over for the ballgame?" Dad asked.

"He said 2:30," I said.

"Speaking of Conrad," Dad said, "what kind of reaction do you think he's going to get when his school chums see those new teeth of his?"

"I don't know," I said. "But I think we may find out today. From what he said, everyone in town goes to this game every year. It's a tradition."

"Well, you be nice to him," my mother said. "I don't want you to make fun of him or join in with anyone who does tease him. What is it that I've always taught you?"

I stared into my bowl of corn flakes and muttered, "If you can't say anything nice, don't say anything at all."

"That's right. So please don't forget that."

"I just hope he doesn't show up in a wool sports jacket and his dad's shoes again," I said. "If he does, I swear I won't go!"
\

* * * * *

Conrad arrived at 2:15. To my relief he was wearing jeans, a dark green polo-shirt and sneakers. At least I didn't have to worry about his father driving up and ripping the shoes off his feet.

Janet had spent an hour deciding what to wear to the game because she wanted to look her best for Scott. After she'd modeled about a dozen different combinations so I could help her choose, we settled on the tan shorts and a blue-and-tan checkered blouse. That was after I'd nixed the tan shorts with the black tank-top, white T-shirt and pink shell. I was happy when Janet finally ran out of clothes, otherwise she probably still would have been trying on things after the game was over.

It didn't take me even two minutes to decide what I was going to wear. I threw on my denim shorts, blue T-shirt and white sneakers. The shorts and T-shirt probably could have used a good scrubbing or an iron, but I didn't care. I, unlike Janet, wasn't trying to impress anyone. In fact, I'd purposely chosen an outfit I thought might have some B.O. on it, just so Conrad would keep his distance.

As usual, my mother looked ready to attend a tea party. She'd donned a black-and-white sundress, dainty white shoes, nylon stockings and earrings. In her hand was a white purse.

My father eyed her purse and frowned. "I'd leave the pocketbook here," he said. "After all, you're going to be out in a field. You don't want to leave it somewhere or lose it."

"But I need my lipstick, my mirror, my tissues, my..."

My father sighed. "Never mind. Take it."

* * * * *

The game was held in a big field behind the town's grammar school. It wasn't even a baseball field, as Conrad had said it was. It was just a field. There were no bleachers; nothing to sit on but the grass. Most of the people there had brought folding lawn chairs or blankets, but we'd brought nothing. I didn't know which was worse: having to stand during the entire game, or risking sitting on an anthill.

Hundreds of people of all ages already were there when we arrived. We had to park about a half-mile away and hike to the field. We'd been there less than a minute when Tweaky, Jake and Scott came over to us. I was really pleased to see them, mainly because they were carrying blankets.

Scott greeted Janet with a hug and a big smile. I'd never seen her look so happy, or quite so flustered. Her cheeks turned the color of my mom's lipstick and she giggled and stammered when she said hi to her Prince Charming.

When Scott hugged Janet, I noticed there was someone standing behind him. It was that Tim Argent guy we'd met on Wyatt Road a few days before when he was out riding his bike. He was the one with the nice teeth and the father who was Sergeant Argent. It was the first time I'd been able to get a close look at him. I thought he was cute, very cute.

"Tim, this is Sally and that's Janet," Tweaky said. "The girls I was telling you about."

"Hi," he said, nodding at us.

"Hello, Tim!" I responded, flashing my brightest smile.

He smiled back at me, and I noticed that his eyes were bright blue. He then apparently got his first good glimpse of Conrad. His smile faded.

"Um, hi, Conrad," he said. There was no question where his gaze was centered.

"Yeah, I got some new choppers!" Conrad said, anticipating what Tim's next words would be. "I figured it was about time."

Tim remained silently staring for a few moments, then turned to me and said, "So, I see you haven't gotten sick of Arrowwood and run screaming back to the big city yet."

I was surprised he knew where I was from. I wondered just how much information Tweaky and Jake had told him about me. I silently prayed they hadn't told him Conrad and I were going steady or anything like that.

"We're here for another week," I said.

"Then you'll be here for the Old Home Day dance Saturday night," he said. "You planning on going?"

I turned to look at Conrad. I wondered why he hadn't even mentioned the dance. Could it be he'd invited someone else before he'd met me and was still obligated to take her? I felt a smile creeping across my lips.

I looked back at Tim. "Oh, I might go."

"Good! Save a dance for me, then!" he said.

"If I go, I definitely will!" I said.

Even after Tim and Jake walked off to go greet some other friends, I still was smiling. Unfortunately, Conrad noticed.

"Tim's a big wolf and a two-face!" he said. "He flirts with all the girls, then makes fun of them behind their backs. It's all just an ego thing for him!"

I turned to look directly into Conrad's eyes. "So, are you going to the Old Home Day dance?"

He looked down at the ground. "No."

"Why not?"

He shrugged. "I just don't want to, that's all."

"He doesn't know how to dance!" Tweaky cut in. "When he goes to dances, he just sits there all night like a bump on a log."

"We can still go to Old Home Day," Conrad said. "There is plenty to do there – a parade, games, a craft fair, music, rides, food stands. We just won't go to the dance."

I couldn't believe he was telling me what I could or couldn't do. If I wanted to go to the dance, I'd go, and it didn't matter one bit to me whether he went or not.

Just to spite him, I blurted out, "Well, unlike you, I love to dance. So maybe I'll go. I can always dance with Tim."

At that moment, I saw something I'd never seen in Conrad before. His eyes narrowed and his lips tightened – well, as much as they possibly could over his new teeth. Through all of my teasing, nearly setting him on fire and basically treating him like dirt, I'd never once seem him get angry. But this time it was obvious I'd pushed him too far. He looked as if he wanted to choke someone. And I was pretty sure I was that someone.

"Conrad!" my mother's voice came from behind him. "Do you have anything we can sit on?"

"I brought an extra blanket," Tweaky answered. "You can use it if you want." She held up a crookedly folded tan blanket.

My mother hesitated before she walked over and took it. I imagined she probably was wondering how she was going to comfortably sit on a blanket through nine innings while wearing a dress and nylons...without showing her underwear to everyone at the game.

"The game is going to start," Scott said. "Let's find a place to sit before we're stuck out in left field somewhere."

As we walked across the field, I noticed that what looked like sacks of sand had been place where the bases normally would be. Tweaky spread out her blanket facing first base and we sat down. There wasn't enough space on the blanket for the five of us to sit side by side, so Scott and Conrad sat directly behind Janet and me. Conrad planted a leg on each side of me and then put his hands on my shoulders and pulled me back against him. He felt like a human armchair. When I leaned against him, he put his arms around my shoulders.

I really didn't want him clinging to me that way, especially in 88-degree heat, but I didn't dare move, mostly because I was afraid to make him even angrier than he already was. Besides that, he made a pretty good backrest.

"The teachers are going to play against the town officials," Scott explained to Janet. "Everyone's hoping Mr. Ryan, the science teacher, will fall off the donkey and maybe get trampled. He's a real jerk."

As he spoke, the players, each one riding a donkey, headed out to the field...or at least tried to. Half of the donkeys refused to move.

Several of the players dismounted and tried tugging the donkeys by their reins, which resulted in the donkeys plunking their butts down on the ground and refusing to budge. I had the feeling it was going to be a very long game.

"The teachers are in the blue shirts and the town officials are in yellow," Scott said. "We want the teachers to win."

"Even Mr. Ryan, the jerk?" Janet asked.

"At least he doesn't raise taxes in town and make our parents worry about money all the time," Scott said.

The game actually turned out to be pretty entertaining. When it came to running bases, the donkeys had minds of their own. One guy who was trying to get to third base, ended up out in the woods somewhere, where he lost his baseball cap on a low-hanging branch. And another player, who was just about to make it to home plate, got tagged out when his donkey suddenly stopped to go to the bathroom.

There was one poor guy assigned to clean up all of the donkey poop during the game. He, with a shovel and cardboard box in hand, spent a lot of time running around the field, trying to keep it clean.

A few of the players, like the pitcher, who had to let go of the reins so he could toss the ball, ended up falling off their donkeys. No one seemed to get hurt, except for one teacher who kept rubbing his wrist. One of the guys who fell landed right in a pile of donkey poop that the cleaning guy hadn't picked up yet. The spectators roared with laughter.

And there was a town official who was so tall, his feet kept dragging on the ground when he was on his donkey. So every time the donkey refused to move, he'd dig his heels into the ground and push. One time, when he pushed forward, the donkey jerked backwards and the guy went flying right over its head.

Nearly three hours later, the game finally ended. The teachers won by a score of 1-0, but according to Conrad, it was only because they'd cheated. He said one of the teachers actually had taken four swings while up at bat – that the umpire had thought he'd checked his swing when he hadn't. I didn't know what that meant, but I wasn't about to ask. The fact was, I really didn't care, nor did I want to hear any lengthy explanation about it. But according to Conrad, that fourth swing was the one that had hit the winning ball.

"Boy, the teachers get all upset if we cheat in school," Conrad said, "but it's fine if they cheat? That's not fair!"

His tone told me he still was angry, not so much at the cheating teachers, but at me. He probably considered me to be a potential cheater, too, because I'd flirted with Tim Argent. But Conrad wasn't my boyfriend, even though he believed he was in that little fantasy world of his, so I figured I could do whatever I wanted and he had no say in the matter.

When I finally stood up, my back felt soaked with sweat. I wasn't sure if the sweat was mine or Conrad's, but I decided I'd probably be better off never knowing.

"That was a great game!" Scott said, stretching.

"Not as good as last year's, though, when the ambulance had to come for Mr. Goodman!" Tweaky said.

I helped Tweaky fold the blanket. When I turned around, two guys were standing there watching me. They were older, like seniors in high school.

"Hey, Conrad!" the huskier guy said. "Is this the girl you've been hiding from us?"

Conrad's expression was far from welcoming when he turned to look at them. "These are two of my older brothers," he said to me. "Michael and Benny."

"Pleased to finally meet you," Benny said with a swoop of his arm and an exaggerated bow. "Conrad talks about you all the time."

I wanted to say that Conrad never talked about them, other than to say his brothers all were pains in the neck. Instead, I just smiled.

"So how do you like his new teeth?" Michael asked. "We have to make him stand in the middle of the living room so they won't accidentally scrape the wallpaper off the walls!"

"And Conrad, you better pray you don't sneeze while you're here!" Benny said. "Your teeth might go flying right into a pile of donkey crap!"

He and Michael dissolved into laughter. Conrad's scowl told me he wasn't amused. In fact, if looks could kill, I was pretty sure his brothers' ashes would already be in jars on a mantel somewhere.

Jake, who'd returned to our group just a few minutes earlier, seemed to think the brothers' comments were pretty funny. "Yeah, I told him if he tries to kiss Sally, he'd better be careful or his teeth might end up in her mouth!" he added between guffaws. Conrad's brothers laughed even harder.

I saw the tendons in Conrad's neck tighten. He grasped me by the arm. "Come on, let's go find your parents."

We spotted my parents over near third base. My mother was brushing the back of her dress with her hand. My father was rubbing his lower back.

"So?" Conrad greeted them. "Was I right? Wasn't the game great?"

My father's smile looked forced. "It was a lot of fun. But next time, I'm going to bring my folding lounge-chair. My back is killing me from sitting on that hard ground for so long."

"And I think I felt something crawl up my dress!" my mom added, squirming.

"It's probably a black ant or a tick," Conrad said. "The field is loaded with them."

I'd seen the tight girdles with the hooks on them my mom wore to hold up her nylon stockings. There was no way an ant or a tick could ever squeeze up into one of those things, not unless it was carrying a miniature crowbar. Sometimes when

126

she was putting on her girdle, I could hear it snap like a mousetrap when she let go of the waistband.

"I'm going to hitch a ride home with my brothers," Conrad said. "No need for you to go out of your way taking me home."

I had to stop myself from cheering. I'd spent enough time with him for one day, so every second I didn't have to spend with him seemed like a gift.

"Well, if you're sure you want to go with them," Dad said. "Thanks again for giving us the tickets to the game, Conrad. It was a lot of fun."

"No problem," he said. He turned to face me. "Before you go, can I have a word with you...in private?"

I wanted to scream "Noooo!" and bolt in the other direction, but instead I allowed him to lead me by the hand over to a cluster of trees at the edge of the field.

"I really enjoyed sitting so close to you all afternoon," he said, not letting go of my hand. "I mean, it was the highlight of my day. But you really hurt my feelings when you flirted with Tim Argent right in front of me like that. You made me feel invisible."

I had no idea what to say. Part of me wanted to tell him he'd brought the hurt upon himself by reading something into our relationship that just wasn't there. But another part of me thought of what my mom had said about saying nothing if I couldn't say anything nice.

"I'm sorry, Conrad," I said, my own words surprising me. "I was only joking around with Tim. I'm not interested in him."

I felt like adding, "I'm not interested in you, either," but once again, my mom's words stopped me.

Conrad smiled and hugged me. The hug happened so fast, I hadn't even seen it coming. After he let me go, he reached into the back pocket of his jeans and pulled out a sealed envelope that was folded in half.

"Here," he said, handing the envelope to me. "Open this only when you get back to the camp." He then ran off, turned to wave at me and shouted, "See you tomorrow!"

I clung to the envelope and headed back to my parents.

"All set?" Dad asked.

"Yeah, let's get out of here," I said. "I've seen and smelled enough donkey poop for one day."

We'd driven about a half-mile when it dawned on me that the back seat seemed a little empty. "Dad! Stop!"

My father slammed on the brakes.

"We forgot Janet!"

"Oh, jeez!" he said. "How the hell did we do that?"

My mother immediately began to panic. "Ohmigod! I'm responsible for her safety! What if she's wandering lost and alone somewhere? Or what if she's been trampled by one of those stampeding donkeys? How would I ever explain that to her parents? What kind of mother am I?"

My dad made a U-turn right in the middle of the road and we sped back to the field. Except for the clean-up crew and a few guys putting donkeys into horse trailers, the field was pretty much empty. There was no sign of Janet anywhere.

"Dear Lord!" my mother fanned herself with her hand, as if to ward off an impending swoon. "What if she's been kidnapped by some sleazy donkey wrangler?"

I rolled my eyes. "Mom, she was with Scott, Jake and Tweaky. They wouldn't let any sleazy guys near her!"

"And how well do you know this guy, Scott, anyway?" Mom asked. "Those farm boys are so used to seeing animals mating, they probably think nothing of doing it themselves!"

"Now don't go getting yourself all upset with crazy ideas," Dad said. "I'm sure Janet is fine."

"Then where is she?" Mom cried.

"Probably back at Scott's," I said. "She has a mad crush on him, in case you haven't noticed!"

"Well, we'll head over to his house and check," Dad said.

During the ride to Scott's, I ran my fingers over the envelope Conrad had given me. It had a hard lump in it. I held the envelope up to the back window to see if the sunlight might help me see what was inside. Whatever was in there, he'd wrapped in either a tissue or paper of some sort so I couldn't see even an outline of it. I was tempted to tear open the envelope right then, but decided to wait. Actually, I thought it was kind of fun to prolong the mystery.

A scary thought suddenly occurred to me. What if the lump in the envelope was a personal souvenir from Conrad...like one of his extracted teeth? Visions of a rotted stump with a blood-covered root caused me to toss the envelope onto the floor of the car. I vowed not to touch it again unless I used something like spaghetti tongs or two sticks. It would be just like Conrad to think one of his yanked-out teeth might have some sort of romantic meaning or symbolism.

Dad pulled into Scott's driveway at the old farmhouse. There were no signs of life there. "Run up and knock on the door," Dad told me.

Just as I got out of the car, a gray-haired man wearing dirt-covered overalls came out of the barn. "Help you?" he asked.

"I was wondering if Scott was back from the donkey ballgame yet?"

He shrugged. "Ain't seen him."

"Do you know how he got over there?" I asked. I knew he'd gone with Jake and Tweaky, but I wasn't certain if maybe Tweaky's parents had given him a ride in their car, they'd all hitchhiked, or what.

"On his bicycle," he said.

That meant if Janet was with him, she either was running alongside his bike, or riding on it with him. It also meant they probably wouldn't be getting to the farm for a while.

"Thank you," I said. I got back into the car.

"Scott's on a bicycle," I told my parents.

"Then wouldn't we have passed him somewhere on the road?" Dad asked. "There's only one main road from here to the school grounds."

"There are dozens of trails and shortcuts through the woods, though," I said.

"*Woods?*" my mother's hand flew up to her chest again. "Do you mean to tell me that Janet could be alone in the woods somewhere right now with a strange boy? Dear Lord!"

"What I'd like to know is how you forgot her in the first place, Sally!" Dad said. "I mean, she's your friend! Didn't you even miss her?"

"I was too deep in thought about an envelope Conrad gave me at the field and told me not to open until I got back to the camp!"

"Conrad gave you an envelope?" my mother asked. "What was in it?"

"I don't know. I'm not back at the camp yet!"

"I thought this vacation was supposed to be relaxing!" my mother said. "So far it's been anything but!"

My father was just about to back out of the driveway when I spotted three bicycles heading up the road. "Dad! I think they're coming!"

I got out of the car and waited for the bikes to get closer. Sure enough, it was Scott, Jake and Tweaky. Janet was so thin, I didn't see her at first, and felt panic rising in my throat. But when Scott turned into the driveway, I finally saw Janet on the back of his bike. Her arms were wrapped tightly around Scott's waist and her head was resting against his back.

I ran over to them. "Thank goodness you're okay! We were worried about you!"

"Thanks for driving off without me!" Janet said. Her tone sounded angry, but her eyes told me she really wasn't upset at all. "If it hadn't been for Scott, I'd have had to hitchhike back to the camp!"

"We went back for you right away," I said. "But you were already gone."

"We kind of got thrown out," Scott said. "The guys didn't want anyone getting kicked by a donkey when they were trying to put them back in their trailers, so they told us to get moving."

"Hurry up, kids!" my mom called out of the car window. "I'm starving!"

If there was one thing my mother was a stickler about, it was her meals. She had an internal alarm clock that told her when it was time to eat, and heaven forbid should anyone interfere with that clock. I couldn't count the number of times she'd made my father stop what he was doing so she could get something to eat, like when they were in the middle of a lake fishing, or at a Golden Gloves boxing match. When her internal alarm clock went off, she had to eat and that was that. The worst part was that every time she complained about "starving to death," she usually ate only a couple bites of food and then pushed the plate away, saying she was full. It drove my dad crazy sometimes.

Janet gave Scott a quick hug and then bounced into the back seat of the car.

"What a great day!" she said as we drove off. She rested her head against the back of the seat and sighed. "I wish it didn't have to end! Scott is such a super nice guy."

"Conrad seems nice, too," my mother said. "It's a shame he had such a bad dentist. He really would be handsome with some nice dentures that fit him right."

Her words made me think about the envelope lying on the floor. I bent over and picked it up. "Conrad gave me this envelope before he left with his brothers today," I told Janet.

She stared at my hand. "What's in it?"

"I don't know, I haven't opened it yet."

"Well, go ahead! What are you waiting for? Christmas?"

I hesitated as my emotions bounced from fear and revulsion to curiosity. Curiosity finally won. I decided to tear open the envelope, come what may. But if a bloody old tooth fell out and landed in my lap, I was pretty sure I'd let out a scream that Conrad himself would be able to hear all the way to his house.

Inside the envelope was a note written on notebook paper. The handwriting, in red ballpoint pen, was beautiful – neat and flowing in a style similar to the script on a store-bought greeting card. It read:

"Hi Beautiful! I saw this ring in the window at a store next to the dentist's office. It reminded me of the one that you liked so much in the comic book. I hope you like it. And I hope every time you wear it you will think of me and my love for you."

Conrad had signed his name, followed by a long row of X's and O's for kisses and hugs. His signature was fancy, with a lot of sweeping lines and curly things on it, kind of like John Hancock's signature on the Declaration of Independence. And underneath his name he'd drawn some sort of artistic swirl with two diagonal lines crossing through it and a small circle in between each line. I was surprised, not only at the flawless penmanship, but also by the fact that his spelling and punctuation were excellent. I would have expected any note from him to be written in pencil, full of eraser smudges and spelled exactly the way the words sounded.

I removed a piece of folded tissue from the envelope and unfolded it. Inside was a wide silver band with a raised flower design encircling it. On the front was a small loop from which two tiny silver hearts hung. I loved it. But, I wondered, if I wore the ring, what would it mean? That Conrad and I were going steady? That I officially was his property?

Janet reached over and grabbed the ring from my hand. "Wow! Do you think he stole it? It looks expensive!"

The word *stole* immediately grabbed my mother's attention. Her upturned palm appeared in the back seat. "Let me see it."

Janet placed the ring in her hand.

"It does look expensive," she said. "I don't think you should accept expensive gifts from boys at your age."

"But it was only $2 in the comic book," I said.

Mom handed the ring back to me. "Well, I still don't like it."

I studied the ring for a few more seconds and then slid it onto the ring finger on my right hand. It went only as far as my first knuckle. I then tried it on my left hand. It fit perfectly.

"Looks just like a wedding band!" Janet said.

I took off the ring so fast, I nearly tore off a fingernail.

CHAPTER TWELVE

"I think we should have a special Sunday dinner today," Dad said right after we'd finished eating breakfast. "There's this nice-looking restaurant I saw about five miles from here when I drove up Friday night, called the Fieldstone. From what I've heard, it hasn't been open very long. How would you like to go out to eat?"

Janet and I jumped out of our chairs and danced around while shouting, "Yay!" I guess that pretty much answered his question.

Even my mother couldn't conceal her delight. "A meal without having to cook on a dollhouse-sized stove or heating up water to wash the dishes?" she said. "You don't have to ask me twice!"

Just the idea of getting away from the camp for a while was enough to make me happy, even if we didn't stop anywhere to eat. The weekend had flown by much too fast, and already Dad would be heading back to the city in the morning and we'd be stuck at the camp for another week. So I intended to grab as much civilization as I possibly could while he was with us. Maybe after we ate at the restaurant we could even take a ride somewhere – somewhere far away from Arrowwood – somewhere where there were crowds of people, tall buildings and lots of traffic. Somewhere where there was no Conrad.

No sooner did I think of Conrad was there a knock on the door. Janet and I bolted into the kitchen, jumped into the bottom bunk and pulled the covers over our heads. We were still in our pajamas and not in any condition to entertain guests, especially uninvited ones at eight o'clock in the morning.

"Boy, couldn't Conrad wait?" I said to Janet underneath the blankets. "Pretty soon he'll be camping out on the porch all night!"

I heard my dad go to the door and open it. The voice that greeted him didn't sound familiar to me. Janet and I poked our heads out from under the blankets so we could hear more clearly.

"I'm Officer Carrignan from the Arrowwood Police Department," the deep male voice stated. "I'm investigating a couple burglaries in the area."

Burglaries? I wondered what on earth anyone possibly could steal in this neck of the woods – a squirrel's stash of acorns?

"The Harmons' house and the house next door to theirs were robbed on Friday night," the officer said. "They took cash and jewelry, mostly. What I want to know is if you saw or heard anything around ten o'clock, like someone running by here or a car racing up the road?"

There was a moment of silence before I heard Dad's voice answer, "No, things were pretty quiet around here."

"Well, if you do remember anything or happen to find any clues on your property, be sure to contact me," the officer said. "I'll give you my card." He then added, "So, are you folks up here for the whole summer?"

"No, just for another week," Dad said. "Actually, I'm heading back to the city in the morning. But the wife and girls will be staying here all week."

"Girls?" he asked.

"My daughter and her friend," Dad said.

"Well, if you'd like, I can drive by here a couple times a night and keep an eye on the place, especially now, since there have been break-ins just down the road."

"That sounds like a good idea," Dad said.

After I heard the door close, I lay in bed for a moment, thinking about what I'd just heard. For one thing, I wondered what had happened to the Harmons' big, shaggy dog. Why hadn't he attacked the thief, or at the very least, barked like crazy? Was the burglar someone the dog knew?

My eyes grew wider and my heart began to thump in my chest. Conrad had mentioned the Harmons' dog several times, saying the mutt seemed vicious until you got to know him, then he was just a great big, lovable puppy.

"Janet!" I whispered. "What if Conrad was the one who robbed those houses?"

"That's crazy!" she whispered back. "Why would you even think such a dumb thing?"

"Because he gave me a ring on Saturday, the day after the burglary! Even *you* asked me if he stole it when I first showed it to you!"

"But it looks just like the ring in the comic book," she said. "What are the odds he'd be able to find a ring exactly like that one to steal?"

She had a point. Still, I persisted. "Well, what if he stole the cash to buy the ring with?"

"His note said he bought it while at the dentist's. When would he have had the time to go shopping if he stole the money on Friday night and then went to the donkey ballgame the next day?"

"There was time! There was all morning! He didn't get here until 2:30!"

Janet sighed and shook her head. "He was still feeling crummy from having his teeth out and felt woozy on Friday, remember? Why would he suddenly be full of energy and running around at ten o'clock at night robbing houses? Sometimes I wonder where you come up with these crazy ideas of yours!"

"I don't care, I'm still going to ask him to show me the receipt!"

* * * * *

Conrad showed up about noon. By then, my head was aching from all of the skeet shooting going on at the Rod and Gun Club across the river. I'd heard "Pull!" *Blam!* so many times, I was ready to march over there and personally introduce all of the shooters to the deadly, poisonous water "mossican."

The first thing Conrad did when he greeted me was look at my hands. When he saw no ring on any of my fingers, he looked up at me and frowned. "Did you open the envelope?"

I had stepped outside when he knocked at the door. We walked over to the picnic table and sat facing each other. The day was sunny and hot, and two blue jays were squawking in the high branches of a maple tree right near us.

"The ring is beautiful," I said. "Thank you for it. But my mom thinks it's too expensive for me to accept."

"It was only $3," he said. "That's not expensive. I wish I could afford to buy you a 10-carat diamond."

I abruptly changed the subject. "So, where were you Friday night at about ten o'clock?" I asked, narrowing my eyes at him.

"Pull!" *Blam!* "Pull!" *Blam!* The shooters drowned out his answer.

"I was in bed," he repeated during a pause in the shooting. "After your dad drove me home, I took some painkillers the dentist gave me and they made me so drowsy, I couldn't stay awake. Why are you asking me about Friday night?"

I shrugged. "Just wondering. I had this strong feeling that at precisely ten o'clock you were in trouble of some kind."

"And you didn't mention it to me yesterday at the ball game?"

"Well, you seemed fine, so I figured I was worrying for nothing and didn't say anything. But I still can't get it out of my mind."

He smiled. I noticed that at least part of the hideousness of his new teeth was gone. There was no blood on them anymore.

"You were really worried about me?" he asked.

"Yeah," I lied again. "It was kind of spooky the way the feeling just hit me like that."

The screen door creaked open and my father and Janet came out of the camp. They walked over to the picnic table and Janet plunked down next to me on the bench. Dad sat next to Conrad.

"What do you know about that new Fieldstone Restaurant?" he asked Conrad.

"Not much," he said. "No one I know has been there yet."

"Well, we're thinking of going there for dinner tonight," Dad said. "You want to join us?"

Normally, such a request would have made me want to leap across the table and put my hands around my father's throat, but I knew Conrad wouldn't go out to eat with us, not until he had his stitches out. So my dad's invitation didn't create the usual urge to kill that his past ones had.

136

"I'd like that," Conrad said. "I can have some soup and hot tea or something light. My dad always told me that it's not the food that's important, it's the people you're eating the food with!" He winked at me across the table.

I opened my mouth to say something, but no words came out. What I wanted to say, I decided, would be best left unsaid until a couple more "pulls" and "blams" were able to drown me out.

"What's Scott doing today?" Janet asked Conrad.

"He was supposed to go to his grandmother's with his family," he said. "They usually visit her every Sunday. She lives in Massachusetts."

"Oh." Janet let out a long sigh. She then added, "Did Sally tell you the police were here this morning? The Harmons' house and the house next door got robbed Friday night. They wanted to know if we heard anything or saw anything around here. Do you know anybody who'd do something like that?"

I tried not to show any reaction to her statement, but I was gritting my teeth so hard, I was afraid I was going to crack them all and when I opened my mouth to talk, they'd fall out like broken glass.

Conrad instantly locked eyes with mine. "A robbery, you say? No, Sally didn't mention anything. About what time did that happen?"

I silently promised God I'd become a nun if He would strike Janet with a severe case of laryngitis at that very moment.

"About ten o'clock," she said.

Where, I wondered, were the "pulls" and "blams" when I needed them?

"Ten o'clock, eh?" Conrad said. He frowned at me. A maple leaf floated down onto the table. I picked it up and studied it as intently as if it were part of my final exam in science class at school.

"Well, I've got some fishing to do," my dad said, rising from the bench. "Didn't get a chance yesterday, what with the ball game and all. We'll probably be leaving here for the restaurant at five o'clock or so, so if you kids go wandering off somewhere, be sure to be back by then."

Dad headed down to the shed, where he kept his old fishing rod, seeing that his new one probably was swimming with the sharks near Cuba somewhere by then.

I finally dared to look up at Conrad. His eyebrows were creased together into a single brow and his eyes looked as if they were about to shoot sparks. It didn't take a genius to figure out he was really ticked off.

"Janet!" he snapped. "I want to talk to Sally...alone!"

"No, Janet, you stay right here," I said. "Don't let us chase you away."

"I want to go watch your dad fish anyway," she said, rising from the bench. "If he needs someone to help him dig up worms, I'll do it. I don't mind worms."

Before I could stop her, she took off running after my father. Some friend she was.

"You think I robbed those houses, don't you?" Conrad asked. I detected a distinct shakiness in his voice.

I stared down at the table and envisioned what his face probably looked like at that moment – glassy eyes, flaring nostrils and his lips pulled back around his huge teeth – kind of like Godzilla. I didn't dare look at him.

"Well," I said, "the cop said jewelry and money were stolen...and you did give me that ring the next day."

"So that makes me a crook?" he asked, his voice rising a few octaves. "Don't you know me better than that?"

I lifted my head and allowed my eyes to meet his. I swore I saw steam coming out of his nose. "No, actually I *don't* know you!" I said. "It's only been a week, Conrad. You could have robbed the whole town before I got here, or spent the last year in reform school, for all I know! I don't live around here, remember?"

"But in the time you've known me, have I ever given you any reason to think I'm the kind of guy who goes around robbing houses?"

I shrugged. "Well, no, it's not like you walk around with a crowbar tucked down your pant leg or anything like that. But a girl just can't be too careful nowadays."

"I make good money mowing lawns," he said. "And I also get 25 cents an hour picking vegetables at Ramsey's farm. I have no reason to be a crook!"

When I didn't respond, he shook his head and put his hand over mine on the table. "I love you," he said. "And I'm really trying to do everything I can to make you love me. What is it about me that you don't like? Just say it and I'll change it for you."

I honestly tried to think of exactly what it was about him I didn't like. He treated me like a queen and was always complimenting me, which wasn't bad. But he was much too clingy, which I didn't like. There also was something about him that gave me a creepy feeling, but I couldn't quite put my finger on what it was – aside from his teeth, that is.

Before I could stop myself, and for reasons even I couldn't explain, I blurted out, "You're too boring."

The minute I uttered the words, I wished I could take them back. I knew how Conrad was. He'd probably show up in a clown costume the next morning and juggle bowling pins for me.

"You think I'm boring?" he asked, his eyes widening. "We've done so much since you've been here! How can you think I'm boring?"

"Well, compared to the city guys, you are."

It was true. The guys I went to school with were...well, cool. They played the guitar or did tricks on their bicycles. They swam in clean, chlorinated public pools and did back dives off the diving board. And they knew how to dance all of the latest dances, like the Twist. Just the thought of Conrad doing the Twist made me chuckle.

"What's so funny?" he asked.

"I was just picturing you dancing the Twist!"

He released a long sigh and slowly shook his head. "Look, I know I'm not fancy like your city friends, and maybe I know more about catching fish than I do about the latest dances, but that's no reason to make me feel like a loser. Have you ever stopped to think that out here in the country, you're the one who's considered a loser? I bet you don't even know there's a $100 fine for picking a pink lady's slipper!"

"What the heck is a pink lady's slipper?"

"Those pink wildflowers your mother was planting near the porch here the other day!"

My head snapped in the direction of my mother's flowers. There must have been two dozen pink lady's slippers there. I wondered if the cop who'd come to the camp earlier had seen them and was at this very moment drawing up the paperwork to send my parents a bill for $2,400...or even worse, haul all of us off to jail.

Conrad got up from the bench. "I'm going to head home now."

I figured he had to be really mad at me if he was leaving, especially when Dad had offered him a free meal at a restaurant.

"I want to change my clothes and get cleaned up before we go out to dinner," he added. "Do you think you can pick me up at my house so I won't have to walk all the way back here? I'm still not back to my old self yet." He paused before adding, "I guess all of that house robbing I did the other night must have been too much for me."

His sarcasm didn't amuse me. "I'm sure my dad won't mind picking you up," I said in a monotone. At least, I thought, Conrad wouldn't have sweaty armpits from walking all the way back over here.

As I watched him walk away, all I could think about was how, thanks to my dad, our family dinner wasn't going to be the fun-filled getaway from Conrad I'd anticipated. In fact, just thinking about it gave me a bad case of heartburn. I'd always considered my dad to be the smartest person I knew, but when it came to Conrad, he sure seemed dumb. If he thought for a single second I actually wanted to eat a meal sitting next to a guy who was slurping soup and straining the noodles through his giant teeth, then he had a lot to learn.

* * * * *

Conrad, to my surprise, looked pretty nice when we picked him up later that afternoon. He was wearing khaki pants and a brown and beige striped shirt. He also smelled like Old Spice cologne. I could identify that scent from a block away because it was my dad's favorite after-shave.

"I'm starving!" Conrad said when he slid in next to me in the back seat. I felt his knee poke the side of my thigh.

"Me, too!" Janet said.

140

That was nothing new. Janet was always hungry. I usually was, too, but rarely for what my parents would classify as "good" food. To me, food wasn't good unless it was coated with sugar or chocolate...or both.

I was impressed with the Fieldstone restaurant from the moment we walked in. The dining room had wood-plank floors and a big fieldstone fireplace. The tables also were made of wooden planks and were dotted with red placemats set with real silverware. The only thing that wasn't impressive was the lack of customers. Only one table was occupied. I silently hoped the previous diners hadn't all dropped dead from food poisoning.

We were seated at a table by a window facing the road. Conrad immediately grabbed the chair next to mine. The thought of practically rubbing elbows with him throughout the meal didn't appeal to me, but I figured it was better than having to stare at him across the table while he struggled to eat with his new teeth and slobbered food down the front of his shirt.

The waitress, wearing a white bib-type apron over a gray cotton dress that came down to her ankles, and a little white hat that kind of looked like a doily, cheerfully greeted us and handed a menu to each of us.

After she walked off, Dad said, "Nice place! Very Colonial looking. I hope the food is as good as the decor."

I scanned the list of dinners – chicken, steak, baked ham, turkey. I also noticed that the soup of the day was clam chowder. My first thought was that Conrad was in big trouble. There was no way he'd be able to chew a bunch of rubbery clams. And the last thing I wanted was to watch him try. The only items on the menu I figured he would be able to handle were mashed potatoes, Jell-O and ice cream. At least my dad wouldn't go broke paying for his meal.

I ended up ordering the baked-ham dinner, which the menu described as a thick slice of fresh, country ham, mashed potatoes and corn. Conrad ordered the clam chowder and a glass of tomato juice. Mom, Dad and Janet all chose the turkey dinner.

As we waited for our food, the waitress delivered a basket of rolls to the table. My father smiled with satisfaction. Dad had to have bread with everything he ate, mostly because he used it like a kitchen sponge to wipe up everything on his plate –

gravy, egg yolk, meat juice, melted butter. His plate always ended up looking squeaky clean, as if it had just been washed.

The rolls turned out to be so hard, the Rod and Gun Club probably could have used them for skeet. I was pretty sure they'd been sitting out back in the kitchen since the restaurant's grand opening.

My father took a bite of one of the rolls and then scowled at the others in the basket. "I hope the rest of the food is fresher than this! I think I just cracked a molar!"

Even my glass of water had a faint fishy smell to it. I imagined the cook scooping water out of some swamp out back because the place was like our camp – no running water. I held up my glass to the light to check for pollywogs.

When our meals finally were served nearly an hour later (after my dad had said, "What are they doing? Hunting in the woods behind here for a wild turkey?" about five times), the food on our plates reminded me of the cafeteria food at school. All I needed was Mrs. Ludwell, the cafeteria lady, who always wore a hairnet and carried a huge metal spoon solely for the purpose of banging it on our tables when we were too noisy or refused to eat our vegetables, to appear, and I'd have sworn I was back at school.

My "thick slice of fresh, country ham" looked more like a thin slice of dried-up cold cuts. I took a bite of the mashed potatoes and felt a golf-ball sized lump in my mouth. Even worse, the food was cold. And the corn was creamed corn. I'd always hated creamed corn, mainly because I thought it looked like throw-up.

I glanced at everyone else's meals. They didn't look any better than mine. The turkey dinners had paper-thin slices of meat that didn't look much like turkey, buried beneath some bright yellow gravy that wasn't the natural color of any meat I'd ever seen. Mom's baked potato was wrapped in foil, and when she unwrapped it, something that resembled a giant raisin was inside.

Conrad seemed to be the only one who was enjoying the food. The clam chowder I'd grown up eating had always been thick and creamy. A spoon could stand up in the middle of a bowl of it. But this chowder was thin and watery, which worked in Conrad's favor because it was easier to slurp. He paused from his slurping only to spit the clams into his cloth napkin. I imagined what names the guy who did the laundry for the restaurant would be calling him when all of those clams fell out.

"Is the clam chowder hot?" my mother asked him.

He shook his head. "No, it's lukewarm, but good."

My father finally said what all of us probably had been thinking. "This food is terrible! I had better food in my C-rations kit in the war!"

At that moment, the waitress approached. "How is everything?" she asked, smiling.

"Fine," my father and mother said in unison, smiling back.

I realized my parents tried to live by the "if you can't say anything nice, don't say anything at all" rule, but if it meant needing to be rushed to the hospital to have our stomachs pumped, I thought maybe it might have been a good idea to speak up.

At least the dessert was better. I had chocolate ice cream that actually tasted like chocolate ice cream. It had a couple chunks of ice in it, but I sucked on them until they melted. Conrad had vanilla ice cream, which he downed in about two bites. I thought he was lucky the chowder hadn't been piping hot because eating ice cream right afterwards might have made his new teeth crack. And knowing Conrad, he'd still have worn them for years with big cracks in them.

The bill came to a little over $15 for the five of us.

"That's outrageous!" Mom said to Dad. "I can buy a whole week's worth of groceries for that! At least if the food had been good, it wouldn't be so bad, but even the old alley cat back home would have turned up his nose at this stuff!"

She was wrong. I'd seen the old alley cat eat everything from dead birds to horse poop left behind by the old nag that pulled the rag wagon around the city. No one knew why the guy who drove the wagon collected rags or what he did with them, but he must have gathered a whole mountain of them over the years. In fact, most of my old pajamas with holes in the crotches had been donated to the guy.

"Um, now that we're done eating," my dad interrupted my ragman thoughts, "I have an announcement to make."

All heads at our table turned toward him.

"Considering the robberies the other night," he said, "I wouldn't feel right leaving the three of you here alone while I go back to the city. So, when we get back to the camp, I want you to pack up your things. We're heading back home tonight. We can come back on weekends and for another full week sometime when I can get time off from work and stay with you. I can understand the city having crime, but I didn't expect it way out here in the country. I'm really sorry to disappoint you."

Disappoint me? If I had been old enough to drink, I'd have ordered a bottle of champagne. I had to stop myself from leaping out of my seat and turning cartwheels across the old plank floor. Not that I knew how to turn cartwheels. My "lard in the can" weighed down my bottom too much to get it into the air.

I glanced at Conrad and Janet. They couldn't have looked more nauseated if they'd have just eaten another helping of the restaurant food.

"Tonight?" Janet finally managed to ask. "You mean I won't even be able to say goodbye to Scott?"

"Afraid not," my dad said. "I really hate to upset you girls, because I know how much fun you were having here, but I think it's for the best. I wouldn't be able to sleep at night if the three of you were to stay here another week alone. I mean, there's not even a phone where I could call to check on you."

"I can keep an eye on them for you," Conrad offered. "And I can call you every night from my house and let you know how everything is going."

My dad shook his head. "Thanks, Conrad, but my mind is made up."

"But what about Old Home Day next weekend?" Conrad asked. "Scott and I were planning to take Sally and Janet to it...and to the dance!"

"No problem," Dad said. "We'll come back for the weekend, so everyone can still go."

Janet flashed a smile so wide, her teeth looked bigger than Conrad's. "Scott wants to take me to Old Home Day?"

Conrad nodded. "And the dance, too."

I strongly suspected he was making up the whole thing just to get us to come back next weekend. Scott hadn't mentioned anything about taking Janet to Old Home Day, and Conrad had admitted he couldn't dance and would rather roll naked in a field of poison ivy than go. Yet now, just because we were leaving, he suddenly was going to turn into Fred Astaire?

I decided to make my dad feel better about his announcement. "Don't worry, Dad, I'll be more than happy to go back to the city. I don't mind giving up another week here if it means I can have TV, a hot bath and a flush toilet again! In fact, what are we waiting for? Let's go!"

Janet and Conrad both turned to give me looks that made me feel as if I'd just announced I was the one who'd killed Janet's beloved frog, Butchy.

"Gee, you could at least act a little sorry about leaving me," Conrad said. "I know I'm going to be missing you like crazy. In fact, you'll have to give me your address and phone number so we can keep in touch while you're in the city."

I immediately tried to think of someone I really disliked so I could give her phone number to Conrad.

"I have a pen right here in my pocket," Dad said. "I'll jot down the information for you." He grabbed the pen, then removed a book of matches from the same pocket, tore off the cover and proceeded to scribble down our address and phone number on the back of it.

I stared in disbelief at my father. Why on earth, I wondered, would he give my personal information to a guy he knew I couldn't stand? I was convinced Conrad's father must have known my dad from back in their school days or maybe the war, and he had some really embarrassing information he was using to blackmail my father into making certain Conrad and I were inseparable. There was no other explanation.

"Here you go," Dad said, handing the matchbook cover across the table to Conrad. Conrad snatched it out of his hand so fast, he reminded me of a magician doing a card trick.

"Thanks!" Conrad said. "I promise I'll write or call every single day!"

The look I shot at my father had "voodoo doll with pins stuck in it" written all over it.

During the ride back to the camp, Conrad slid his arm around my shoulders. Cringing, I made a mental note to personally track down the guy who'd robbed the Harmons' house and thank him. Thanks to him, I wouldn't have to spend one more day at the camp. No more snakes, no more blood-sucking mosquitoes, no more outhouse...and best of all, no more Conrad.

CHAPTER THIRTEEN

My first day back in the city was, in my opinion, *heavenly*. I slept in my nice big bed all alone without Janet's knees in my back, and was able to sprawl out in any direction I pleased. I finally crawled out at noon and watched three straight hours of television. I even soaked in the tub for an hour, enjoying the feel of hot water, even though it was 90 degrees outside. And I flushed the toilet at least a dozen times...just because I could. I would have flushed it another dozen times but my mom yelled at me that I'd better be doing all of that flushing because I had diarrhea and not because I was just wasting water.

The only thing that ruined my nearly perfect day was the phone. It rang three different times, and each time it was Conrad.

"Hi honey, whatcha doing?" he began every phone call. "I miss you."

Each time, I told him what I'd been doing – except for soaking in the tub. The last thing I wanted was for Conrad to picture me in any state of nakedness. And I certainly wasn't going to tell him I missed him. I'd barely even thought of him since I'd been back home.

"I'm really excited for this weekend," he said. "Can't wait for you to get back here, and for Old Home Day. It seems like years until then. It's really boring without you here. I mowed a couple lawns for extra money this morning, so we can have fun at Old Home Day. And then I wrote you a letter and mailed it. You should get it in the mail tomorrow."

I stifled a groan. I could only imagine what he'd written. Probably a lot of mushy stuff that would make me want to fake

147

some kind of terminal illness by the weekend, just so I wouldn't have to go back to the camp.

Actually, I was pretty good at faking illnesses – or so I'd thought. Through the years, my extreme dislike of the dentist had forced me to fake everything from the black plague to leprosy, just to get out of going. And it had worked...until the day my mom finally called my bluff.

I knew I was in for real torture at the dentist that day because I was scheduled to have an extraction. One of my baby teeth hadn't fallen out, and the permanent tooth already had grown in behind it, so the baby tooth had to be pulled. Just the thought of having something yanked out of my head had made me quiver with fear. My mother, however, told me that short of my getting hit by a bus, I was going to keep the appointment.

So I came up with what I'd thought was the perfect plan. I went into the bathroom, patted bath powder all over my face to make myself look pale, and then put some of my mother's pink lipstick around my eyes to make them look sickly. When I was satisfied I'd achieved the perfect too-sick-to-go-to-the-dentist look, I stretched out on the bathroom floor and groaned. It took a few groans, each one louder than the previous one, to make my mom finally come check the bathroom.

"Ohhhhh, I'm so sickkkkkkk," I'd moaned. "Call the dentist and cancel my appointment!"

My mother had hesitated only long enough to take a closer look at me, then said, "No time for that! I have to call an ambulance right away!"

I ended up going to the dentist and having the baby tooth pulled. Looking back, I think I might have been a little too heavy handed with the bath powder on my face. The effect I'd wanted was to look pale, not like a mime.

"I put a little gift for you in with the letter," Conrad was saying on the phone. "Hope you like it!"

"I have to hang up now," I said. "I promised Mom I'd go grocery shopping with her. We need absolutely everything since we got back."

Actually, my mom had done all of the grocery shopping the minute the grocery store opened that morning...and I'd already eaten my way through at least half of what she'd bought.

"Okay, but I'll call you again tonight. Talk to you then! I love you!"

I hung up and muttered some unkind words about my dad for giving Conrad our phone number. Then I dashed across the street to see Janet.

Janet looked as if she hadn't slept much the night before. Her eyes were ringed with dark circles, her hair was sticking up everywhere, and she was still in her bathrobe.

"Are you okay?" I asked.

She shrugged. "Yeah, I guess. I'm just upset I didn't get to talk to Scott before we left. All I've done since being back is listen to my brother complain about stuff and my mother yell at him for complaining. And my mom's watching all of her soap operas, so I can't even watch TV. And I really miss Scott a lot. I keep thinking about all of the fun we had swimming, going to the drive-in and the ball game. There's nothing to do around here."

"There's plenty to do around here!"

"Like what?"

"Well, the ice cream man will be coming around later and we can walk over to the corner store for some penny candy."

"Eat?" she said. "Is that all there is to do in the city? Eat? Did you notice that the kids at the camp hardly ever think about eating? They're too busy having fun!"

"We could go bowling," I said. "Or to a movie. Or we could go downtown and hang out in the record store and listen to the new records. I heard that Ricky Nelson has a new one coming out."

"Nah," Janet said. "I think I'll just stay here."

Finally, I came up with an idea I was pretty sure she'd go for. It had to do with sewing, one of her favorite hobbies. The past year in school, we'd had to take one semester of sewing, followed by one of cooking. During the sewing semester, we were supposed to make a bibbed apron, a tote bag with our name embroidered on it and a hand towel that buttoned onto the apron – all in preparation for the cooking semester. Janet had completed all three projects in record time and even went on to make a skirt, vest and blouse for extra credit. I, on the other hand, was still struggling to make the apron, the first item on the mandatory list, at the end of the semester.

149

But it wasn't my fault. Every time I brought my work up to the sewing teacher so she could examine it, she'd say the same thing, "Rip it out! It's crooked!"

I used my stitch-ripping tool so often, the tip eventually broke off. Part of the problem was the sewing machines we were forced to use in class. They were so old, I was certain they had arrived with Christopher Columbus. They had these platforms under them that had to be pumped by foot to make the sewing needle go up and down. I never was able to get the rhythm right, so my stitches always ended up resembling Morse code. I managed to pull a D in sewing class. Janet got an A+. That's when I developed my motto, "If I can't glue it, I won't do it!"

Anyway, I decided to use Janet's love of sewing to get her out of her current slump.

"Why don't we go downtown and pick out some nice material and you can make a dress for the Old Home Day dance this weekend? Scott would be really impressed if you showed up in a dress you made all by yourself!"

Actually, I didn't think Scott would know the difference between a flour sack and a hand-sewn dress, or even care, but my mission was to make Janet feel less miserable.

Her eyes widened and a smile slowly spread across her face. "That's a great idea! Scott said his favorite color is blue, so I could make a blue dress just for him!"

I was pleased to see the sparkle in her eyes again, but a thought crossed my mind that made me feel uneasy. What if, I wondered, the Old Home Day dance was a big barn dance like I'd seen on *The Rifleman*, where everyone wore checkered square-dancing skirts? Or what if the girls in Arrowwood were all like Tweaky and dressed like guys for the dance? Janet probably would be embarrassed showing up in a fancy blue dress. I decided we probably should postpone our shopping trip for fabric until I talked to Conrad again, which, according to my calculations, would be in another hour or so.

Conrad turned out to be no help. "I don't know what girls wear to those things," he said during his next phone call. "I guess they're the kind of dresses you'd see in school. Nothing real fancy."

"Do any of the girls wear jeans or pants?" I asked.

"Yeah, they wear those – and shorts, too."

That really narrowed it down. It sounded as if anything, as long as it could be classified as clothing, was fine at the dance.

"Are you and Scott still planning to take us to the dance?" I asked.

There was silence on the other end of the line. Immediately, I felt my muscles tense.

"Um, yeah, I guess so," he said. "I know we're taking you to the Old Home Day celebration during the day, but I'm not really sure about the dance at night. I haven't talked to Scott about it."

"I was right!" I said. "You lied about you guys taking us to the dance just so my dad would bring us back to the camp this weekend!"

"No, I didn't lie. I just haven't talked to Scott about it recently. He could have changed his mind, or had a family emergency or something."

"Well, if I were you, I'd hang up right now and call Scott. I don't want Janet to spend all week making a dress for nothing! I'm the one who suggested she make her own dress, you know!"

When he didn't say anything, I did what I was famous for doing...I blurted out the first thing that came to mind.

"Well, it doesn't matter if you guys take us or not because Janet and I are still going to go to that dance, no matter what! I'm sure Tim Argent will dance with us!"

It wasn't as if Janet and I were strangers to dances. When we were younger, we rarely missed the weekly fifth-and-sixth-grade dance parties at the local YMCA. Kids from all over the city attended. Some nights, so many kids would show up, dozens had to be turned away because of the fire laws. Janet and I had danced with plenty of boys – boys who were dressed in suits and ties and who did the box step and looked at their feet and counted out loud when they danced. And we'd been carefully watched by the chaperones, who made sure that during waltzes, we remained an arm's length from our partners at all times. Cheek-to-cheek and bear-hug dancing were strictly taboo.

There was this one guy, Maurice, who always asked me to dance. He seemed to have radar when it came to knowing when

151

the chaperones wouldn't be looking, and he'd pull me so close to him, I could hardly breathe. The thing I didn't like about dancing that close to Maurice was it always felt like he had a roll of quarters in the front pocket of his pants. I couldn't help but wonder why he just didn't switch over to paper money. I mean, it would have been a lot less bulky.

But Janet and I had always had fun at the YMCA dances, so I was determined we would have fun at this Old Home Day dance, too, no matter what.

"I wish you would stop mentioning Tim Argent!" Conrad said. "I never liked the guy, and now I really can't stand him, thanks to you. I'll call Scott, ask if he still wants to go to the dance, and then call you back!"

I hung up and frowned. For Janet's sake, I hoped Scott and Conrad were taking us to the dance. But for my sake, I hoped Janet and I could go alone and dance with any guys we wanted to and not be stuck with just one guy all night...especially a certain clingy guy with huge teeth.

Conrad called back about 20 minutes later. "Scott said he'll go," he said. "I had to do a little arm twisting, but he's going."

I wondered what the arm twisting had involved. Blackmail? Threats? Or maybe Conrad had been forced to promise Scott something, like help him shovel manure all next week?

"And what are you going to wear?" I nearly didn't dare ask him. If he said the white bucks and woolen tweed sports jacket, I was going to head straight for the bath powder and fake another illness.

"I don't know. I guess jeans and a shirt."

That sounded safe enough to me. Before I could comment, I heard what sounded like his father's voice shouting in the background. "Conrad! Are you on that damned phone again? If you're running up a big long-distance bill, I'll take it out on your hide!"

I could tell that Conrad had covered the phone with his hand because his voice was muffled when he shouted back at his father, "Don't worry! It's not a long-distance call!"

I hated to break the news to him, but it was. Whenever my dad had to call Arrowwood to talk to someone at the town hall about the property-tax bill, or whatever, he always complained afterwards that it cost more to call there than it did to call his sister in Connecticut.

"It *is* a long-distance call!" I shouted over the phone, hoping Conrad could hear me. This, I thought, just might put an end to his constant phoning. If it did, it would be the answer to my prayers.

"I didn't think it was," Conrad's voice wasn't muffled any longer. "I guess I'm going to have to stick to letter writing, then. I'll call you Friday night, though, to set up the time and plans for Saturday."

* * * * *

His letter arrived the next day. I happened to be sitting on the front steps and listening to my radio when the mailman came. He smiled and handed me an envelope that had hearts drawn in red ink all over it.

"Someone has an admirer, I see," he said with a wink.

I glared at the envelope. Not only did it have hearts drawn all over it, the hearts had arrows through them and Conrad's initials and mine on them. I felt like crawling underneath the porch.

The letter was just as I'd expected it would be...as mushy as a bowl of oatmeal. In it, Conrad talked about the drive-in and how badly he'd wanted to kiss me, which, he said, was why he'd gulped so much. He said he really regretted that he hadn't been brave enough to just lean over and do it.

My only thought was that if he had, he'd probably have ended up needing a lot more than just a new set of teeth.

He also talked about his newborn nephew and how cute he was, and how he'd like to have a baby someday...with me. And then he rambled on about how much he missed me and how he could hardly wait to see me again. He ended the letter with, "There better be a kiss waiting for me when I get to the camp on Saturday!"

"In your dreams!" I said out loud.

His signature was the same swirling, fancy one he'd used in the note with the ring. And the same design was under it – two curved lines with two straight lines through them and the two little circles. He'd actually enclosed two gifts in the letter. One was a ballpoint pen in my favorite color, orange. The other was a dollar bill, onto which he'd paper-clipped a note that said he wanted me to go to Woolworth's and buy a turtle with it.

To heck with the turtle, I thought, greedily eyeing the crisp bill. I was going to use the money to buy twenty Fudgesicles or twenty Hershey bars. Or maybe ten of each. Or maybe five candy bars, twenty-five penny candies and ten Popsicles. The possibilities were endless.

"If you write back to me," Conrad's P.S. on the letter said, "don't put your return address on the envelope. And write real sloppy on it, like a guy's writing. My older brothers will open your letter and read it if they know it's from a girl, just so they can tease me about it."

I figured he didn't have anything to worry about because I had no intention of writing to him, especially if he was expecting mushy stuff in return. I didn't want to encourage him even one little bit. And if he really thought there'd be a kiss waiting for him at the camp, then he was setting himself up for a big disappointment. I had more of a chance of kissing Troy Donahue than Conrad ever had a chance of kissing me.

When I showed the letter to Janet later that day, she didn't laugh at it as I'd expected she would.

"He's so romantic!" she said, sighing. "I sure wish Scott would write me a letter like that. I would read it over and over again. Maybe I'd even sleep with it under my pillow."

"I wouldn't dare sleep with anything Conrad sent me," I said. "It probably would give me nightmares."

"Oh, I have to show you the material and pattern I bought to make my dress for the dance!" she said.

"You went shopping already? And without me?"

"Yeah, Mom took me to Arden's House of Cloth early this morning. I figured you were still sleeping anyway."

She'd figured right. Once again, I hadn't crawled out of bed until noon. There was something about the city that made me want to stay in bed, unlike at the camp, where I was up with the birds – and the snakes – every morning.

When Janet showed me her dress pattern, I thought the dress pictured on the package looked so simple, even I might be able to sew it. It consisted of two straight pieces of cloth sewn up each side with holes cut out for the arms and neck. No belt, no sleeves, no collar, no shape. I was willing to bet Janet could make a dress like that in less than 30 minutes. The material she'd selected also was fairly plain – light blue cotton with tiny navy-blue dots all over it.

My expression must have told Janet I wasn't quite as excited about her selections as she was.

"I know the pattern looks kind of plain," she said, "but I'm going to add things to the dress, like a belt made out of the same material and maybe a ruffle at the neckline."

"I'm sure it will look nice," I said.

"So, what are you going to wear?" she asked.

"My gray sleeveless dress."

The dress had always been one of my favorites. It was fitted, but gave me curves where I didn't usually have them. Mom said it was because of something called darts in the right places. I probably should have known what darts were after taking sewing classes, but the only darts I knew about were the kind with metal points on them that people threw at targets...and I was pretty sure my dress didn't have any of those in it.

"It still fits you?" Janet asked.

Her question caught me off guard. I had no idea if the dress still fit me, mainly because I hadn't worn it in a long time. I didn't feel as if I'd gained any weight, but I knew, from past experience, that the scale usually proved me wrong. For that reason, I treated most scales as if they were contaminated with radiation.

"I guess it fits," I said. "Everything else I have still does, so why wouldn't it?"

She shrugged. "I guess because the last time you wore it, it looked kind of tight in the hips."

I gasped. I was sensitive about my hips because they were wider than any other part of my body. Whenever I gained weight, it went straight to my hips. I figured if all of the fat on my hips could be lifted up to my chest, I'd have a body like Marilyn Monroe's.

And while I was thinking about my chest, there was something that had been happening during the past week or so I hadn't mentioned to anyone, especially my mother, because I was afraid she'd drag me to the doctor's. My breasts, in all of their training-bra glory, were tender. I hadn't even been able to lie on my stomach because they hurt so much. The thought had crossed my mind that if there were no chaperones at the Old Home Day dance and Conrad decided to dance bear-hug style with me, the pain probably would cause me to do something rash, like punch him.

"You okay?" I hadn't realized Janet had been staring at me.

"Yeah...I guess." I paused before I decided to confess my problem to her. After all, if I had something wrong with me and I suddenly dropped dead, I thought someone should be able to tell my parents what had caused my early demise. "It's just that my breasts have been really sore lately and I'm afraid something is wrong with them."

"Did you do something to hurt them?" she asked.

"I haven't done anything but sleep lately. I don't think I could hurt anything in bed."

Janet's mother, who, to my embarrassment, obviously had been eavesdropping, stepped into the kitchen and smiled at me. "They're just growing," she said. "You're at that age...your breasts are growing."

Had the genie from Aladdin's lamp just appeared and granted me three wishes, I couldn't have been more delighted.

I looked down at my chest. "So how soon will I get them? Do you think I'll have them in time for the dance this weekend?"

Janet's mom laughed. "I don't think so. But some girls grow them fast, while others grow them slowly, over a period of a couple years."

I silently prayed mine were the fast-growing kind. The problem was, I was slow at everything I did – getting up in the morning, getting to school on time, getting my homework done. The odds were I'd still be wearing a training bra when I was forty. But on the bright side, there was my grandmother with the three huge breasts. If I took after her, I'd end up in a DD cup by the time I was thirteen.

"Well, I'm anxious to get started on making my dress," Janet said, picking up the pattern. "I want it to be perfect so Scott will fall madly in love with me when he sees me in it!"

"I have to go home and try on some stuff," I said. "I sure hope something fits."

* * * * *

A half-hour later, my bed was heaped with clothes I'd taken out of my closet, tried on and cast aside. The full-length mirror on the back of my bedroom door had become my enemy because it made me look bottom heavy in everything I tried on. Maybe, I thought, the mirror was like one of those carnival mirrors, distorted in some way to make me look like a giant pear, when in reality, I actually looked like Jayne Mansfield.

I was still wearing my gray dress when my mom walked into my bedroom. She stared critically at my outfit, then said, "I think it's time to donate that one to charity. You've outgrown it."

"No, it's fine!" I protested. It was the dress I wanted to wear to the dance – the dress with the darts in it that made me look curvy instead of chunky. It didn't matter that it made my ribs feel as if they were being pushed through my lungs, I wanted to wear it. "This is what I'm going to wear to the dance Saturday night."

Mom slowly shook her head. "Honey, it's too tight everywhere, especially in the hips. If you sat down in that dress, it would split right up the seams."

"I'm sure Conrad wouldn't mind," I muttered.

"Why don't you wear your green dress? That's really pretty."

The dress was a yucky green color and had white lace all over it. When I wore it, I looked like a giant piece of asparagus wrapped in a doily.

"I don't think any dance in Arrowwood ever would be fancy enough for a lace dress," I said. "Conrad said the dresses the girls wear are kind of like school dresses."

"How about your maroon skirt and your pink shell? Pink has always looked good on you."

I hadn't even considered a skirt and a top. I'd been too fixated on finding a dress. I rushed to my closet, dug out the maroon skirt and pink shell and tried them on.

"Perfect!" Mom said. "There's even a little extra room in the seat of the skirt! All you need now is a necklace and you'll be all set."

I stared at my reflection. I still thought I looked like a pear, but at least I could exhale without popping a button and sit down without cutting off the circulation to my intestines. That was good enough for me.

CHAPTER FOURTEEN

Being back at the camp made me realize just how much I hadn't missed the place. The minute I stepped out of the car, bugs swarmed around me, probably searching for the fattest and juiciest parts of my body to attack.

From the driveway I could see my least favorite building in the world, the outhouse. I hadn't thought once about it since leaving it, but now I realized I would be spending some time in there this weekend, unless I suddenly developed bowels and kidneys of steel.

"Oh, it's so good to be back!" Janet said, taking a deep breath and slowly exhaling. "The fresh country air, the sounds of the birds, the clear blue sky! Isn't it great?"

I grimaced. I thought no one our age should be that excited at nine o'clock in the morning...it just wasn't normal. I'd still be asleep if Dad hadn't wanted to get such an early start so he could do a little fishing. Actually, he'd wanted to leave before sunrise, but the only thing that would have made me get out of bed at that hour was a stick of dynamite planted in my mattress to blast me out...and well, maybe Troy Donahue wearing only his underpants.

"The Old Home Day parade starts in an hour," I said to no one in particular.

"Are we supposed to pick up Conrad and Scott and drive you guys to the parade?" Dad asked.

"Yeah," I said. "Conrad said the parade kicks off the whole Old Home Day celebration, which lasts all day. Then there's a dance in the school gym tonight, followed by fireworks at ten."

"That sounds like a really long day," Mom said. "You'll have to come back here and change for the dance, won't you?"

I wanted to tell her I'd be happy to come back to the camp at noon and stay there until the dance because the thought of spending 12 hours with Conrad made me want to develop a sudden case of malaria, but Janet seemed so excited about the day ahead, I decided I'd better keep my opinions to myself.

"I guess we should come back here about four," I said. "It'll give us time to relax a little, freshen up – especially after being out in the hot sun all day – and get ready for the dance."

"Well, after we pick up Conrad and Scott for the parade, we'll figure out a time and place to pick you up later this afternoon so you can come back here," Dad said.

"I'd like to see the parade," Mom, who'd been unloading groceries from the car, said. "It's been ages since we've been to one."

My dad's expression had "Noooo! I want to go fishing!" written all over it. It was clear he'd much rather be in his waders, standing in the river and hooking brook trout, than watching some crummy old parade. But very rarely, if ever, did he say no to my mother.

"I suppose we can stay for the parade," he said.

His tone sounded about as enthusiastic as mine did whenever I talked about seeing Conrad...or going to the dentist.

"I can't wait to see Scott!" Janet said.

I could wait forever to see Conrad, especially since, according to his letter, he was expecting a kiss when he saw me. I could just picture him trying to force his lips to pucker over those huge teeth. I thought if I ever developed temporary insanity and actually did allow him to kiss me, I'd probably end up kissing nothing but ceramic or porcelain, or whatever fake teeth were made of. What really bothered me, however, was I had a strong feeling he was planning a sneak attack at some point during Old Home Day. That meant I'd have to keep a close eye on him all day and night, which would be exhausting. I still harbored the small hope that Conrad had developed a bad case of chicken pox since our last phone call the night before. Someone, just someone, might have said a prayer or two that he would.

"Well, put everything in the camp, so we can get going," Dad said. "We want to get a good spot so we'll be able to see the parade."

I reached into the trunk of the car and grabbed my suitcase, in which I'd carefully packed my skirt and shell for the dance, and headed into the camp. At any other time, a parade, carnival, dance and fireworks would have excited me, but not on this day. All I felt was dread.

* * * * *

I had expected the parade to be like the big parades in the city, with precision marching bands and flower-covered floats. The Arrowwood Old Home Day parade turned out to be something entirely different.

For one thing, it took place on a narrow, winding road that was in desperate need of repaving. My dad, per Conrad's directions, had parked the car in a grassy clearing on the side of the road. The six of us stood leaning against the car as the parade passed. Groups of people had gathered on each side of the road, but they were spread far enough apart to allow everyone a clear view. Back in the city, so many people always lined the streets downtown when there was a parade, anyone who wasn't over six feet tall usually ended up looking at the backs of people's heads for two hours.

The Arrowwood parade moved along at a leisurely pace. There was a hay wagon pulled by two gigantic horses, a beat-up old tractor decorated with balloons, a bunch of kids on bicycles covered with crepe-paper streamers, a fire engine with its siren blasting, and a group of flag-bearing members of some local organization who all seemed really happy for so early in the day. As they marched past us, they made whooping sounds, waved at everyone and everything, including the bushes, and appeared to have trouble walking straight. When the guy leading the group suddenly stopped dead, all of the guys behind him crashed into each other. I heard Dad comment to my mother that the guys probably had added a hefty dose of liquid courage to their orange juice that morning, whatever that meant.

Then there was a high-school marching band that wasn't too bad. At least their songs were recognizable. And they were playing actual instruments, not the plastic whistles or aluminum-pot-lids cymbals I'd anticipated.

Conrad, Scott and Janet seemed to be enjoying every second of the parade. For one thing, Scott and Conrad apparently knew everyone who was in it, judging by the way they were shouting

161

and waving at all of the marchers as they passed by. They even knew the names of the horses. And, naturally, Janet was having a good time because she was standing shoulder to shoulder with Scott. Heck, the parade could have been nothing but a couple of guys walking their dogs and carrying a portable radio and she'd have thought it was the best parade on earth.

Conrad actually looked pretty good, I thought. In the week since I'd last seen him, his hair had grown a little and his tan looked deeper. His clothes – jeans and a blue polo-shirt – looked as if they'd been freshly washed and pressed. I almost, just almost, could overlook his face-consuming teeth. Out in the bright sunlight, however, they were nearly impossible to ignore. Every time the light hit them, I was afraid their reflection might blind pilots in low-flying aircraft.

The parade lasted all of twenty-five minutes, which I figured would please my dad. I knew how eager he was to get back to his awaiting brook trout.

"Hop in!" Dad shouted at us as he flung open the car door. "I'll drop you off at the fair."

"We can walk from here," Conrad said. "The field is just up the road on the left."

Dad didn't need any further convincing. "Okay then, I'll be back to pick you up at four o'clock. You kids have a good time."

Before we even could respond, he and mom sped off, leaving us in a cloud of soft-shoulder road dust.

I was concerned that if the Old Home Day fair was anything like the parade, I'd be bored within twenty minutes. And there was no way to contact my father to come get me any earlier, so I knew I was going to be stuck at the fair all day, whether I liked it or not. I'd never hitchhiked before, but I swore if I got desperate enough, I just might give it a try.

"So, what did you think of the parade?" Conrad asked as we walked up the road. Scott and Janet were a few steps ahead of us and involved in a conversation of their own.

"It was nice," I said. "I expected it to last a little longer, though."

"Yeah, it was kind of short this year, for some reason. I think maybe it's because the Bell Family moved away over the winter. They always entered at least three or four floats in the parade. Mrs. Bell was a high-school art teacher so she had some great ideas for floats."

I wanted to say, "Like what? A goat being pushed in a shopping cart?" but I just smiled and nodded.

"I really, really missed you," Conrad suddenly said. "I never realized how empty this town was until you weren't in it. I couldn't even sleep last night, I was so excited, thinking about seeing you today."

"I didn't sleep much, either," I said.

Thinking about seeing him had been the reason for my insomnia, too, but it certainly wasn't because I was excited.

"I waited for a letter from you all week," he said. "I was real disappointed you didn't write."

"Well, we talked on the phone so much, I didn't have anything left to write about. And then I figured we could talk today about anything new that happened."

"But you could've written me a love letter," he said, "like the one I wrote to you. I really wanted to have something I could read over and over again until we could be together."

I was becoming very uncomfortable with the direction in which the conversation was taking. My discomfort mainly was due to the fact I wanted to shout at him to stop being an idiot and realize we were not boyfriend and girlfriend, nor would we ever be, and to stop waiting for something to happen that never would. There would be snowmen living on the sun before I ever wrote him a love letter.

At that point we rounded a corner and came to a field that was filled with people, food booths, game booths, carnival rides and entertainers. A guy riding on a unicycle and juggling four bright red balls passed in front of us.

"Wow! This is pretty cool!" I said.

I had been expecting something much more primitive, like people demonstrating how to milk cows or yodel. And when Conrad had told me there would be rides, I'd pictured a seesaw made from a board and a barrel, and a swing made from a rope and an old tire. But in the distance, to my surprise, I saw a modern-looking Ferris wheel towering over the crowd.

"I love Ferris wheels!" I said, unable to control my enthusiasm.

"Good! We'll have to ride on it, then," Conrad said, smiling.

My own smile faded as I thought about being trapped next to him on the small seat a hundred stories in the air with no means of escape.

Janet and Scott had stopped walking, allowing us to catch up to them.

"Isn't this great?" Janet said. "I don't know what to do first!"

As if answering her question, a woman who was wearing a button that said "Old Home Day Committee" on it walked over and handed each of us a sheet of paper with the day's schedule of events listed on it.

"Ooh, look!" Janet pointed to the list. "There's a horseshoe tournament, a petting zoo and a pie-eating contest!"

The only thing that appealed to me out of the three was the petting zoo. I loved animals that were small enough and friendly enough to pet.

"Let's head over to the petting zoo," I said.

Scott led us to a fenced-in area that had a gate in front. Inside the fence were goats, sheep, chickens, a small pig and some rabbits. Next to the gate was a table stacked with paper cups filled with what looked like cereal. A man behind the table was shouting, "Feed the animals! Only five cents a cup!"

I dug a nickel out of my shorts pocket and handed it to him. Then I grabbed a cup and entered the fenced-in area. Before I even was able to close the gate behind me, at least five goats charged at me. One goat, a tall, skinny one with a white beard, rammed my hand with its nose and knocked the cup right out of it. Within seconds, my nickel's worth of food had been inhaled. I thought of all the things I could have bought with that nickel – a bag of M&Ms, a Milky Way bar or an orange Popsicle. Suddenly, I really wanted to see that goat roasting on a pole over a barbecue pit.

When I turned to look at Janet, Scott and Conrad, I felt even more annoyed because they were laughing at me.

"You should have seen your face when the goat knocked the cup out of your hand!" Janet managed to stop laughing long enough to say. "We were afraid you were going to kick him!"

I stomped out of the pen and slammed the gate behind me. "I should ask for my nickel back! If the guy can't teach his animals some manners, then he shouldn't bring them out in public!"

Conrad slipped his arm around my waist and pulled me toward him for a hug. "It's okay, honey, don't let that old goat ruin your day!"

"Let's go on the Ferris wheel!" Janet said. "It's not crowded yet."

The four of us headed in that direction. It was twenty-five cents per person for a ride. Conrad paid for my ticket, but Scott bought just one, for himself. Janet didn't seem fazed at all by his cheapness. She took her change purse out of her shorts pockets and bought her own ticket.

As soon as Conrad and I were seated, I realized that going on the Ferris wheel with him probably was a big mistake. For one thing, my rear end barely had touched the seat when he slid his arm around me and cupped his hand around my shoulder. Then he just sat there, silently staring at me. I could feel his eyes boring into the side of my head, so I looked straight ahead. Nothing, I vowed, was going to make me turn to look at him. There was no way I was going to give him any opportunity to lean in for a kiss.

The Ferris wheel lurched to a start, and I was surprised at how fast it turned. The ones I'd been on in the past had moved pretty slowly so the riders could enjoy the view, but on this one, the scenery seemed to go whizzing by.

Each time our car neared the very top, Conrad would rock back and forth, making the whole thing swing. And each time, I grabbed his arm and screamed. He obviously enjoyed terrifying me because he continued to make the car rock...even harder. I swore I could hear the bolts on each side loosening as he did. I dared to glance down, wondering where my innards were going to splatter when the car crashed to the ground. Immediately, I clamped my eyes shut.

I heard Janet's screams, a combination of fear and delight, coming from above us. I opened my eyes, looked up and saw her sneaker-clad feet swinging back and forth overhead. Obviously Scott, just like Conrad, was rocking their car. And as he did, he was laughing an evil-sounding laugh, kind of like Snidely Whiplash's in the Dudley Do-Right cartoons.

After about twenty revolutions on the fast-moving Ferris wheel and Conrad's constant rocking of our seat, despite my pleas for him to stop, my breakfast – scrambled eggs, bacon, cinnamon toast, orange juice and half a banana – began to talk to me. The grumbling and rumbling sounds coming from my stomach grew so loud, they nearly drowned out Janet's screams.

"Conrad!" I shouted at him. "Stop rocking the seat! I'm going to be sick!"

He smiled at me. "Aw, come on, you know you're having fun!"

"No! I'm serious! I'm going to be sick!"

Either he didn't hear me or he pretended he didn't, because he seemed to put renewed effort into his rocking. Panicking, I turned toward him so I could shout directly into his ear.

When I opened my mouth to plead with him, that's when he decided to lean over for a kiss.

That's also when I lost my breakfast.

My first reaction when I saw my bacon, eggs and cinnamon toast all over the front of Conrad's shirt wasn't guilt or embarrassment, it was anger. I was so mad at him for making me sick, I honestly wanted to shove him off the ride. I'd put up with a lot of crap from him during the past two weeks, all because I knew how much Janet wanted to be with Scott. But this was the final straw. I vowed that the second the Ferris wheel stopped, I was going to get off and walk away, and keep walking all the way back to the camp. I never wanted to hear Conrad's name or see his fake-toothed face again. Never.

"Hell, Conrad," Scott said when the four of us once again were safely on the ground. "Don't tell me you puked on yourself! I thought you had a stronger stomach than that!"

Conrad's eyebrows drew together as he stood stiff and unmoving with his arms extended at his sides. He reminded me of a Gumby doll.

"I did it," I said before he could answer. "He was rocking the seat and I told him to stop because it was making me sick, but he kept rocking it harder and harder. So I lost my breakfast on him. And you know something? It serves him right! I hope the three of you will have a good time because I'm leaving!"

I turned and walked off. I didn't care how Conrad was going to clean himself off or what he was going to do the rest of the

166

day. I didn't care if the horse-drawn wagon ran him over. I just wanted to go back to the camp, lie down and try to forget my terrible morning.

"Sally, wait!" I heard Conrad's voice behind me. "I'm sorry!"

I kept walking.

"Sally!" This time it was a female voice to my right. I turned and saw Tweaky coming toward me.

"How's it going?" she asked.

"Crummy!" I said. "Do you know anyone who can give me a ride back to the camp?"

"She's not going anywhere!" Conrad had caught up with us. I noticed a clump of paper napkins in his right hand, which he'd obviously used to wipe off his shirt. A big wet stain was all that remained on the front of it – no more chunks.

"I'm going back to the camp!" I snapped, narrowing my eyes at him. "And I'll hitchhike if I have to!"

"Hmmm," Tweaky said. "Do I sense trouble in paradise here?"

"Paradise?" I repeated. "That's a joke! I never want to see him again!"

For a moment, I thought Conrad might cry. He just stood there with his head hanging, and I could swear I saw his bottom lip quivering. Never had I seen anything more pathetic...and the vomit-stained shirt didn't help much.

For some reason even I couldn't understand, my anger began to lessen. I even felt kind of sorry for Conrad. He'd been so excited to see me, so eager for me to arrive, he hadn't been able to sleep, and here I was, leaving him after barely an hour.

Still, I thought, frowning, he hadn't listened to me on the Ferris wheel and had acted like a jerk. He'd ruined what could have been a fun day. He deserved to be left by himself with his puky shirt.

"Aw, come on, Sally," Tweaky said. "Conrad spent all week talking about how he could hardly wait to see you. He was even counting the hours. He drove us crazy! I don't know what he did to make you so mad, but can't you forgive him?"

I glanced at Conrad, who lifted his eyes, but not his head, to look at me.

167

"We can't just go on and have fun like nothing happened!" I said. "His shirt is a mess – and smelly! I'm not going to hang around with him like that!"

"They're selling Old Home Day souvenir T-shirts over there," Tweaky said, pointing. "They're only two dollars each. Maybe he could get one of those to wear." She paused before turning to Conrad and asking, "What'd you do to your shirt anyway?"

"If he's smart, he won't answer that," I said through gritted teeth.

Conrad finally dared to look directly at me. "If I go buy one of those T-shirts and change, will you stay?"

I looked past him and spotted a carousel. I loved carousels even more than Ferris wheels, and I was pretty sure Conrad couldn't make me sick on a carousel horse...unless he made me sit on it on his lap while he nuzzled my neck or nibbled my ear or something.

I sighed. "Okay, I guess I'll stay." The fact that I'd just spotted Tim Argent standing near the carousel just might have had something to do with my decision.

Conrad smiled his huge smile. "Great! You wait right here! I'll be back in a minute!"

Before I could respond, he disappeared into the crowd.

I could feel Tweaky's eyes burning into me. I turned to look at her.

"You don't really like him much, do you?" she asked. "He might be too dumb to know it, but anyone else would have to be blind not to notice."

I hesitated before I answered. "No, I don't like him...I mean, not the way he likes me. The most the two of us could ever be is friends...and even that's a stretch."

She slowly shook her head. "He's already got the two of you married and living in a house he's planning to build for you on part of his brother's land."

"Oh, for cryin' out loud, I'm not even thirteen yet! You know, that's one of the reasons why I don't like him! He has all these fantasies he thinks are really going to happen. And he's too pushy!"

"That's 'cause he's a guy," Tweaky said, giggling. "They're all too pushy."

"Are you here with Jake?" I asked, eager to change the subject.

"Yeah, and Tim Argent. They're around here somewhere. Jake's going to enter the pie-eating contest. It should be a riot to watch! Last year he missed winning by only two bites. The prize was five dollars, so he was pretty upset when he didn't win. He'd already had that money spent on some model airplane he'd been eyeing at Woolworth's."

"I think I could win that contest," I said, rubbing my stomach. "I'm feeling kinda empty right now."

I couldn't help but notice that Tweaky still wasn't wearing a bra. Her beige T-shirt, which had two holes near the bellybutton area, clung to her and highlighted what looked like two Hershey's kisses stuck to her chest. Before I could stop myself, I blurted out, "Don't you ever wear a bra?"

She shrugged. "Ain't no reason to in the summer. But when I go back to school I have to because the school is strict. I think bras are dumb and uncomfortable."

"My mom always says if you don't wear one, your breasts will sag down to your waist when you're older and you'll have to tuck them in your belt."

Tweaky laughed. "I don't think mine could ever stretch that far, even if they got run over by a steamroller!"

I giggled, already feeling better about my decision to stay.

"What's so funny?" Conrad's voice came from behind me. I turned and nearly was blinded by the bright chartreuse color of his shirt.

He obviously read my expression. "It was either this color, bright yellow or pink," he said.

"Well, at least you'll be able to find him if you lose him!" Tweaky said.

The color was bad enough, but the design on the front, a sketch of the Ferris wheel with *Arrowwood Old Home Day 1962* printed under it, made it even worse. Every time I looked at the darned thing, I knew I'd be thinking about Conrad's childish rocking on the Ferris wheel and I'd get mad at him all over again.

"Hey, guys! How's it going?"

I had been so busy glaring at Conrad's T-shirt, I hadn't even noticed Tim Argent until he was standing next to Tweaky.

Immediately I felt my breath catch in my throat. Tim looked almost as good as Troy Donahue, I thought. His sky-blue shirt made his thick-lashed eyes look even bluer, and the sunlight made his golden hair sparkle as if it had specks of mica in it. I could have stared at him all day.

"So, are you having a good time?" Tim asked, looking directly at me. "Last year it started pouring out right after the parade, but this looks like it's going to be a good day. The fireworks should be great tonight, too, seeing there's no clouds."

"Well, the morning got off to a rocky start," Conrad said, "but I think we'll have a good time now."

I thought the only way I'd have a good time would be if Tim stuck with us for the rest of the day. I was certain that just being able to stare at him whenever I wanted to would make me forget how miserable I was.

"Hey, the pie-eating contest is starting in ten minutes," Tweaky said, looking at her watch. "Let's go cheer my brother on!"

"The pie-eating contest is pretty cool," Tim said. "Somebody always ends up puking!"

Conrad glanced at me and I could tell he was trying hard not to laugh.

I vowed that if he dared to breathe even one word to Tim about my accident on the Ferris wheel, I'd head right back to the city and never come back to the camp again, even if he sent me a gazillion letters begging me to. And Conrad didn't know it, but I was determined to hold Tim to his promise to dance with me at the Old Home Day dance that night – in fact, I'd been thinking of nothing else since he'd mentioned it at the donkey ballgame. But I had the feeling if Tim found out I'd upchucked, he probably wouldn't be in any hurry to have me breathing in his face on the dance floor, even if I brushed my teeth and gargled. So it was imperative that Conrad keep his mouth shut.

The four of us walked across the field to an area that had been set up with three long tables covered in plastic. Behind the tables sat four females and nine males, one of whom was Jake, all wearing paper bibs. A crowd had gathered in front of the tables. I spotted Janet and Scott as soon as we approached.

"Hey, where'd you two disappear to?" I asked Janet.

"We went on the octopus," she said. "It was pretty scary, but Scott protected me!'

The octopus was a ride that looked like a big metal octopus with a seat on the tip of each arm. The arms went up and down and the seats twirled around. Just the thought of it made me feel queasy all over again. But Janet's smile told me she probably would have ridden on the octopus a hundred times if it meant she'd be sitting close to Scott.

Janet stared at Conrad's T-shirt. "I see you changed," she said to him. "What'd you do with your other shirt?"

"I tossed it," he said. "It was a hand-me-down from one of my brothers anyway."

Out of the corner of my eye, I could see Tim looking at Conrad. I was certain he must be wondering why he'd thrown away his shirt and was going to ask him what happened to it. I braced myself for the inevitable.

"Ladies and gentlemen," an announcer's voice suddenly boomed at us, "welcome to the fifteenth annual Arrowwood Old Home Day pie-eating contest!"

Tim turned his attention to Jake at the table. I allowed myself to exhale. At least for the moment, my secret humiliation would remain exactly that.

One of the committee members wheeled a cart of golden-crusted pies over to the contestants. From what I could tell, they were blueberry, which I thought was a pretty obvious choice as far as entertainment value went. What other type of pie would stain everyone's teeth and lips a brilliant shade of purple?

"The rules of the contest are hands behind your back at all times," the announcer said. "The first one to finish the entire pie, crust and all, will be the winner! On the count of three, the contest will begin!"

He'd barely uttered "three!" when the feeding frenzy began. The contestants resembled a row of pigs lined up at a trough, their faces buried in their plates as they snorted and slurped, causing pie to fly everywhere. Jake, from what I could tell, considering his entire face was in his plate and all I could see was the top of his head, appeared to be doing well. In what seemed like only seconds from the start of the contest, Jake's arm flew up and his head popped up, a signal to the judges that

171

he'd finished the pie. Blueberry pie-filling covered everything from the roots of his hair to his neck. I thought if the judges scraped off everything that still was on his face, they'd probably disqualify him for not eating half of the pie.

"The winner!" the announcer shouted, lifting Jake's arm as if he were a prizefighter who'd just won a match. "Your prize is a crisp $5 bill and a beautiful trophy!"

We cheered, whistled and whooped. Jake smiled broadly, displaying a bunch of purple teeth. His celebration was short-lived, however. One of the other contestants, a guy about Jake's age, stood up from the table and keeled over backwards. We heard a loud thud when he hit the ground.

"What's wrong with him?" I asked Tweaky. "I didn't think eating too much pie could cause someone to pass out!"

"Oh, that's Ronnie," she said matter-of-factly. "He did that at school once when he accidentally ate something with peanuts in it. He's real allergic to them. He can die if he eats them."

"But there's no peanuts in blueberry pie," I said. "Is there?"

"Could be peanut oil or something in the crust," she said. "Or if the person who made the pies also made something that had peanuts in it and her hands just touched the blueberry pie, that would do it, too!"

Tweaky's words scared me. I'd never heard of people being so allergic to food they could drop dead from eating it. It was terrifying to think I might be allergic to some food I hadn't even tried yet. Just to be safe, I vowed I'd never eat a new food again. Even if Mr. Breen at Breen's Apothecary back in the city came up with some new ice-cream flavor for his soda fountain, I'd stick with just plain vanilla or chocolate. After all, I wouldn't want to take my final breath with my face in a dish of mocha-banana-pistachio ice cream, just for the sake of trying something new.

All of the police and firemen who'd been in the parade rushed over to help the fallen pie-eater. I wondered which was more embarrassing: throwing up on the Ferris wheel or having to be rushed to the hospital with mashed-up blueberries all over your face.

Janet seemed to read my thoughts. "I guess you don't feel so bad now that you threw up all over Conrad on the Ferris wheel!" she said.

I cast a panicked glance at Tim Argent. Had he, I wondered, heard her? His amused smile told me he had.

I made a mental note to have a little talk with Janet later on. She seemed to have a knack lately for spilling things I wanted to keep secret, like my dream about naked Conrad, or the fact I suspected he'd robbed the Harmons' house. And now, here she was, blabbing about the puking incident. If I didn't know better, I'd think she had something against me.

CHAPTER FIFTEEN

The school gymnasium where the Old Home Day dance was held didn't look anything like I'd expected it would. The hay bales sitting on sawdust-covered floors I'd envisioned turned out to be potted artificial trees decorated with colored crepe-paper streamers and paper flowers. The walls were covered with glittery stars of all sizes, bathed in soft blue lighting. A four-piece band was warming up on a makeshift stage at the far end of the gym when we arrived.

I honestly thought the four of us had never looked better. The dress Janet made was sewn so well, it looked store-bought, and the fabric-covered belt and little cape she'd added, using her leftover material, were just the right touches to spiffy it up. I also thought I didn't look too shabby in my cranberry skirt and pink shell accessorized with Mom's pearl necklace with the rhinestone clasp.

The boys had cleaned up nicely, too. Scott's hair, which usually hung in his eyes, was combed and parted, and it looked as if a healthy dose of Brylcreem had been added to help tame his cowlick. He was wearing brown corduroy pants and a pale yellow dress-shirt. Conrad had on black slacks, a white shirt with a button-down collar, and black-and-white high-top sneakers. I didn't think sneakers were a very good choice for dancing, but at least they were better than his father's white bucks.

The perimeter of the gym was lined with folding chairs, many of which already were occupied. Everywhere I looked, groups of people of all ages were gathered, talking and laughing. I guessed the crowd numbered about a hundred or so.

"Is this a good turnout?" I asked Conrad.

"Not bad for so early," he said. "But by the end of the night it'll be wall-to-wall people."

I checked out what other people were wearing. The fashions ranged from shorts and T-shirts to fancy party dresses and suits and ties.

"There's Tweaky, Jay and Tim," Conrad said, pointing toward the entrance door.

My head snapped in the direction of his finger, and my eyes instantly made a head-to-toe sweep over Tim. I thought he looked absolutely dreamy in his tan chinos, white dress-shirt with the top button unbuttoned, navy sports jacket and black loafers. In fact, his outfit looked exactly like one of the outfits Troy Donahue had worn in *Parrish*. I felt my heartbeat quicken.

"You can put your eyeballs back in your head now," Conrad said, frowning at me.

"I'm staring at Tweaky!" I lied. "I nearly didn't recognize her in a dress!"

"And shoes," Scott said. "She never wears shoes during the summer."

The way Tweaky was walking as she moved toward us pretty much told me, and everyone else at the dance, that she rarely wore shoes, and that her Mary Janes were killing her. Her legs seemed stiff, as did her feet, giving her a robot-like gait. Her flowered sundress in yellow and white looked a little long for her and a little too roomy, causing me to suspect she'd probably found it in her mother's closet. As she came closer, I spotted something that made my mouth fall open.

She was wearing a bra!

Actually, when Tweaky pulled up her breasts to where they belonged, I thought she really looked stacked. I never would have guessed that the bouncy, T-shirt-covered breasts she'd flaunted around town all summer actually were Marilyn Monroe-esque.

But the last thing I would have expected was a tomboy like Tweaky to get all dressed up for an Old Home Day dance. In fact, I hadn't expected to see her at the dance at all. She hadn't expressed even the slightest bit of interest in it when Janet and I had talked about it earlier at the field. Her lack of interest had come as no surprise to us, however, because Tweaky just didn't seem like the dancing type. I couldn't help but wonder what had happened to change her mind and her appearance so quickly and so dramatically.

My eyebrows rose as the answer hit me...she had a crush on Tim Argent! That had to be it! Tim was so cute and so charming, I figured no girl, not even a tomboy like Tweaky, could resist him. They'd been together at the Old Home Day events all day and now they were at the dance together. Could the feeling on Tim's part, I wondered, be mutual? Did he like her, too? A pang of jealousy suddenly stabbed me.

"My girdle is killing me!" Tweaky greeted us. "Isn't there an easier way to hold up nylons?"

"There's garter belts," Janet said. "They're just a wide band with hooks."

"The hooks are what's killing me!" Tweaky said. "They keep twisting sideways and digging into the backs of my thighs! If I sit down I'm afraid they'll slice me open like razor blades!"

I couldn't believe she was talking about such intimate things as girdles and hooks in front of the boys. I silently prayed she wouldn't blurt out something even more embarrassing, like her bra was crushing her nipples. I'd never be able to face Tim again if she did.

"You girls look nice," Tim said. He looked directly at me. "So how's your stomach feeling?"

I felt the heat rise to my cheeks. "I'm fine. It wasn't like I was sick or had the flu or anything. It was just Conrad shaking me up on the ride that made my stomach upset. I was fine the minute the ride was over."

"I just like to make boring rides more exciting," Conrad said, shrugging.

"What do you do on roller coasters?" Janet asked. "Unlock the bar that holds you in?"

He narrowed his eyes at her. "No, I wouldn't go that far."

"I hate dances," Tweaky interrupted. "They're just a poor excuse for guys to cop a cheap feel. If any guy tries to feel me up while we're dancing, he'll be picking up his teeth off the floor!"

I caught Jake giving Conrad an amused glance. I was pretty sure the "teeth off the floor" comment had made him think of Conrad's new, removable smile.

176

"I'm actually kind of surprised you came," I said to Tweaky. "I mean, you never said you were coming when we were with you all day."

"I just want to see the fireworks," she said. "They're going to shoot them off out back here right after the dance. I was just gonna come over for the fireworks and skip the dance, but Jake and Tim talked me into coming with them."

"My parents are coming for the fireworks," I said. "Then they'll drive us back to the camp."

"Well, it's going to be the longest three hours of my life," Tweaky muttered, scrunching up her face and twisting her body at the waist, as if trying to free herself from the confines of her girdle.

Conrad moved closer to me and slipped his arm around my waist. I was pretty sure he was giving a not-so-subtle signal to Tim that I was his, so to keep his distance.

Tweaky was right, I thought dismally. It was going to be a very long three hours.

"Well, I'll catch you guys later," Tim said. "I see some of my buddies from my baseball team over there and I want to say hi."

As I watched him walk away, I had mixed emotions. First of all, I was happy he'd left Tweaky because that meant he probably wasn't interested in her and I just might have a chance with him. But I also was sad because he'd taken off so fast. I'd been hoping he'd hang around with us all night and make the evening more bearable. He'd left the Old Home Day fair early, too, forcing me to spend a long afternoon alone with Conrad because Scott and Janet wanted to ride every ride there...at least three times each. The only ride my stomach had allowed me to ride on was the carousel, and even then, I'd chosen one of the stationary horses, not the ones that went up and down, just to be safe. I'd thought the day never would end.

"Let's go find some seats and I'll get us some punch," Conrad said. "I sit more than I dance, so I want to get a seat that has a good view of the dance floor. You coming, Scott?"

"Sitting is for wallflowers," Scott said. "I'm fine standing."

"Me, too!" Janet said almost too quickly. She had mentioned at the camp that her new white T-strap shoes were pinching her toes, so I knew she probably was dying to get off her feet.

"I don't know if I dare sit!" Tweaky said. "This girdle will probably stop my circulation and I'll pass out!"

I knew exactly how she was feeling. My own girdle wasn't exactly loose, and it was the long-leg variety that went nearly down to my knees. To make matters worse, the heat and humidity in the gym were making my skin feel sticky and clammy, which contributed to an uncomfortable affliction known as girdle suction. I expected to take off my girdle when I got back to the camp and have a gallon of sweat come pouring out. I also expected my thighs to end up looking like two rolls of white crepe paper.

Conrad grabbed me by the hand and led me over to a row of seats near the stage. "Stay here," he said. "I'll be back in a second with the punch."

I sat there alone, wondering if I was going to be stuck with him all night. I told myself there was no law that said I had to stay with him through the entire dance. After all, he wasn't my boyfriend, as much as he liked to think he was. So if I wanted to dance with someone else or hang around with Janet and Tweaky...or Tim Argent, then I'd do it.

My eyes scanned the gym until they came to rest on Tim, who was standing and talking with a group of guys about his age. I enjoyed watching him, no matter what he was doing. Just looking at him in all of his gorgeousness was enough to please me. I allowed myself to daydream about what it would be like to have him hold me in his arms as we danced, and I felt a shiver travel up the entire length of my body. I had my fingers crossed that he wouldn't forget his promise to dance with me.

"Here's your punch." Conrad's voice put an abrupt end to my daydreaming. He thrust a Dixie cup filled with a red liquid at me.

"Thanks." I took the cup from him and tasted the punch. From what I could tell, it was canned Hawaiian punch mixed with ginger ale.

Conrad plopped down next to me and studied the crowd of people. "There's two of my brothers over there," he pointed out. "And that's my sister to the left of them."

He had way too many brothers and sisters for me to ever remember any of them or their names, so I didn't pay much attention to him when he talked about them. I supposed he was thinking they'd all be my in-laws someday, so I should get to know them, but I was thinking that the less I associated with anyone related to him, the better. The last thing I wanted was to be considered a part of Conrad's family.

The overhead lights dimmed, so only the blue lights were illuminating the dance floor. According to a poster on the wall, the theme of the dance was "Blue Moon," which I guessed explained all of the stars and the blue lighting. If the idea had been to create a romantic atmosphere, the crowd of now blue-faced people just wasn't having that effect on me. In fact, I thought everyone looked kind of eerie...as if they desperately needed oxygen.

One of the members of the band welcomed everyone and said they were going to start off with a slow song, "for all of you young lovers out there!"

Conrad turned to smile and wink at me. Did he, I wondered, seriously believe we were young lovers? Could he possibly be that blind?

The band then began to play *Smoke Gets in Your Eyes*.

"They're not too bad," I had to say louder than I wanted to because we were sitting so close to one of the speakers. "I wonder if the lead singer will be able to hit the high note at the end of the song?"

"They can sing and play just about anything," Conrad said. "They play at most of our functions here in town, from school dances to weddings."

The band members were a far cry from the foot-stomping, harmonica-playing group I'd expected them to be. I'd even imagined one of them would be playing a washboard or blowing into a jug. The fact they were playing electric guitars and wearing matching tan suits surprised me.

A few of the older couples, who were about my parents' age, waltzed out onto the dance floor. It was obvious that some of them had been dancing together for years, the way they matched each other's steps perfectly and added fancy stuff like twirls and dips. I couldn't picture Conrad twirling me or dipping me. If he did, I'd probably end up flat on my back on

179

the floor with my skirt hiked up and my long-leg girdle showing.

The slow song ended and the band launched right into The Twist. Janet and I loved doing the Twist, so I wasn't surprised when I saw her heading across the floor toward me.

"Mind if Janet and I do the Twist?" I asked Conrad – not that I cared whether he did or didn't.

He shook his head and smiled. "No, go right ahead! I think I'll enjoy watching you shake your hips!"

Janet and I picked a spot only a few feet from Tim and his buddies and started to dance. A crowd of mostly females also joined us and we all gyrated to the music. If nothing else, the Twist was good exercise for the waistline, which I needed. Janet, however, certainly didn't need to whittle anything off her waist. It was bad enough the kids at school already teased her about her thinness, calling her Skinny Minnie or saying things like if she stood sideways and stuck out her tongue, she'd look like a zipper.

"Look at her with the cape out there," I heard one of Tim's friends say. He was looking directly at Janet. "Who's she supposed to be, Zorro?"

"Yeah," another guy in the group joined in. "And that must be Sergeant Garcia dancing with her!"

They all burst out laughing...including Tim.

I bit at my bottom lip. Sergeant Garcia? The hugely overweight, bumbling foe of Zorro on the TV show? I knew I could stand to shed a few pounds, but Sergeant Garcia must have weighed over 300 pounds. Was that really the way I looked to guys, I wondered? Or was it just that Janet was so thin, she made me look bigger when I was next to her?

"I'm going to go sit down," I said to Janet, who still was smiling and dancing, apparently oblivious to what I'd just overheard. "I have a pain in my side."

Before she could respond, I rushed back to Conrad and sat down next to him.

"You looked great out there!" he said. "I was really enjoying watching you. Why'd you stop so soon?"

I wanted to tell him it was because I'd danced in front of Tim, thinking I'd attract him, but all I did was set myself up to be the brunt of his and his buddies' insulting jokes. I wanted to tell him I was a fool for ever thinking someone like Tim possibly could find me attractive, and I was regretting all of the time I'd wasted daydreaming about him. But most of all I wanted to tell him he'd been right about Tim when he'd warned me back at the ballgame that he had a big ego and was two-faced.

"I had a pain in my side," I said. "I guess I'm not used to doing the Twist, it's been so long."

Conrad handed me my cup of punch, which he'd been holding while I danced. "Here, take a drink. Maybe it will help."

I took the cup and sipped from it as I looked back toward the area where Janet and I had been dancing. Janet was still twisting, but now with a group of other girls who'd been dancing next to us. Tim and his pals no longer were standing nearby. For the first time all night, I found myself not caring where Tim was. I figured he'd probably checked out all of the girls at the dance and had decided that none met his high standards, so he'd left. The thought of him heading home actually appealed to me.

The band then switched to a slow song, Roy Orbison's *Crying,* which just happened to be one of my favorites. I looked down into my empty cup and stared at the little bits of pulp left in the bottom. An overwhelming urge to cry threatened to embarrass me even worse than I'd already been embarrassed on what had turned out to be a completely humiliating day. I struggled to hold back my tears. The last thing I needed was for Conrad to see me crying because knowing him, he'd endlessly bug me about the reason why. I supposed I always could tell him the song was so sad it made me cry.

"May I have this dance?"

I raised my eyes up the length of tan chino pants and a white shirt, to the face of Tim Argent, who was flashing one of his best heart-melting smiles. He, in all of his gorgeousness, was standing only inches from me, his hand extended toward me.

When I managed to catch my breath, I said something that even I hadn't expected. "No, thank you."

Tim's eyes widened and his smile faded. "You promised me a dance, remember?" he said.

"Maybe I did...but I changed my mind."

His eyebrows drew together in a deep crease. "Later, then?"

I shook my head. "Sorry, I don't think so."

His expression clearly displayed his bewilderment. I imagined he wasn't accustomed to being turned down by girls, particularly by one whose score on his potential-girlfriend rating chart probably was only a five out of a possible ten.

"Okay, then," he said. "Talk to you later."

The moment Tim was out of sight, Conrad grabbed me and hugged me so hard, I was afraid he'd cracked one of my ribs – or crushed one of my already tender, budding breasts.

"That was fantastic!" he said, releasing his grip and pulling away from me just far enough so I could see his ear-to-ear smile, which glowed an iridescent white in the blue light. "You put down the mighty Tim Argent! You showed him that I was more important to you! I'm so proud of you, darling!"

I wanted to groan. Conrad had it all wrong. He thought I'd shot down Tim because I was his girlfriend and wanted to exclusively be with him. But as wrong as that was, I wasn't about to tell him the real reason why I'd rejected Tim. I never wanted to think about or mention Sergeant Garcia again.

"Let's dance!" Conrad suddenly said.

He stood up, grabbed me by the hand and pulled me out of the chair. The action happened so quickly, I was wrapped in his arms in a bear hug with his cheek pressed against mine before I even had time to take a breath.

Conrad's dancing consisted of rocking back and forth from one foot to the other while clinging to me like Saran Wrap. We never moved from the spot where we started. Over his shoulder I spotted Tim waltzing with some blonde who looked older, high-school age. She was petite, probably a size four, and was wearing a short, very fitted white dress. I tried to imagine how I'd look in that dress. First of all, my mom had always told me white wasn't my color because it made me look too pasty. She'd also said white was unforgiving and showed every bulge and ripple. Black, she claimed, was slimming and concealed bulges. Yet when I told her I wanted an entirely black back-to-school wardrobe, she refused to buy it for me, saying, "Don't be ridiculous! You'll look like a mortician!"

I suddenly hated the girl in the white dress. She looked too good in it – sleek and shapely. On my body, that same dress would have looked like a bag of marshmallows...that's if it even came in my size – jumbo petite.

I tore my eyes from Tim and his dance partner and caught a glimpse of Janet and Scott dancing. The "in heaven" look on Janet's face as she clung to him made me envious. I wanted to feel the same way about a guy, kind of like the way I felt about Troy Donahue. I thought I'd experienced some of those same feelings with Tim, but now he just made me feel...well, stupid.

The sound of Conrad making gulping noises in my ear snapped me back to reality. I was familiar with that gulping sound, thanks to my night of hell with him at the drive-in. It meant he was trying to gather the courage for another attempt at a kiss. He probably thought I'd let him now, seeing he was convinced I'd turned down Tim because I wanted to be solely with him.

I pulled away from Conrad. "It's really hot dancing," I said, fanning my face with my hand. "Could you get me another cup of punch?"

He just stared at me for a moment, then sighed. "Yeah, okay. I'll be right back."

I walked over to my seat and plunked down. I'd had just about enough of the Old Home Day dance. The only reason I'd wanted to come in the first place was to dance with Tim, not to be stuck with Conrad gulping into my ear all night. At least at the YMCA dances I'd been able to dance with different guys, which always made the evening fun and interesting. Here, if I so much as thought of dancing with another guy, I'd no doubt have to put up with a tantrum from Conrad. I wished the telephone fairy would drop off a phone at the camp so I could call my parents and tell them to come rescue me.

Conrad returned with my punch...and Janet and Scott.

"Isn't this great?" Janet fairly gushed. "Today has been so much fun, I hate to see it end!"

I wondered if she and I had attended the same events because I certainly wouldn't have classified any part of my day as being fun. I also wondered how she'd feel if I told her that Tim and his buddies had called us Zorro and Sergeant Garcia. Would she still be acting as if she'd swallowed a handful of happy pills?

Probably, I thought. She was so excited to be with Scott, dumb remarks wouldn't bother her – unless, that is, Scott was the one who was making the dumb remarks. I, on the other hand, was so miserable with Conrad, even someone telling me I had a run in my stocking probably would make me burst into tears.

The band started to play the Bristol Stomp, a dance Janet and I loved to do...and most boys had no clue how to.

"Come on," Janet said to me. "Let's go stomp!"

I took a couple sips of punch, handed my cup to Conrad, and said, "I'll be right back after this song!"

Within seconds, Janet and I were out on the dance floor, doing the stomp in synchronized steps. A few of the other dancers stopped to watch us, then copied what we were doing. In spite of myself, I smiled.

"Mind if I join you?"

It was Tim Argent. Not even waiting for an answer, he jumped between Janet and me and fell into perfect step with us. He was the first guy I'd ever seen do the stomp so effortlessly, so smoothly. As much as I hated to admit it, I was impressed. After all, I was pretty sure the only stomping Conrad had ever done probably involved killing ants in his house.

Still, a part of me wanted to walk off the dance floor and leave Tim and his fancy footwork out there. But a bigger part of me wanted to keep dancing and not return to Conrad even one second sooner than absolutely necessary. Finally, I decided to just keep dancing and try to enjoy myself. To heck with what Tim or Conrad or anyone else thought. They all could go jump into the Abenaki River for all I cared.

A group of girls gathered to watch us – or, should I say, to watch Tim. Their goo-goo-eyed expressions as they stood gaping at him made it pretty obvious he was the object of their desire. I couldn't help but wonder if I'd looked that pathetic during the times I'd stared at him.

When the song ended, Janet made a beeline for Scott. I started to walk away when I felt a hand grasp my arm. I turned and looked directly into Tim's big blue eyes.

"I want to know why you're suddenly acting like you can't stand me," he said.

184

I stared at the floor and took a deep breath before I answered. "I overheard you and your pals making fun of Janet and me. You know, Zorro and Sergeant Garcia? I didn't think it was as funny as you obviously did."

Tim released his grip on my arm. His silence made me look up at him. The expression on his face – his lips taut, his eyebrows drawn together in a crease – told me I had caught him completely off guard with my response.

"You can't blame me for what my friends say," he said. "I had nothing to do with it."

"Maybe not, but I looked directly at you and you were laughing."

"Yeah, but not *at* you. I was laughing at how ridiculous the comment was. I mean, you don't look any more like Sergeant Garcia than I do!"

Oh, Tim, you're such a cool one! I'd expected him to come up with some excuse to make himself look good, but not so effortlessly. The guy obviously was a real pro.

"No problem," I said, shrugging. "I'd better get back to Conrad now."

"I'm right here." I felt an arm slide around my waist. Conrad pulled me against him in another not-so-subtle display of possessiveness.

"See you guys later," Tim said and disappeared into the crowd.

I looked at Conrad and instantly guessed he wasn't pleased, so I waited for the inevitable lecture. I didn't have to wait long.

"It was too hot to slow dance with me," he said, "but not too hot to fast dance with Tim Argent?"

"He cut in on us. I didn't invite him. Honestly, I can't even stand the guy. He thinks the world revolves around him."

"Then you should have come back and sat down with me," he said.

"And leave Janet alone with Tim? I wasn't about to abandon her."

Conrad shook his head and sighed. "Look, I don't mean to sound so jealous all the time, but it's just that I get kind of crazy when I think of you with anyone else. I'm scared I'm going to lose you. I can't compete with guys like Tim."

185

I wanted to yell at him, *"You can't lose something you've never had, you idiot! And you'd better start getting used to being without me because the minute I head back to the city, you won't ever hear from me again!"*

As far as I was concerned, this one-sided summer romance had been overdue for a decent burial ever since the day it began. If it hadn't been for Janet liking Scott so much, Conrad's entire relationship with me would have begun and ended when he first flashed his black-eyed-peas smile at me at Cutter's swimming hole.

I felt a small sense of peace in knowing that by late the next afternoon I'd be on my way back to the city and could forget about my summer vacation from Hell...and Conrad.

"I need more punch," was all I said to him. "It really is hot in here."

CHAPTER SIXTEEN

Conrad showed up at the camp at sunrise on Sunday morning, probably because he wanted to make certain we didn't head back to the city before he could say his goodbyes.

He had nothing to worry about. Dad was in no hurry to leave. To him, going home meant returning to his two jobs, taking care of the tenement building, and leaving the forest, fresh air and fish behind. So he probably wanted to make his day at the camp last as long as possible. I, on the other hand, had been packed and ready to leave since the moment I'd returned from the Old Home Day fireworks.

I climbed down from the bunk at eleven and found Conrad and my dad fishing in the river. I figured Dad had found him sitting out on the porch and had taken pity on him, so he'd invited him to join him. Dad never would have considered waking me to tell me Conrad was there – not unless he wanted to risk being permanently disowned as my father. I'd actually been awake since about nine anyway, mainly because of the Rod and Gun Club's weekly skeet-shooting event. I wondered if I lived at the camp year-round if I'd ever get used to the shooting and be able to tune it out and sleep through it.

I, however, had no intention whatsoever of ever finding out.

Janet also was in a hurry to return to the city. She and Scott had said their farewells after the Old Home Day fireworks because he always visited his grandmother on Sundays and wasn't going to be around. Janet had asked him to write to her, seeing she didn't have a phone, but he said he wasn't the letter-writing type. Then she'd given him a quick kiss on the cheek, hoping he'd reciprocate with a kiss, too – maybe even one on the lips. But he hadn't. In fact, he'd dashed off right afterwards, then stopped and turned to wave at Janet and shouted, "It's been real nice knowing you!"

To Janet's disappointment, he'd gone home with Tweaky, Jake and Tim instead of riding with us, which had deprived her of some valuable backseat closeness time. And Scott's words had seemed much too final – a verbal form of a "Dear John" letter, in her opinion. So ever since then, she had been moping around, looking and acting as if she'd just been jilted at the altar.

"Can we go for a short walk?" Conrad asked me after Mom had fed us a lunch of ham-and-cheese sandwiches and chocolate-chip cookies with half a walnut pressed into the top of each. "I want to talk to you before you leave."

The last thing I wanted was to be alone with Conrad, but I knew I had to talk to him, too. I had tossed and turned most of the night, trying to think of the least painful way to tell him he wasn't going to see or hear from me again. I'd concluded there was no painless way to do it, so I was just going to have to blurt out whatever came to mind and let him deal with it. Still, I dreaded the thought of what his reaction was going to be.

Conrad and I walked in silence up Shepherdess Road until we came to a narrow trail on the left that I was surprised I hadn't noticed before, seeing it wasn't very far from Big Rock.

"Have you been here before?" he asked.

I shook my head. "I didn't even know it was here."

"Follow me. I want to show you something."

I wasn't certain what it was he wanted to show me, but I prayed it wasn't going to be something really stupid, like his teeny white weenie. If he ever tried to show me that, I swore I'd kick it so hard, he'd walk with a limp for the rest of his life.

The trail was so narrow, we had to walk in a single file, but after only a few yards, it opened up into a wide, weed-covered dirt road...that led to a half-built two-story house. I blinked, thinking I was seeing things.

As we moved closer to the house, I could tell it must have been years since anyone had been there. The wood was gray and weathered and three birds flew out of the house as we approached. There were no walls, just the wooden framework and a plywood roof and floor. A wooden plank, rather than front steps, led up to the first floor.

Not far from the house was a small shack that looked as if a strong wind would topple it. The wood was rotted all the way through in spots and a portion of the roof was missing. I walked over and tried the door. It was locked. I peered through a dirt-covered window that was about the size of a record album. I could see a cot covered with newspapers inside. I also could make out a shelf with some rusted cans of food and several half-burned candles in holders on it.

"What is this place?" I turned to ask Conrad.

"A guy named McCreedy started building this house as a surprise for his fiancée years ago," he said. "He was going to have it all finished by their wedding day and then bring her here and give it to her as a wedding gift. He did most of the work himself, and would stay here most weekends in the little shack."

"So what happened?" I asked. "He obviously never finished the house. Is it because he ran out of money?" I gasped as another thought struck me. "Did his fiancée break off their engagement?"

"Even worse...she died. McCreedy never came back here after that. I guess he must have kept paying the taxes on the land because otherwise the town would own it by now. I think my dad once told me McCreedy owns about 20 acres here."

I wasn't able to utter a word. I couldn't believe there was a two-story house, or the frame of one, so close to the camp and I hadn't even known it. The fact that the place was surrounded by broad, thick evergreen trees might have been the reason why. Even in the winter when most trees were bare and provided views of things that had been hidden in the summer, evergreens never shed. So the house was well concealed year round.

I felt sad for poor McCreedy and what he must have gone through, building the house for the woman he loved, thinking how surprised and delighted she would be when he revealed his surprise. And now, here sat all of his hard work, decaying and serving as a home only for the birds and bugs.

Conrad and I walked up the ramp and onto the first floor of the house. There were two overturned metal buckets near the center of the floor.

"Have a seat," he said, pointing to one of the buckets. He sat on the other one. "I come here sometimes when I want to be alone. It's my think spot. I don't know why, but I find it kind of peaceful, even though the history of the place is so sad."

I sat down and studied my surroundings. McCreedy seemed to have done a professional-looking job of framing the house, I thought, even though I knew nothing about construction. I tried to imagine how the house would have looked if he'd have finished it. I was pretty sure it would have been beautiful, like a mansion.

"There are a lot of wasps' nests in here," Conrad said, looking up at one of the corners. "I bet there are a lot of mice, raccoons, skunks and who knows what else living in the basement, too."

"There's a basement? I hadn't even noticed!"

"Yeah, it's concrete blocks with a dirt floor. But you can stand up in it."

"How come you never mentioned this place or brought me here before?" I asked him. "I mean, why did you wait until now?"

He shrugged. "As I said, it's my private place."

He slid his bucket closer to mine and sat facing me. "I brought you here because I wanted to talk to you alone before you leave."

I avoided his eyes. "Yes, we do have to talk."

"I can't stand the thought of not seeing you once school starts," he said. "While we were fishing this morning, your dad told me he'll be coming up here on weekends during pheasant-hunting season and deer-hunting season, and he said he'll bring you with him so we can see each other. But it's going to be torture in between those times."

I made a mental note to officially disown my father. The pained look on Conrad's face, however, gave me a glimmer of hope. Maybe, I thought, just maybe, he was going to tell me he couldn't bear the separation and had decided we should end our so-called relationship right then to prevent his inevitable, future pain.

"I just want you to know," Conrad said, "that no matter what – no matter how long we're apart or how many days or weeks we can't be together – I'll wait for you. In fact, I'll wait a whole lifetime for you because you're worth it. And when you're back in the city, I'll write to you every day, even twice a day, and call you at least twice a week. Just hearing your voice will make me happy. You are the best thing that's ever happened to me and I'd never do anything to ruin what we have."

I opened my mouth to respond, but nothing came out.

"And I just found out some good news last night!" he continued, smiling his gigantic smile. "My brother Eric is supposed to be moving to the city the beginning of next year so he can go to trade school. These two guys he knows have an apartment there and said he could move in with them. When he does move, I'll be able to stay with him whenever I want. You and I can be together every weekend then, and during school vacations! Won't that be great?"

My mind was reeling, trying to absorb everything he'd just said. I knew I had to tell Conrad that my feelings for him weren't on the same level – actually, not even in the same solar system – as his feelings for me, and they never would be. And above all, I had to stop him from coming to the city. It was bad enough he hung around the camp all of the time, uninvited. But having him hanging around in the city, too, would mean I'd never have a weekend without him. There was no way I could allow that to happen. And if, heaven forbid, he showed up wearing that get-up he'd worn to the drive-in, especially his dad's shoes, my friends never would let me live it down. I'd probably be forced to move to another state.

"To be honest, Conrad," I said, looking down at my lap. "I think we're way too young to be talking about stuff like love and seeing each other all the time. For one thing, my parents would never allow it."

He vigorously shook his head. "They like me. And they know I'd never do anything to hurt you. They trust me, I know they do."

"Even if they do, that still doesn't mean they want me to spend all my time with you. They'll keep reminding me that I still have high school and college ahead of me!"

When he remained silent, I allowed myself to look up at him. His eyes locked with mine.

"All that really matters to me," he said, "is the answer to this question...what do *you* want?"

What did *I* want? The answer was simple. I wanted to be rid of him once and for all and return to the city and never think about him again. I wanted him to disappear from the face of the earth or, at the very least, move to Siberia.

But I said nothing. I didn't understand why, but I just couldn't bring myself to say something mean to him, at least not to his face. It would be easier, I decided, to write him a letter when I got back home. That way, I'd be able to carefully compose my words and get them exactly right. And that way, I wouldn't have to look at him when I broke his heart and turned him into a woman hater for the rest of his life.

I stood up. "I think we should be getting back to the camp now. It's rude to leave Janet, especially since she's kind of depressed that she can't see Scott today before we head back."

Conrad rose to his feet, grasped my arm and pulled me toward him. "Can I have a goodbye kiss?" His voice came out sounding like a croak. "Please? It would make me the happiest guy on earth."

I clamped my eyes shut and prayed for a sudden earthquake or hurricane. I silently cursed myself for allowing myself to get into such an awkward situation – all alone in the woods with kiss-craving Conrad. What had I been thinking?

Before I could answer him, I saw his lips swooping in for the attack. At the last second, I turned my head and the kiss landed on my cheek. I felt nothing but teeth against my skin.

Conrad pulled away from me. His expression clearly was one of disappointment.

I didn't wait for him to comment. I yanked my arm from his grasp, bolted down the ramp and headed back down the overgrown road.

"Well, come on!" I called over my shoulder. "Unless you want to stay in there with the birds all afternoon!"

A vision of him sitting on the bucket with a big pile of bird poop on his head made me giggle.

* * * * *

The ride back to the city that night was a quiet one. My dad was suffering from a headache, which he said had been caused by being out in the sun too long, fishing. But he said it had been worth it, seeing he'd snagged four fat brook-trout. I didn't have to guess what our first meal back in the city was going to be.

Janet sat sulking in the corner of the back seat because she was silently mourning the loss of Scott. She said she knew she'd never see or hear from him again, and that ending what had been a magical summer romance was tearing her apart.

Mom wasn't her usual chatty self, either, because she said she was tired. She blamed it on the sleepless night she'd been forced to suffer thanks to the lumpy mattress on the bottom bunk. It was the same lumpy mattress she'd slept pretty soundly on just a week before, but for some reason, last night she thought it felt as if it had been stuffed with corncobs. She sat with her head leaning against the car door and her eyes closed.

I was the only one who seemed to be happy, even though my efforts to break things off with Conrad before I left had been unsuccessful. Already, I mentally was composing the words I would put to paper the next morning – my Dear John letter to him that would end things once and for all. I knew the letter would take a couple days to arrive in his clammy little hands, so I'd probably have to endure a phone call or two from him beforehand. But then the nightmare would be over and I'd be free of him forever. I couldn't wait for that moment.

The minute we set foot in the apartment, the phone rang. Before I even picked up the receiver, I knew who was calling.

"Hi, sweetie," Conrad's voice greeted me. "I'm sitting here missing you already. I sure wish we were back at the dance, where I could be holding you in my arms again."

"Hello, Conrad," I said, with no expression whatsoever. "The ride home made me really tired. Can't wait to take a hot bath and crawl into my nice comfy bed."

"I wish I could be a fly on the wall in when you take your bath!" he said.

His words made my skin feel as if it had bugs crawling all over it. I shuddered. To heck with waiting until morning to compose the Dear John letter, I thought. I was going to write it as soon as I hung up the phone.

When I didn't respond to his bath comment, Conrad was silent for a few seconds, then said, "Well, I guess you want to get settled in, so I'll let you go. I just wanted to hear your voice and tell you I miss you like crazy already and can't stop thinking about you. I'll call again tomorrow night. And in the meantime, I'll be writing to you!"

The thought of receiving another letter with hearts and kisses drawn all over the envelope made me wish even more that I'd been able to end things before I'd left. I made a mental note not to be anywhere near our mailbox when the mailman arrived. The last time had been humiliating enough.

"Well, take care," I said. "I have to help my parents unload stuff from the car."

"Bye, honey," he said. "I love you."

I hung up the phone. Only a few more days, I thought, and I'd never have to talk to him again. It was going to seem like a century until then.

* * * * *

By eleven o'clock that night, I was dozing off on my desk. I'd rewritten the Dear John letter to Conrad five times, but finally, on attempt number six, I'd achieved what I felt was perfection...a letter that was short and to the point, and said everything I wanted it to say:

Dear Conrad,

I want to thank you for showing me such a nice time during my stay at the camp. I enjoyed meeting you and your friends and going to all of the fun places I wouldn't have gone to otherwise. So this is very hard for me to write, but I know I have to. I don't want to hurt your feelings, but I do want to be completely honest with you because I don't want to lead you on or give you the wrong impression. I know you think of me as your girlfriend, and you have all these plans for us to be together in the future, but the truth is, I just don't think of you in a romantic way at all. And I definitely don't think of you as my boyfriend, and I never will. Therefore, I don't think it would be fair to be in any kind of a relationship with you. I was going to say we could still be friends, but I don't think you could handle being "just friends" with me. So I've decided it would be best for both of us if we don't have any contact of any kind any more. You are a nice guy, and I'm sure you'll make a great boyfriend for some girl someday, but that girl isn't me. I don't have feelings for you the way I know you would like me to, and I'm sorry about that. I wish you all the best of luck in your future...

Sincerely,
Sally"

I carefully folded the sheet of notebook paper and stuffed it into an envelope. Then I dug Conrad's previous love letter out my desk drawer and copied his return address onto the envelope. The first thing in the morning, I'd ask my mom for a stamp and then I'd run to the corner mailbox and mail the letter.

I smiled at the envelope in my hand. I had the feeling I was going to sleep very peacefully that night.

CHAPTER SEVENTEEN

"My goodness! How long have you been hiding *those*?"

My mother's voice startled me when she, carrying a stack of folded laundry, came into my bedroom the next morning just as I was removing my pajama top. I was up and getting dressed much earlier than I normally would, especially considering I was back home in my own cozy bed, but I wanted to mail my letter to Conrad as soon as humanly possible. I was a bit apprehensive, however – not about sending the letter, but about trusting the mailman not to lose it after he removed it from the mailbox. After all, once it left the mailbox, it would be in his mail sack for maybe hours. Then when he was finished walking his route, he'd hop a bus back to the main post office downtown. A lot could happen between the mailbox and the post office.

"How long have I been hiding what?" I asked.

"Those breasts!" my mother said, her eyes wide. "Have you been stuffing them into your training bra all summer?"

Now that she mentioned it, I actually had noticed that the training bra seemed to be getting more and more difficult to squeeze into, but I thought it was because I was gaining some ice-cream-induced summer weight. My training bra was kind of like a wide elastic band, so it had a lot of stretching power. It covered my chest but didn't do much else, like make me have two big points in front like Sophia Loren's.

"I guess it's kind of tight," I said, shrugging. "It makes me feel a little sore, too."

"Well, no wonder! How long were you going to keep wearing a bra that's obviously too small for you? Until it ripped open and your breasts exploded out of it? Here you are, always complaining about how flat you are, when the only thing flat is that bra! It must be like wearing a tourniquet!"

I opened my mouth to comment, but she interrupted. "We are taking the next bus downtown to buy you your first real bra, young lady!"

I didn't know whether to celebrate or run and hide. Mom's favorite store for shopping for ladies' unmentionables was LaRue's Corset Shop, a place where I had accompanied her on more than one occasion during our shopping excursions. At LaRue's, the female employees were famous for knowing everything there was to know about underwear and where to get it. If a customer wanted purple silk panties with pink bows down the front, they would find them for her even if they had to breed their own silkworms to spin the silk.

But what I didn't like about LaRue's was I'd also seen the employees fling open the dressing-room curtains while women were trying on bras, just to ask them how they were doing. I'd even seen employees escorting women into the dressing rooms so they could measure them for bras and girdles.

"I don't want some strange woman measuring my chest!" I said.

"Well, how do you expect to get a proper fit otherwise? They are experts! Are you a bra expert? Do you know what cup size you take? Is it AAA? AA? A? B?"

All of those letters confused me. The only A's and B's I knew about were on report cards. Stuff to wear usually came in numbered sizes, not lettered. It would be easier, I decided, just to keep wearing the training bra. After all, I figured it had to have some major purpose and was training my breasts for something. So common sense told me that the longer I let it keep training, the better off my breasts would be.

"What's a training bra training my breasts to do anyway?" I asked as I pulled it on over my head.

Mom looked up at the ceiling and sighed. "Finish getting dressed. We can make the nine o'clock bus downtown."

The bus stop was on the same corner as the mailbox, which was only two houses up from ours. I'd tucked my letter to Conrad into my pocketbook so I could pop it into the mailbox the minute Mom and I set foot on the curb. Soon, I thought, with a shiver of anticipation, the letter would be on its merry way to the wilds of Arrowwood.

But when Mom and I reached the corner, a bolt of realization struck me. Fate, I concluded, was sending us downtown that morning – fate in the form of a bus that would deliver me to within just one block of the city's main post office. I could mail the letter there – inside the safe confines of the building's sturdy brick walls. I prayed that in the meantime, a mugger wouldn't sneak up behind me and snatch my pocketbook. I found myself regretting that I hadn't made a carbon copy of the letter, or at the very least, written it twice so I could have a duplicate for myself. After all, if I lost it, what were the odds I'd ever be able to reproduce its perfection again?

The first thing I noticed when we entered LaRue's was there was only one other customer in there. It wasn't a very large store in area, but it was crammed with every type of lingerie imaginable – and even some I never could have imagined.

"May I help you?" a thin, gray-haired saleslady immediately greeted us.

"Yes," my mother said. "I'd like my daughter to be fitted for her first bra."

The only customer in the store looked at me and smiled. I wanted to turn and run back out the door. This shopping experience, I was certain, was going to be one of my most, if not my most, humiliating ever.

"Well, then," the saleslady said, smiling. When she did, I noticed she had a smear of red lipstick on her front teeth. "Why don't you follow me into the dressing room and we'll see what size you take. Then you can pick out a bra you like in that size."

As I followed her into the dressing room, I felt the same sense of dread I usually felt whenever Mom made me go for a physical exam and I knew the doctor was going to ask me to take off my clothes.

The dressing room was small and very pink, which matched the light pink and dark pink stripes of the store's wallpaper and sign. I wasn't surprised when the curtain in the dressing room also was striped.

The three of us squeezed into the room. Had I been in there all alone, I still would have been squished, so I was surprised that Mom, who often complained about her claustrophobia, wasn't gasping for air.

"Okay, take off your top and we'll see what we have here," the saleslady said. Her tone was so casual, she sounded like someone ordering takeout food.

I unbuttoned my sleeveless, flowered blouse and removed it.

"That training bra is much too small for you," the saleslady said. "You should have been here shopping for a bra long before this! Now, let's remove it so I can measure you. She reached into a pocket in her polka-dotted skirt and pulled out a yellow tape measure.

I didn't move. She and my mother were just standing there staring at me, as if awaiting the unveiling of a nude sculpture in an art gallery. I didn't want to take off my training bra. After all, I wasn't a young kid any more. I was too old to be standing around half-naked in front of anyone, especially a complete stranger.

"Hurry up, Sally," my mother said. "This woman hasn't got all day."

I folded my arms in front of my chest and shook my head.

"Don't be embarrassed," the saleslady said. "I have seen thousands of breasts during my years working here. To me, looking at them is no different than looking at cantaloupes in the grocery store!"

I wondered whose breasts were big enough to look like cantaloupes and if mine would ever get that big. Frowning, I yanked off the training bra and tossed it onto the floor.

In a flash, the cold tape-measure was wrapped around me – first, underneath my breasts, and then across the front of them.

"I'd say she's in a 34B," the lady said.

"Are you certain?" my mother sounded surprised. "She's already skipped all of the A's?"

"I'm afraid so," she said. She turned to me. "Do you want to get dressed and come pick out a bra, or would you like me to bring in a few of our most popular styles and let you try those on?"

I didn't feel like getting dressed and undressed again. I also didn't care what the dumb bra looked like, just so long as it supported my budding cantaloupes and didn't flatten me like the training bra did.

199

"You and my mom can pick out one for me," I said. "I'm not fussy."

They disappeared back into the store, while I crouched in the corner of the dressing room, my arms covering my breasts. I didn't want the saleslady to return, fling open the curtain and reveal my bare breasts to any customers who might have entered the store. After all, I wasn't a striptease act.

"We have three lovely bras, I'm sure you'll like," the saleslady said when she and my mom returned. She held up a plain, white cotton one with a small satin bow on the front. Before she handed it to me, she adjusted two sliding metal things on the straps. "Try this one on first."

I took the bra, slipped my arms through the straps and then reached behind my back to hook it.

"No, no!" the saleslady scolded me. "You have to bend over and allow your breasts to fall into the cups before you hook it! Otherwise, the bra will slide up to your chin!"

I just stared at her, not believing what she was saying. Did she really want me to flop my breasts into the bra?

"Go on, do what she says," my mother said.

I leaned over, allowed my breasts to fall into the bra and then I fumbled with the two hooks on the back of it. No sooner had I hooked the last hook did the saleslady practically leap at me and attack. She tugged on the bra, pulled the straps and poked at my breasts.

"Looks like a good fit," she said. "Turn sideways and look at yourself in the mirror."

I did as she said and nearly gasped. Suddenly, I had breasts! They were pointy and high up on my chest. I looked like a woman!

"I like it!" I said, smiling.

My mother studied me for a moment. "I think the other bra, the silkier one looks more comfortable. Try that one on, too."

The second bra was more lightweight and had a lace trim across the top. I "flopped" into it and hooked it. It felt more comfortable, but didn't give me the stick-out points like the first one did.

"I like the other one," I said. "Can we buy that one, Mom?"

She didn't respond immediately. Finally she sighed and said, "Okay, I guess we'll take that one." She turned toward the saleslady. "Is it okay if she wears it home?"

The saleslady nodded. "Come with me to the cash register while she gets dressed."

After they left, I put on the first bra and then my blouse. I had trouble buttoning the button between my breasts because the two sides of the blouse barely met in front, now that I wasn't flattened out any more. When I finally did get it buttoned, I was worried that if I stepped out of the dressing room and exhaled, the button would go flying off and pop someone in the eye.

Once I was dressed, I spent a few minutes posing in the mirror and admiring my new bustline. The whole ordeal may have been embarrassing, but I was pleased with the results. I was positive that if I'd had this bra in time for the Old Home Day dance, Tim Argent would have been chasing after me all night.

"Too bad, Tim," I said out loud as I took one last look at myself in the mirror. "You missed out!"

When Mom and I emerged from LaRue's and headed down Main Street, I was surprised to discover I was walking much straighter, with my shoulders back. I figured it was because I unconsciously wanted to show off my newly discovered assets to their full advantage.

"Want to go grab something to eat at Woolworth's lunch counter?" Mom asked me.

She didn't have to ask twice. Woolworth's, with its frosted donuts, grilled-cheese sandwiches and greasy burgers, was one of my favorite places to stuff myself. In the past, Mom and I always had gone to Newberry's lunch counter, which was directly across the street from Woolworth's...but that was before "the incident" about six months ago. Mom and I had just been served two big pieces of chocolate-cream pie, heaped high with whipped cream. I'd shoveled about three forkfuls of the pie into my mouth, when I noticed that my mother wasn't eating hers. She was sitting motionless, staring at a portion of the counter just beyond where I was sitting. Her expression sort of looked as if she'd just smelled some week-old fish.

"What's wrong?" I asked her.

She said nothing, just pointed. My eyes followed her finger and I spotted, walking across the counter, a big cockroach...covered with whipped cream.

We never ate at Newberry's lunch counter again.

"Before we go to Woolworth's," I said, "can we go to the post office? I have to mail a letter to Conrad."

Mom's eyebrows rose. "Oh? You wrote to him already? Do you miss him that much?"

"It's a Dear John letter," I said. "I don't miss him at all."

She stopped walking. "Are you really sure you want nothing to do with him ever again? The camp might be pretty boring for you without Conrad and his friends around. And remember, once you write down something and he receives it, it will be there for him to read over and over again forever. You can't change it."

"I'm sure. Even if there were no other people in the whole world, I still wouldn't want to be with him. He gives me the creeps."

Mom shook her head and started walking again. We changed direction and headed toward the post office. "I don't understand what it is about Conrad that you dislike so much. He seems like a perfectly nice young man to me."

"I can't explain it," I said. "There's just something about him – something I can't put my finger on – that makes me not like him."

"You weren't cruel to him in your letter, were you? I mean, I hope you let the poor boy down easy."

"I wrote it a bunch of times until I got it just right," I said. "It's not cruel at all, just very honest. If he can't take the truth, then it's not my fault. Heaven knows I've been trying to tell him all along that I don't want to be his girlfriend. He just refuses to listen."

I hand delivered the letter to the clerk at the window in the post office and then breathed a sigh of relief. I figured in two more days, at the most, I'd be rid of Conrad. I knew there probably would be whining phone calls or desperate letters from him for a while, begging me to reconsider, but soon he'd have no choice but to give up.

The post office was located in a sprawling building that housed other offices. In a corner of the spacious, marble-floored lobby was a booth where people could buy candy, newspapers, magazines and bottles of soft drinks. I headed over to the booth to see if any new movie magazines were out yet, where I might find a pin-up of Troy Donahue.

I was flipping through the pages of a magazine when I heard someone behind me say, "Is that you, Sally?"

I turned to face Ronnie and Mike, two guys who were in my class at school.

"Hi, guys," I greeted them, smiling.

Four eyes immediately settled on my chest. Ronnie turned to look at Mike and then back at my chest again. Suddenly, he began to violently cough.

"Are you okay?" I asked, concerned he might be choking.

He patted his chest and cleared his throat. "I'm fine," he said with a wheeze so dramatic, a few people turned to look at him. "It's just that I'm allergic to foam rubber!"

He and Mike then burst out laughing.

It took me a few seconds to understand the meaning of his words. He thought I was wearing *falsies*! I could feel my cheeks turning tomato red.

"Well, if you're allergic to foam rubber, then Mike must be wearing it, because there's none on me!" I turned and walked off.

The minute I emerged from the building, my mother, who was waiting for me at the bottom of the steps, took one look at my face and asked me what was wrong.

"Two guys from my class were in there and they made jokes about foam rubber!" I snapped. "They think I'm wearing falsies! If this is what I'm going to have to deal with when I go back to school, then I'm taking this bra back to LaRue's right now!"

Mom looked as if she might laugh. "Honey, you'll get teased a lot more if you bounce around school braless. Do you want to look like Tweaky? And there is no way you're going to squeeze back into a training bra. So I guess you're just going to have to get used to the comments."

"Boys are all creeps!" I said as we headed back toward Woolworth's. I thought about Conrad and his clinginess and Tim and his conceit, and now Ronnie and Mike with their nasty jokes. "I wouldn't give a penny for any one of them! And I'll tell you another thing – I'm *never* going to get married!"

* * * * *

Just as he'd promised, Conrad called that night.

"Hey, beautiful! It's so good to hear your voice!" he said, his tone cheerful. "So, what did you do all day?"

I knew I wasn't ever going to have to face him again, so I decided to be honest. "Mom and I went shopping for a bra for me. I got a 34B!"

Conrad didn't respond. I could just picture his expression as he sat there, imagining me in my new bra. I had to hold my breath so I wouldn't giggle in his ear.

"Um...gee, I bet it looks great on you," he finally said.

"Yeah, I look like Sophia Loren!"

"Well, I can't wait to see you again – not because of your new bra, but because I miss you so much! When do you think you'll be coming back? This weekend?"

"I don't know," I said. "But I don't think it will be this weekend."

"That's too bad." His voice sounded heavy with disappointment. "I sent you two letters today, by the way."

"I sent you one, too."

"Wow, really? Already? I can't wait to get it!"

He sounded so genuinely excited, a small pang of guilt struck me. But it vanished just as quickly as it struck. The letter I'd written to him had been a necessity, I reasoned. Conrad was the type who never would take a hint, so I had no choice but to be blunt and put everything in writing. I just hoped he wouldn't twist my words around in his fantasy-fueled little mind and read something into them that wasn't there.

"So what did you do all day?" I asked. "Did you see Scott?"

"No, I didn't see anyone. I spent all day missing you and writing to you. I didn't leave the house, except to put the letters out in our mailbox for the mailman to pick up. He came about three o'clock."

"I didn't see Janet today, either. Maybe she's still too depressed over having to leave Scott."

"Are you depressed you had to leave me?"

His question made me wish I'd hired someone to drive straight to his house and deliver my letter in person that morning. "I don't get depressed very often," I said. "I try to stay happy."

"Well, my dad is going to yell at me if I run up the phone bill any higher," Conrad said with a sigh. "So as much as I hate to, I'm going to hang up now. I miss you and love you. And I promise I'll write to you every day. I'll call you again either Thursday night or Friday."

I was pretty sure he'd be calling me before then, once he received my letter. "Okay, I'll talk to you then."

No sooner did I hang up was there a knock at the door. I opened it to see a broadly smiling Janet.

"You're not going to believe what happened today!" She walked right past me and into my bedroom.

I followed her into the room and closed the door.

"Wow!" she said, staring at my bustline. She sat on the edge of my bed and continued to stare. "Where'd you get those? Did you grow them overnight?"

"Mom took me to LaRue's today. Turns out my training bra was badly squishing some size B-cups."

"B? Really?" She seemed impressed. "Can I have your training bras, then?"

I shrugged. "Sure. I won't be needing them...unless I want to make a slingshot or something. I saw Ronnie Porter and Mike O'Brien downtown after I got the bra today and they started coughing, saying they were allergic to foam rubber!"

"They said that to Suzanne Tanner, too...so she showed them that hers were real – out behind the baseball field!"

"Well, if they think I'm going to prove anything to them, they're gonna have a really long wait!" I took a seat next to Janet on the bed. The bed was double-sized, a hand-me-down from my parents. The walls of my room were painted light blue, and then Mom, during one of her creative moods, had decided to try something she'd read about in one of her women's magazines. She'd dipped a sponge into some maroon-colored paint and pressed the sponge all over the blue walls in an overlapping pattern, giving them a kind of spider-web effect. All of her hard work had been in vain, however, because as soon as the paint had dried, I'd covered the walls with fold-out posters from my teen magazines. There was Bobby Rydell and the Everly Brothers, and about a dozen of Ricky Nelson. I vowed that as soon as I found some of Troy Donahue, I'd be hanging up those, too. Maroon curtains with dark blue flowers on them completed the decor in the room. I wasn't particularly fond of maroon and blue. In fact, orange was my favorite color. But when I'd asked my mom to paint my room orange, she couldn't have been more appalled if I'd asked her to paint it with real blood.

"So, what is it you did today that you're so excited about?" I asked Janet.

She clasped her hands over her heart. "I spent the whole day with Rusty!"

"Rusty, from the apartment building next to yours? Rusty, the guy who kissed you on the cheek last year?"

"Yep! He is so cool! And he likes me! We rode our bikes all over town and stopped at this golf course at the country club by the river to pick up golf balls out of the pond there. He turns them in at the clubhouse for cash and makes good money. After that, he bought a Popsicle and gave me half!"

There I'd thought she'd been hibernating in her room all day, crying over the loss of Scott, when she'd actually been gallivanting all over town with Rusty. "So I guess you've forgotten about Scott?"

She shrugged. "Well, I like Scott and all, but he doesn't want to write to me and he can't call unless we get a phone. And you're not going to be going back to the camp too often now, so why not have a guy who's only a shout away? Oh, and guess what? Rusty has a friend named Jerry who lives right next to the golf course. I met him today and he is soooooo cute!"

She paused to smile at me before adding, "Now here's the exciting part! Rusty and Jerry want to know if we want to go to the golf course with them tomorrow morning to look for more golf balls!"

Her statement caught me completely off guard. "Jerry wants me to go? You told him about me?"

Janet nodded. "He seemed really interested, too!"

My mind reeled. A blind date, picking up golf balls? I pictured my broad posterior up in the air all day as I bent over picking up balls in front of this Jerry guy. Not exactly a pretty sight or my best side, I thought. Heck, he wouldn't even be able to see my newly discovered assets – not if they were pressed against my knees all day. I had no idea what to say.

"Jerry has long, dark-blond hair, he's kind of thin, and he has all of his teeth!" Janet said. "He's really into sports, too. He plays golf, baseball and is on a bowling league."

I'd always thought Rusty was a pretty cool-looking guy, with his crew cut, broad shoulders and high cheekbones. So I figured the odds were his friend Jerry might not be so bad, either.

"Okay, I'll go," I said. "Sounds like it might be fun. By the way, I sent Conrad a Dear John letter today."

Janet's eyes widened and she let out a long whistle. "Good luck with that. Knowing him, he'll probably hitchhike over here to throw himself at your feet and beg you not to leave him!"

I'd never considered the fact Conrad might actually show up on my doorstep. He had my address, so what would stop him from rushing to the city in an act of desperation?

"Maybe I can talk my parents into buying me an attack dog," I said.

CHAPTER EIGHTEEN

I was glad I'd done so much walking at the camp, otherwise, I never would have been able to make the trek to the golf course the next morning. For one thing, it was about a hundred million degrees outside, and another, the golf course was at least three miles from my house...all uphill.

Trying to carry on a conversation with Jerry wasn't easy when I was huffing and puffing like a locomotive, so I considered myself fortunate he was the quiet type. Janet had been right about his looks. He was a nice-looking guy – not quite as nice as Tim Argent or Troy Donahue – but still cute. He was wearing something I never would have imagined a guy would wear, yet on him, it looked good. It was a pale pink, long-sleeved dress-shirt. He had the top two buttons unbuttoned and the sleeves rolled up to his elbows. He wore the shirt tucked into jeans that were worn out on the knees, but looked freshly washed. A black leather belt with the buckle resting on his hip completed the look. He'd smiled at me when we were introduced, and I was pleased to see straight white teeth, all of which were the appropriate size for his face.

Rusty and Janet walked ahead of us, and I could hear Janet chattering away, but I couldn't understand what she was saying.

I eyed the hill ahead of us and was concerned I'd end up passing out before we reached the top. It was one of the steepest hills in the city, maybe even in the entire state. At that moment, it looked even bigger to me than Mount Everest. Not exactly a great hill to try to tackle on a first date when I wanted to look feminine and fresh.

When we finally made it to the top of the hill, I felt like kneeling down and kissing the pavement. My heart was hammering in my chest and I could feel rivers of perspiration running down my back.

After a few minutes of walking on a level, non-hilly surface, I was able to breathe without sounding like the Orient Express. I figured while I had the opportunity, before we came to another hill, I'd try to initiate a conversation with Jerry.

I turned to my left and looked at him. "So, you live down by the river?"

"Yeah," he said, "right next to the country club."

"That's a different school district. You must go to Wright School, then?"

He shook his head. "Not any more. I'm starting high school this year."

"I'm going into the eighth at Elm Park," I said. "I think I'm going to miss the school when I leave it, though. After all, I've been there most of my life."

"I think high school is going to be cool," he said. "I'm going to take shop so I can learn to fix cars. I want to own my own repair shop someday. There's real good money in it."

We came to a wooded area on the outskirts of the city. To the right of the woods was a street that led down to the river and the country club. Janet and Rusty, however, headed into the woods.

Jerry must have noticed the puzzled expression on my face.

"There's a path through there," he said. "A shortcut. And it's a lot cooler than walking out in the heat."

The woods were pretty sparse compared to the woods at the camp, especially the woods that led to Little Paradise. I recalled how dark they'd been when Janet and I had explored them, making mid-afternoon look like midnight. But at least these woods provided some shade. I didn't want Jerry to see me with armpit sweat stains like Conrad's, all the way down to my waist. What concerned me was the wide-open space of the golf course. I knew I'd be out in the blazing sun while searching for golf balls and probably would sweat so much, I'd look as if I'd been dunked in a vat of grease. If worse came to worse, I supposed I always could accidentally trip and fall into the pond. That way, I'd not only cool off, my sweaty clothes would be so wet, the armpit stains would blend right in.

As we followed the path through the woods, Jerry, who was walking behind me, tapped me on the shoulder. I turned around and he handed me a wildflower – a dainty white blossom on a thin stem. When I took it from him, he cocked his head and smiled at me.

At that very moment, I fell in love.

* * * * *

Two letters from Conrad arrived later that afternoon. The envelopes, originally plain white, were decorated with so many hearts, hugs and kisses in red ink, the white barely showed through. I'd had so much fun with Jerry that day – laughing, splashing each other with pond water, eating ice cream – just the thought of reading a bunch of mushy stuff from Conrad made me want to toss the letters, unopened, into the trash. But curiosity got the better of me. I poured myself a glass of strawberry Kool-Aid, stretched out on my side on my bed and tore open the envelopes.

Just as I'd anticipated, they contained Conrad's endless rambling about how much he missed me, how wonderful our time together had been, and how he couldn't wait to see me again. He said he was going to spend a lot of time at his private spot at McCreedy's house site so he could be all alone with his thoughts about me and our future. Also, he said, McCreedy's was just a stone's throw from the camp, which he intended to walk by as often as possible because it reminded him of the best summer of his life.

He said he wasn't in the mood to hang around with his friends because he didn't feel like doing anything without me there. Then he wrote about how great it was going to be when his brother moved to the city so he could stay with him and be with me every weekend. He said he wanted to take me on real dates, like to the movies or bowling. Then he asked me to do him a big favor and write him a romantic letter – one where I said I loved him and missed him, and wanted to be with only him – so he could read it over and over again and feel closer to me.

"What planet are you from anyway?" I said out loud to the letter, as if Conrad somehow could hear me through it. "Tell you that I love you? Tell you that you're the only guy for me? Did you get into your dad's booze or something?"

The letters were signed with his usual fancy signature and his now-famous swirl with the two lines through it and two circles dotting it.

I rolled onto my back and felt the coolness of the pillowcase against my sunburned neck. The letters fell from my hand and onto the bedspread. I wondered if Conrad was reading my Dear John letter at that very moment, and how he was feeling. Would he be angry? Hurt? In tears? Would he rush to the phone to call me? All I knew was I wanted whatever was going to happen to hurry up and happen so it would be over and done with. Only when Conrad was completely out of my life would I be able to give Jerry my full attention. In fact, earlier, at the golf course, when I was telling Jerry about the camp, he'd seemed really interested and said he'd love to go there sometime because he enjoyed fishing and catching frogs. I thought it would be fun to bring Janet, Rusty and Jerry to the camp for a barbecue some Saturday or Sunday before school started. But Conrad had to be completely out of the picture by then. I could just imagine him walking up to Jerry and me at the picnic table and saying something like, "Hi, sweetheart! How's my girlfriend today? Who's this guy?" or even worse, having him shout, "Who is *he*? How could you do this to me after all the good times we've had together? I thought you *loved* me!"

Yes, Conrad definitely had to be out – way, way out – of my life before I ever took Jerry to the camp.

* * * * *

Another love letter arrived from Conrad on Wednesday. I figured he must have put it out in his mailbox for the mailman to pick up just as my Dear John letter was being delivered to him, so our letters crossed.

No other letters arrived from him after that one, nor did he call me, which I thought was odd. By Saturday, I was losing sleep, wondering what had happened after he'd read my letter.

"Maybe he tied a big rock onto his ankle and jumped into Bone Swamp!" Janet said. "Or maybe he sacrificed himself to the water moccasin at the Rod and Gun Club, or sat naked in the river and let the leeches suck out all of his blood!"

"Don't be dumb," I said. "He wouldn't kill himself over me. I mean, maybe I could see it if I'd passionately kissed him or told him I loved him and wanted to marry him or something, then my letter would have been super painful, but the way I treated him all the time, I'm certainly not worth jumping into Bone Swamp over!"

"Then explain why you haven't heard a word from him!" Janet said. "You know that's not like him at all!"

"I don't know. Maybe he's trying to calm down and think straight before he puts anything into writing. Or maybe it's taking him a while to mentally organize what he wants to say before he calls me. I mean, it took me ages to word my letter to him just right."

"Or maybe he's lying pale and anemic, covered with leeches, along the Abenaki River somewhere!"

I scowled at her. "Do you have to be so dramatic?"

"Or..." she added, "maybe he rushed right out and found another girlfriend to mend his broken heart, and he's spending all of his time with her!"

The odds of Conrad finding a new girlfriend that fast in the wilds of Arrowwood were pretty slim, I thought. But the images Janet had put into my head of him lying lifeless near the river somewhere disturbed me. Was it possible, I wondered, that he actually could have done something drastic after reading my letter? And would I ever be able to live with myself if he had?

* * * * *

"I'm thinking of going up to the camp tomorrow to do a little fishing," my dad said over supper that night. "According to the weather report, it's supposed to be overcast and cooler – perfect fishing weather."

"Then I think I'm going to spend the day visiting my mother," Mom said. "I promised to give her a perm sometime this month, so if you're going to be fishing, tomorrow will probably be a good day to do it. You can drop me and Sally off there on your way to the camp and pick us up on your way back."

"Can I go with you to the camp?" I asked my father.

Both he and mother turned to stare at me.

212

"You'd rather go to the camp than to your grandmother's?" my mother asked. "Are you sure you didn't get too much sun at the golf course the other day?"

I loved visiting my grandmother, who enjoyed spoiling me…and feeding me. She associated plumpness with being strong and healthy, so she liked to make certain I was well fed at all times. Not only did I enjoy spending the day at her house, I also always looked forward to visiting my aunts, uncles and cousins who lived right across the road from her.

I shook my head. "Believe me, I'd much rather go with you, Mom, but I sent that Dear John letter to Conrad on Monday and I haven't heard a thing from him. I'm a little worried. I just want to make sure he's okay. I thought maybe if I went to the camp, he might walk by or I might spot him during the ride up our road. I *really* need to know if he's okay. Janet thinks he might have tied a rock to his leg and jumped into the swamp or the river after he read my letter."

"That's a terrible thing to put into your head!" Mom said after she'd swallowed a mouthful of macaroni and cheese.

"I'm sure he's fine," Dad said. "You probably hurt his pride, that's all. Maybe he's just not ready to face you or talk to you yet. But if you're that worried about him, why don't you just call him?"

My mother gasped. "Proper young ladies *never* call boys! That's strictly taboo!"

"Even if they're worried they're dead?" my dad asked.

"I wouldn't call his house, no matter what," I said. "One of his brothers probably would answer and give me a hard time. Conrad says they're all jerks and like to pull pranks on him. I'd just feel better if I could see him walking around or something."

"Well, if it will make you feel better and ease your mind," Dad said, "you can come with me tomorrow."

"Thanks." I wasn't certain if I should feel relieved or frightened. Dad didn't know it, but I was going to make him drive by every place where Conrad might be – his house, the swimming hole, Tweaky's, Scott's. All I needed was a quick glimpse of him to assure me he still was among the living, and then I'd be able to sleep at night.

* * * * *

213

Dad and I headed to the camp at eight o'clock on Sunday morning, after we dropped off Mom at my grandmother's. I'd asked Janet if she wanted to go for the ride, thinking she still might jump at the chance to possibly see her beloved Scott again, but she said she and Rusty were going to take a bike riding trip to his uncle's pig farm in Pennford.

"You'd rather go to a smelly pig farm than see Scott again?" I asked her.

"I like Rusty," she answered. "And he lives next door. It makes things a lot easier."

It might make things easier for her at that moment, I thought, but if Rusty ever turned out to be a real creep or a leech like Conrad and she wanted to get rid of him, he'd be right there all of the time, able to watch her every move. I was thankful Conrad lived about forty-five minutes away – but even that seemed too close at times. On the other hand, if he lived next door, at least I'd know whether he was still alive or not.

"You're going to ride all the way to Pennford on your little brother's bike?" Janet didn't have a bike of her own, so she always borrowed her brother's, which was so small for her, her knees practically hit her chin when she pedaled it.

"His bike is just fine," she said. "I get around okay on it."

* * * * *

The ride to the camp seemed to be taking forever, I thought, as I stared at the tree-lined road ahead.

"Dad?" I turned to look at him. "What if we get to the camp and we find Conrad lying on the riverbank like Janet said? We'll have to drive all the way to the police station because we don't have a phone!"

My father's eyes didn't leave the road. "Honey, stop worrying. Conrad is just fine – I'm positive he is. There won't be any need to go to a police station."

I knew my dad probably was right, but I couldn't shake my gut feeling that something bad had happened, otherwise Conrad surely would have called or written to me.

When we reached the main road through Arrowwood, my eyes darted from one side of the road to the other, just in case Conrad might be out walking.

214

"Can we take the back way?" I asked. "That way we'll pass by Scott's and Tweaky's and then be on Conrad's Road."

Dad didn't answer, but when we came to Wyatt Road, he took a right instead of going straight, which was the shorter route to the camp. I felt a lump form in my throat when we passed by Tim Argent's house because it made me think about all of the time I'd wasted having a crush on him, thinking he was the perfect guy. His looks may have been perfect, but as far as I was concerned, his personality had turned out to be pretty ugly.

The thought suddenly struck me that I really wasn't much better than Tim. I'd had a crush on him, just like Conrad had a crush on me. And now, all I felt was dumb for having liked Tim so much. I was willing to bet that Conrad, since reading my letter, probably was feeling dumb, too. I also recalled how hurt I'd felt when Tim laughed at the Sergeant Garcia comment about me...and yet I'd called Conrad "boring" to his face, which was just as hurtful.

No, I decided, as a strong feeling of shame washed over me, I was no better than Tim Argent. And that realization made me feel sick to my stomach.

Soon, Tweaky's house came into view. There were no signs of life there, other than a gray cat lying in the driveway. We rounded the corner by Scott's. Still nothing.

Finally, we headed up Red Oak, Conrad's road. When we arrived at the intersection of the far end Shepherdess Road, Dad stopped the car.

"Do you want me to turn here and go to the camp, or do you want to keep going up to Conrad's house?"

As much as I wanted to drive by Conrad's, the thought of him being outside and seeing us drive past made it seem like not such a hot idea. I mean, we never drove that far up Red Oak, not unless Conrad was with us.

"Turn onto Shepherdess," I said, sighing. "Let's just go to the camp."

The dirt road at that end seemed bumpier and dustier because it didn't get much use. And the thick woods lining it made it appear dark and spooky, especially on an overcast morning.

We passed the trail to Little Paradise, the Minutemen's graves and finally, Big Rock. I could see our familiar driveway up ahead.

"I hope the fish are biting today!" Dad said as he made a left turn into the yard. "If I catch a couple, we can fry some up for lun..."

He slammed on the brakes. I turned to look at him. His eyes were wide and unblinking. His mouth was open.

I allowed my eyes to follow his. "Ohmigod!"

Dad turned off the car and slowly, cautiously, we climbed out.

The camp's windows looked as if they'd been smashed with rocks. The screens on the porch had been slashed and were hanging like peeling wallpaper. The front door was lying on the steps.

I scanned the immediate area, wondering if the person or gang of thugs who'd done this still might be around. I noticed that the picnic table and benches were missing from their spot in front of the barbecue.

I grabbed my dad's arm and together we inched our way toward the camp.

"Dad, I'm scared." I tightened my grip on his arm.

"I don't think anyone's here," he said. "I think this may have happened at least a day or two ago. I wonder why that cop who was supposed to be checking on the place didn't see it and contact us?"

The inside of the camp looked as if a herd of cattle had stampeded through it. The sofa bed had been slashed and the stuffing was strewn everywhere. The oil lamps had been smashed, and condiments, like the ketchup and mustard we'd left in the cabinet, had been squirted all over the braided rug and bunk beds. Glass from the broken windows and oil lamps was scattered all over the floors.

I looked through the kitchen window, which appeared to be the only one still intact, and stared at the river. "Dad, I found the picnic table! It's sticking up out of the water on the other side of the river, caught up on some branches or something."

My father shook his head and let out a long sigh. "I'll bet the same creeps who robbed the Harmons' place broke in here, hoping to find something to steal, then got ticked off and went on a rampage when they found out there wasn't anything of value. Come on, let's go out and check the other side."

We stepped around all of the broken glass and made our way outside, then walked over to the far side of the camp, which wasn't visible from the road. I looked up at the side of the building and suddenly felt as if all of the air had been sucked from my lungs. I couldn't believe my eyes…nor did I want to.

"*No!*" My hands flew up to my mouth and tears sprang to my eyes.

There, written on the wall's white clapboards in huge black spray-painted words was, "Have fun!"

And below the words was a swirl with two lines through it and two circles.

My father and I stood silently staring at the message for a few seconds. So this, I thought, as the all-too-familiar handwriting leapt out at me, mocking me, was my punishment for dumping Conrad. Maybe I could understand him doing this in a fit of anger to spite me, but why hurt my parents? They'd been nothing but kind to him. Heck, they'd even stood up for him when I'd tried to tell them there was something about him I just didn't like.

At that moment, I couldn't think of anyone on earth I disliked more than Conrad.

"Dad, I know who did this." My words came out in a whisper.

I felt his big hand on my shoulder. In a voice I thought sounded much too calm, he said, "I know, honey, I know."

EPILOGUE

I never understood why my dad didn't report the incident to the police. Maybe he thought Conrad already had suffered enough. Or maybe he just didn't want to make him even angrier, for fear he'd retaliate. Over the next few weekends, Dad simply repaired everything that was broken at the camp and then repainted the exterior. Mom and I cleaned up inside and then Mom redecorated both rooms. No one ever mentioned the incident again.

Through the years, the camp turned out to be the site of many good times. Janet and I did bring Jerry and Rusty there, and we repeated our river rafting adventure – but with a bigger and better raft, and the boys at the helm. It was amazing how much less scary the river was when I was leaning against Jerry.

My junior-high graduation party, featuring a big barbecue, was held at the camp. And we even threw a surprise birthday barbecue there for my grandmother.

In the early 1970s a real-estate developer purchased the land surrounding the camp and chopped down most of the trees. Soon, new roads and houses began to pop up, seemingly every week. Even McCreedy deeded his land to the developer. That's when Mom and Dad decided the time had come to sell the camp. After all, their rustic little getaway, their retreat from city life, just wasn't the same any more. Dad complained that every time he blinked, a new house seemed to appear next to the camp, and the area was looking more and more like the city than the country. The sadness he and Mom felt when they signed the final paperwork, however, was somewhat eased by the big wad of cash they received...more than quadruple what they'd originally paid for the place.

I never saw or heard from Conrad again. It was as if he disappeared into thin air...or went into hiding. But not long ago, out of curiosity, I searched his name online and found him on Facebook. His personal information said he's married, has two children, owns his own company...and lives only about ten miles from me. And judging from his Facebook photo, he finally grew into his teeth.

I never saw Scott, Tweaky, Jake or Tim again, either. Sometimes I wonder if they all were part of some alien plot and were beamed down to Arrowwood just to entertain Janet and me during our summer vacation.

By the time I entered my freshman year in high school, my bra size was 34D. Mom and I spent so much time at LaRue's buying new bras, people thought we worked there. And the guys at school kept asking me if my dad had invested in a foam-rubber factory.

And finally, although never in a zillion years would I ever have believed I'd be saying this...I really do miss the camp.

Heck, I even miss the outhouse.

# # #

ABOUT THE AUTHOR

Sally Breslin was born and raised in New Hampshire, where she still resides, so she is a true New Englander through and through.

She knew at a young age that writing was her passion. She started writing poetry when she was only 8. During summer vacations from school, she would sit on the front steps of her tenement building and write books. Each day, groups of kids from the neighborhood would gather and she would read the next installment to them. She also began keeping a journal when she was 12, and has continued to do so every day since. She says her journals are like having her own time machine. She even can tell you what she ate for breakfast back in November of 1963!

For over 20 years, she worked as a newspaper correspondent and photographer for the *Hooksett Banner*. Since 1984, she has been interpreting dreams in her weekly newspaper column, *Dreams...with Sally Breslin,* and since 1994, has been writing a weekly humor column, *My Life*, both of which are published in four New England Newspapers. In 1996, she was named the New Hampshire Press Association's columnist of the year. She also has taught humor-writing classes for Concord Community Education.

Her stories have been published in the bestsellers: *A Second Chicken Soup for the Woman's Soul, Chicken Soup for the Soul at Christmas* and *Belly Laughs and Babies.*

Although she grew up in New Hampshire's largest city, she currently lives way out in the country with her husband and two rottweilers, her faithful hiking companions. She says she loves the country – but can do without the mosquitoes and spiders...and especially the ticks!

To read more of Sally's adventures, visit her weekly blog at:

www.sallythedreamlady.com

Made in the USA
Charleston, SC
13 January 2013